The Longman Companion to

European Decolonisation in the Twentieth Century

Longman Companions to History
General Editors: Chris Cook and John Stevenson

Now available

The Longman Companion to

European Decolonisation in the Twentieth Century

Muriel E. Chamberlain

Longman
London and New York

Addison Wesley Longman Limited
Edinburgh Gate,
Harlow, Essex CM20 2JE, United Kingdom
and Associated Companies throughout the world.

Published in the United States of America by Addison Wesley Longman, New York.

© Addison Wesley Longman Limited 1998

First published 1998

ISBN 0-582-07774-5 CSD
ISBN 0-582-07773-7 PPR

Visit Addison Wesley Longman on the world wide web at
http://www.awl-he.com

British Library Cataloguing in Publication Data

A catalogue entry for this title is available from the British Library

Library of Congress Cataloging-in-Publication Data

Chamberlain, Muriel Evelyn.
  The Longman companion to European decolonisation in the
twentieth century / Muriel E. Chamberlain.
    p.   cm. — (Longman companions to history)
  Includes bibliographical references and index.
  ISBN 0-582-07774-5. — ISBN 0-582-07773-7 (pbk.)
    1. Europe—Colonies—History—20th century.   2. Decolonization—
History.   I. Title.   II. Series.
  JV151.C475   1998
  325'.3'094—dc21   98–14251
                                                                      CIP

Set by 35 in 9½/12pt New Baskerville
Produced by Addison Wesley Longman Singapore (Pte) Ltd.,
Printed in Singapore

Contents

List of Maps

Preface

This book covers only the European maritime empires. Two other great empires were created in the eighteenth/nineteenth centuries. The Russian empire expanded into Central Asia. Arguably this did not differ from the maritime expansion of western Europe and it has dissolved in not dissimilar ways since 1989. The United States, itself the successor state of various European empires, acquired a huge land mass and some overseas possessions in the nineteenth century. This too can be seen as part of the same process of European expansion. Some parts of the American empire have also been decolonised, for example the Philippines in 1946.

Some European empires dissolved or were decolonised before 1945. They were (1) that part of the British empire which became the United States of America in 1783; (2) the Spanish empire in South and Central America, which dissolved during or just after the Napoleonic Wars; (3) the Portuguese empire in South America, which also dissolved in the early nineteenth century; and (4) the German empire, which was divided between other Powers at the end of the First World War.

SECTION ONE

The World in 1945

1 The European Empires in 1945

The British Commonwealth and Empire in 1945

In 1945 the British Commonwealth and empire still covered about one-fifth of the land surface of the globe and about one-quarter of the population of the world, but varying degrees of autonomy had already been devolved to their separate parts. Some, like Canada, were for all practical purposes already independent nations. Others, like Hong Kong, were Crown Colonies, administered by a Governor, with little or no 'unofficial' advice. The rest had differing degrees of 'representative' or 'responsible' government (see Glossary for these terms).

It had been true since late Victorian times that less than one-tenth of the population of the empire/Commonwealth lived in the metropolitan country. By the Second World War the ratio was roughly 46,000,000: 500,000,000.

	Status	Area (in square miles)	Population[1]
Metropolitan Britain			
England and Wales		58,543	39,988,000
Scotland		30,140	4,843,000
Northern Ireland		5,449	1,243,000
Isle of Man		227	49,308
Channel Islands			
Jersey and dependencies		45	50,000
Guernsey and dependencies		30	40,000
Total		94,434	46,213,308

[1] Census taking had been disrupted by the war. In some countries censuses were carried out in 1946. Where possible the 1946 figures are given. In other cases the latest previous census or estimate is used.

	Status	Area (in square miles)	Population
The Commonwealth (in order of seniority)			
Canada	Dominion	3,700,000	11,506,655
Newfoundland (including Labrador)	Dominion (in 1949 Newfoundland became a Province of Canada)	42,750	321,101
Australia	Dominion	3,000,000	6,629,839
New Zealand (plus dependent territories:)	Dominion	104,000	1,702,298
Western Samoa		1,133	59,306
Papua		90,540	301,488
New Guinea		93,000	587,625
South Africa (plus administered territory:)	Dominion	473,000	11,258,858
South West Africa	Mandate	317,725	318,422
Eire	Dominion	26,000	2,986,429
The Empire[2] (in alphabetical order)			
Aden	Colony and Protectorate	80 112,000	80,515 c.600,000
Ascension Island	Colony	38	200
Bahamas	Colony	375	71,850
Barbados	Colony	166	195,398
Basutoland	Protectorate	11,720	562,311
Bechuanaland	Colony and Protectorate	275,000	252,869
Bermuda	Colony	21	34,965
Borneo, North	Colony from 1 July 1946, previously administered by Chartered Company	30,000	270,223

[2] Some small islands are omitted.

	Status	Area (in square miles)	Population
Brunei	Protected State	2,250	30,135
Cameroons	Mandate	34,000	831,103
Ccylon	Colony	25,000	6,633,617
Cyprus	Colony	3,600	462,318
Falkland Islands	Colony	4,618	2,435
Fiji	Colony	7,100	259,638
Gambia, The	Colony and		21,152
	Protectorate	4,070	219,983
Gibraltar	Colony	2	21,000
Gilbert and			
Ellice Islands	Colony	200	35,298
Gold Coast	Colony and		
(including	Protectorate	91,843	3,959,510
mandated territory			
of Togoland)			
Guiana, British	Colony	83,000	375,819
Honduras, British	Colony	8,876	51,347
Hong Kong	Colony and		
	Leased Territory	400	c.1,600,000
India	Empire	1,575,187	388,800,000
'British India'		862,679	295,827,000
Princely States		712,508	92,973,000
Jamaica	Colony	4,411	1,237,063
(plus dependencies:)			
Cayman Islands		100	6,670
Turks and			
Caicos Islands		170	6,138
Kenya	Colony and		
	Protectorate	220,000	4,046,968
Leeward Islands (see West Indies, British)			
Malaya	Colony	(53,222)	(5,278,866)
(see also North	(in process of		
Borneo, Brunei,	reorganisation		
Sarawak, Singapore	after Japanese		
and Straits	occupation)		
Settlements)			
Malta	Colony	122	241,621
Mauritius	Colony	720	428,273

	Status	Area (in square miles)	Population
New Hebrides	Condominium with France	5,700	48,815
Nigeria (including mandated territory of Cameroons)	Colony and Protectorate Mandate	373,000	20,588,840
Norfolk Island	Colony	15	1,059
Nyasaland	Protectorate	48,000	2,049,459
Palestine	Mandate	10,400	1,912,110
Pitcairn	Colony	2	202
Rhodesia, Northern	Colony	288,000	1,656,899
Rhodesia, Southern	'Self-governing' Colony	150,300	1,776,883
Saint Helena	Colony	47	4,710
Seychelles	Colony	156	34,419
Sierra Leone	Colony and Protectorate	250 28,000	122,000 1,770,000
Singapore	Colony	220	769,216
Solomon Islands	Protectorate	11,500	94,965
Somaliland, British	Protectorate	68,000	500–700,000
Straits Settlements ([Singapore], Penang, Malacca, Labuan)	Colonies (in process of reorganisation)	1,356	1,357,854
Sudan	Anglo-Egyptian Condominium	967,500	7,498,000
Swaziland	Protectorate	6,700	186,880
Tanganyika	Mandate	360,000	5,417,594
Transjordan	Mandate	30,000	300,000
Trinidad and Tobago	Colony	1,978	558,605
Tristan da Cunha	Colony	45	224
Tonga (or Friendly Islands)	Protectorate	250	40,668
Uganda	Protectorate	94,000	Over 4,000,000
West Indies, British Leeward Islands: Antigua and Barbuda	Colony	170	42,000

	Status	Area (in square miles)	Population
St Kitts-Nevis with Anguilla	Colony	150	46,200
Montserrat	Colony	32	14,200
British Virgin Islands	Colony	67	6,500
Windward Islands:			
Dominica	Colony	305	47,682
Grenada and Grenadines	Colony	133	72,053
St Lucia	Colony	238	69,088
St Vincent	Colony	150	61,593
Windward Islands (see West Indies, British)			
Zanzibar (and Pemba)	Protectorate	380	250,000

Special cases

Egypt   Egypt had ceased to be a British Protectorate on 28 February 1922 and Britain had formally recognised it as a sovereign state by the treaty of 26 August 1936, but in 1945 Britain still retained treaty rights, which detracted from Egypt's total independence.

Persian Gulf   A number of the small states of the Persian Gulf region had special treaty relationships with Britain. They included Kuwait, Qatar, and the Trucial Coast (i.e. the sheikdoms of Abu Dhabi, Dubei, Sharjah, Ajman, Umm el Qwain, Ras el Khaimah and, after 1952, Fujairah).

Iran (Persia) Iran had never formally been part of the British empire, but in 1907 Britain and Russia had agreed on spheres of influence there. During the Second World War, fearing German intervention, British and Russian troops had entered the country and were still there in 1945.

The French Empire in 1945

The French empire was the next largest maritime empire after the British. Its total area and population in 1945 were roughly 3,791,400 square miles and 65,598,000 people. It had been severely disrupted during the Second World War by the defeat of France by Germany in 1940 and the subsequent struggles for control of the French colonies between Vichy France and the Free French.

	Status	Area (in square miles)	Population
Metropolitan France (excluding Algeria)		212,895	40,517,923 (excluding 312,105 absent on service abroad)
French Empire			
Algeria	Governed as a French Department, i.e. part of metropolitan France, in 1945.	222,120	7,234,684 (of whom 987,252 were Europeans)
French Equatorial Africa			
Chad	Colony	481,000	1,100,000
Gabon	Colony	106,181	387,000
Middle Congo	Colony	160,000	662,000
Ubanghi-Shari	Colony	230,000	1,100,000
French India (Pondicherry, Chandernagore, Karikal, Yanaon, Mahe)	Colony	200	323,000
French West Africa			
Cameroon (part)	Mandate	143,415	2,600,000
Dahomey	Colony	47,144	1,450,000
Ivory Coast	Colony	189,029	4,020,000
Mauretania	Colony	322,344	490,000
Niger	Colony	483,526	2,160,000
Senegal	Colony	77,814	1,720,000
Sudan, French	Colony	582,437	3,790,000
Togoland (part)	Mandate	20,464	750,000
French West Indies			
French Guiana	Colony	35,135	12,000
Guadeloupe	Colony (become Overseas Department of France, March 1946)	583	13,638

	Status	Area (in square miles)	Population
Martinique	Colony (become Overseas Department of France, March 1946)	425	52,051
Indo-China			
Annam	Protectorate	58,000	6,000,000
Cambodia	Protectorate	70,000	3,100,000
Cochin China	Colony	26,000	4,616,000
Laos	Protectorate	90,000	1,500,000
Tonkin	Protectorate	43,000	10,000,000
Lebanon	Mandate	4,300	1,200,000
Madagascar	Protectorate	228,000	3,797,936
(plus dependencies:)			
Comoro Islands		800	123,516
Réunion (formerly Île de Bourbon)		1000	200,000
Morocco (French)	Protectorate	162,000	6,430,000
New Caledonia	Colony	7,200	50,500
New Hebrides	Condominium (see under British empire)		
St Pierre and Miquelon	Colony	93	4,606
Society Islands (Tahiti and dependencies)	Colony	650	14,000
Somaliland, French	Colony	9,000	45,000
Syria	Mandate	55,700	2,000,000
Tunis	Protectorate	45,000	2,608,313 (of whom 219,587 were Europeans)

The Dutch Empire in 1945

Holland (more correctly, the Netherlands) had an ancient trading empire in both the East and the West Indies. Like France, it had been defeated and occupied by the Germans during the Second World War. The Dutch colonies had declared their loyalty to the Dutch government in exile, but the Dutch East Indies had been occupied by the Japanese in 1943. The empire was in a state of flux in 1945.

	Area (in square miles)	Population
Metropolitan Kingdom of the Netherlands	13,514	9,298,889
Colonies		
Dutch East Indies		
(Java and Madura, Sumatra, Riouw-Lingga		
Archipelago, Banka and Billiton, Celebes,		
Moluccas, Timor, Bali and Lombok,		
Borneo (Dutch), New Guinea (Dutch))	730,000	53,000,000
Dutch West Indies		
Curaçao	436	79,395
(including Curaçao, Bonaire, Aruba,		
St Martaans, St Eustatius and Saba)		
Surinam (Dutch Guiana)	54,000	164,085

The Portuguese Empire in 1945

The Portuguese was the oldest of the European maritime empires, dating from the beginning of the sixteenth century. Portugal lost its most important colony, Brazil, in 1822. The empire seemed moribund until revived by the new scramble for colonies at the end of the nineteenth century. Portugal remained neutral during the Second World War and its empire was thus less disrupted than that of some other Powers. Portugal under the authoritarian rule of President Salazar in 1945 had no plans for any major changes in its empire.

	Area (in square miles)	Population
Metropolitan Portugal		
In Europe	34,500	7,954,000
Azores	922	284,755
Madeira	314	249,771
Colonies		
Cape Verde Islands	1,516	181,286
São Tomé and		
Príncipe Islands	372	60,490
Portuguese Guinea	14,000	351,000
Angola	488,000	3,788,000

	Area (in square miles)	Population
Mozambique	297,657	5,081,266
Portuguese India		
(Goa, Damaunın Diu)	1,636	600,000
Macao	5	157,175
Portuguese Timor	7,329	474,363

The Spanish Empire in 1945

The Spanish empire had at one time been Europe's largest maritime empire but Spain had lost most of it when her colonies in South and Central America demanded independence during and after the Napoleonic Wars. She had lost some of the remnants, notably the Philippines, Cuba and Puerto Rico to the United States as a result of the Spanish-American war of 1898. Spain had been neutral during the Second World War and its colonies (apart from the Protectorate in Morocco) had been little affected. The dictatorial government of General Franco had no plans for major reorganisation in 1945.

	Status	Area (in square miles)	Population
Metropolitan Spain			
Iberian Peninsula		196,700	25,240,971
Balearic Islands		1,935	376,735
Canary Islands		2,807	599,712
Spanish Empire			
Ceuta	Colony	5	35,219
Melilla	Colony	8	50,170
Spanish Guinea (including Fernando Po and Rio Muni)	Colony	10,000	170,000
Spanish Morocco	Protectorate	17,631	1,003,900
Spanish Sahara (Rio de Oro)	Colony	73,362	26,000

The Belgian Empire in 1945

Belgium had only one colony. The Congo, founded as a nominally independent state under the Belgian King in 1885, became a Belgium colony on 15 November 1908. Belgium was defeated and occupied by Germany during the Second World War. After the capitulation of Belgium, the Congo government in its capital, Leopoldville, declared its support for Britain and the Free French. It was not a theatre of war. Belgium had no plans to change its status in 1945. It also had one mandated territory.

	Status	Area (in square miles)	Population
Metropolitan Belgium		11,750	8,386,553
Belgian Empire			
Belgian Congo	Colony	909,654	African – 10,500,000; European – 33,786
Ruanda-Urundi	Mandate	20,000	3,400,000

The Italian Empire in 1945

The Italian empire had all been acquired after the unification of Italy in 1871. Italy had fought on the Allied side during the First World War and had expected, but not obtained, significant colonial gains in the Near East. Italy's conquest of Abyssinia (Ethiopia) in 1935 had been condemned, but not prevented, by the League of Nations. Italy had fought on the German side in the Second World War and so emerged from the war as a defeated Power. It was generally accepted that Italy would be required to surrender her colonies, all of which had been captured by the Allies, but their future was still under discussion in 1945.

	Area (in square miles)	Population
Metropolitan Italy (including Sicily, Sardinia and Elba)	193,000	45,645,000
Colonies		
Libya (incorporated into metropolitan Italy in 1939)	810,000	c.1,100,000
Italian East Africa		
Eritrea	64,000	640,000
Italian Somaliland	220,000	c.900,000
(Abyssinia had resumed independence in 1943)		

2 The League of Nations and the Mandate System

The Mandate System

This was established at the end of the First World War and arose from the declared war aims of the Allied Powers. The American President, Woodrow Wilson, in his Address at Mount Vernon on 4 July 1918, further expanding his famous Fourteen Points (which summarised Allied war aims but did not specifically mention self-determination), promised 'the settlement of every question, whether of territory, of sovereignty, of economic arrangement, or of political relationship, upon the basis of the free acceptance of that settlement by the people immediately concerned, and not upon the basis of the material interest or advantage of any other nation or people . . .'. The Allied Powers had declared that there would be 'no annexations' after this war, but at the same time they were determined not to return any of Germany's conquered colonies to her. It was also necessary to make provision for the successor states of the Ottoman (Turkish) empire, which had been allied to Germany and which had now collapsed.

The result was Article 22 of the Covenant of the League of Nations, annexed to the treaty of Versailles of 1919. This provided:

1. To those colonies and territories which as a consequence of the late war have ceased to be under the Sovereignty of the States which formerly governed them and which are inhabited by people not yet able to stand by themselves under the strenuous conditions of the modern world, there should be applied the priniciple that the well-being and development of such peoples form a sacred trust of civilization and that securities for the performance of this trust should be embodied in this Covenant.

2. The best method of giving practical effect to this principle is that the tutelage of such people should be intrusted to advanced nations who by reason of their resources, their experience or their geographical position can best undertake this responsibility . . . and

that this tutelage should be exercised by them as Mandatories on behalf of the League.

3. The character of the mandate must differ according to the stage of the development of the people, the geographical situation of the territory, its economic conditions and other similar circumstances.

4. Certain communities formerly belonging to the Turkish Empire have reached a stage of development where their existence as independent nations can be provisionally recognized subject to the rendering of administrative advice and assistance by a Mandatory until such time as they are able to stand alone. The wishes of these communities must be a principal consideration in the selection of the Mandatory. [Class A mandates]

5. Other peoples, especially those of Central Africa, are at such a stage that the Mandatory must be responsible for the administration of the territory under conditions which will guarantee freedom of conscience and religion, subject only to the maintenance of public order and morals, the prohibition of the slave trade, the arms traffic and liquor traffic . . . [Class B mandates]

6. There are territories, such as Southwest Africa and certain of the South Pacific islands, which, owing to the sparseness of their population, or their small size, or their remoteness from the centres of civilization, or their geographical contiguity to the territory of the Mandatory . . . can best be administered under the laws of the Mandatory as integral portions of its territory, subject to the safeguards above mentioned in the interests of the indigenous population. [Class C mandates]

7. In every case of mandate, the Mandatory shall render to the Council an annual report in reference to the territory committed to its charge.

8. A permanent Commission shall be constituted to receive and examine the annual reports of the Mandatories and to advise the Council on all matters relating to the observance of the mandates.

Article 22 thus created a clear distinction between Class A mandates, applying to the former territories of the Ottoman empire, which were expected to become independent quickly, and the rest, where the obligation was only to provide good government for the foreseeable future.

The obligation to provide annual reports to the League of Nations Mandate Commission was generally faithfully observed by the Mandatory Powers between the World Wars.

The Mandated Territories

These were generally finalised by a variety of agreements, 1920–23.

Category	Territory	Mandatory
A	Iraq	Great Britain
A	Palestine	Great Britain
A	Transjordan	Great Britain
A	Syria/Lebanon (The Lebanon had been carved out of Syria with the intention of giving Lebanese Christians a separate homeland)	France
B	Cameroons	France
B	North West Cameroons	Great Britain
B	Ruanda-Urundi	Belgium
B	Tanganyika (formerly German East Africa)	Great Britain
B	Togoland	France
B	Togoland, West	Great Britain
C	South West Africa	Union of South Africa
C	Pacific Islands, North of the Equator: Caroline, Marianas and Marshall Islands	Japan
C	Pacific Islands, South of the Equator: Nauru and Eastern New Guinea	Australia
	Western Samoa	New Zealand

3 Key Events of the Second World War

Pre-war

1931
Sept. 18   Japan began conquest of Manchuria.

1935
Oct.   3   Italians invaded Abyssinia (Ethiopia).

1936
July   League of Nations abandoned sanctions against Italy.

1937
July   7   Sino–Japanese War began.

1939
Aug. 23   Nazi–Soviet Non-Agression Pact.

War

1939
Sept. 1   Germany invaded Poland.
        3   Britain and France declared war on Germany.

1940
Feb.   Australian and New Zealand troops arrived in Egypt.
May 10   Germany invaded Netherlands and Belgium.
        14   Dutch Army surrendered (Dutch government in exile
                      continued struggle).
        28   Belgium surrendered unconditionally to Germany.
June 4   British completed Dunkirk evacuation (some French
                      troops also evacuated).
        10   Italy declared war on Britain and France.
        15   Soviet Union seized Lithuania, Latvia and Estonia.
        22   France signed armistice with Germany.
        23   General de Gaulle announced intention to continue
                      struggle.
June 24   France signed armistice with Italy.

July	3	British attacked French fleet at Oran and Mers-el-Kebir.
	10	Battle of Britain began.
Aug.	5–19	Italians occupied British Somaliland.
Sept.	3	US President Roosevelt announced intention to 'lend' Britain 50 destroyers in return for lease on naval bases.
	13	Italians invaded Egypt.
	22–25	British and Free French attempted to take Dakar (Senegal).
	22	Japanese forces entered northern French Indo-China.
	27	Japan joined Germany and Italy in Axis Pact.
Oct.		Germany postponed plans to invade Britain.
	28	Italy invaded Greece.
Dec.	29	British under General Wavell launched counter-offensive in Egypt.

1941

Feb.	7	Italian army surrendered to British at Bedafomm (Libya).
	12	German General Rommel arrived in Tripoli to take command of North African campaign.
Mar.	5	British forces arrived in Greece.
	11	US Congress passed Lend-Lease Act.
	16	British forces landed at Berbera in British Somaliland.
	24	Axis forces launched offensive in North Africa and besieged Tobruk.
Apr.	3	A pro-German politician, Rashid Ali al-Gailani, organised successful coup in Iraq.
	6	British occupied Abyssinian capital, Addis Ababa.
	13	Japan and Soviet Union signed neutrality pact.
	17	Indian brigade sent to protect Iraq–Haifa oil pipe-line.
	30	Greece conquered by German forces.
May	2	British forces engaged insurgents in Iraq.
	31	British forces occupied Baghdad; regent, Emir Abdullah, restored.
	31	Germans conquered Crete.
June	8–14	British and Free French attacked and defeated Vichy French forces in Syria.
	22	Germans invaded Russia.
July	23	Japan occupied southern Indo-China.
Nov.	18	British, under General Auchinleck, invaded Libya.
	27	British conquest of Italian East Africa completed.
Dec.	5	German attack stalled 25 miles from Moscow.
	7	Japanese attacked American base at Pearl Harbor.

8	Japan declared war on United States and Britain.
8	Japanese invaded Thailand, Malaysia and mainland territories of Hong Kong, and bombarded Wake and Guam (US).
9	Japanese invaded Gilbert Islands.
10	Japanese seized Guam.
10	British relieved Tobruk.
16	Japanese invaded Burma and British Borneo.
18	Japanese invaded island of Hong Kong.
22	Japanese launched major attack on Philippines.
24	British forces entered Benghazi (Libya).

1942

Jan.	11	Japanese began invasion of Dutch East Indies.
	20	Japanese began major offensive in Burma.
	21	Rommel launched major counter-offensive in North Africa.
	26	First American troops arrived in Britain.
	27	British forces in Malaya began withdrawal to Singapore.
Feb.	4	Singapore surrendered.
	19	Japanese air raid on Darwin, Australia.
	27	Allies defeated in Battle of Java Sea.
Mar.	7	British evacuated Burmese capital, Rangoon.
	7	Japanese invaded New Guinea.
	9	Java surrendered to Japanese.
May	5	British landed in Madagascar.
	6	Philippines surrendered to Japanese.
	20	Japanese completed conquest of Burma and arrived on frontiers of India.
	30	RAF began major air offensive with raid on Cologne.
June	21	Rommel captured Tobruk.
	30	British forced back to El Alamein.
July	1	Germans captured Sebastopol.
	4	First US air operations in Europe.
Aug.	19	British and Canadians made commando raid on Dieppe.
Oct.	23	British forces opened El Alamein offensive.
Nov.	8	British and American forces landed in Morocco and Algeria (Operation Torch).
	9	German troops occupied Tunisia.
	11	German troops moved into 'unoccupied' (i.e. southern) France.
	10	French Admiral Darlan ordered French troops in North Africa to cease resisting the Allies.

	27	French warships in Toulon harbour scuttled to prevent seizure by Germans.
Dec.	16	British began counter-offensive in Burma.
	24	Admiral Darlan assassinated.

1943

Jan.	14	Casablanca Conference (Britain and US) opened.
	23	British occupied Tripoli.
Feb.	2	German troops surrendered at Stalingrad.
	4	British entered Tunisia.
	8	Brigadier Orde Wingates's operations began in Burma.
	9	Japanese surrendered on Guadalcanal.
May	13	Tunisia fell and 240,000 Axis troops surrendered to Allies; Africa now clear of Axis forces.
June	30	Partially successful Allied counter-attack in Solomon Islands and New Guinea.
July	9	Allied forces invaded Sicily.
Sept.	3	British forces invaded Italy; Italy signed secret armistice.
	8	Armistice made public; Italian fleet and air force surrendered.
	11	Germans counter-attacked Allies in Italy.
Nov.	21	Partially successful counter-attack began in Gilbert Islands.

1944

Jan.	16	American General Eisenhower became Supreme Commander of Allied Expeditionary Force.
	25	New counter-offensive began in Burma.
Apr.	22	Further Allied forces landed in New Guinea.
June	6	Allied forces landed in Normandy.
	22	Japanese began to retreat in Burma.
Aug.	15	American forces landed in southern France.
	25	Allied forces entered Paris.
Sept.	16	Arnhem offensive failed.
	30	Russian forces crossed the Danube.
Nov.	24	First American air raid on Tokyo.
Dec.	16	Germans opened Ardennes counter-offensive.

1945

Jan.	17	Russians captured Warsaw.
Feb.	4	Yalta Conference (Big Three: Churchill, Roosevelt and Stalin) began.
Mar.	22–23	British and American forces crossed the Rhine.

Apr. 7	Russians entered Vienna.
23	Russians reached Berlin.
May 2	Fighting ended in Italy.
3	British recaptured Rangoon.
4	Germans surrendered in the Netherlands.
7	Germans surrendered unconditionally to Allies.
9	Hostilities in Europe officially ended.
July 17–Aug. 2	Potsdam Conference.
Aug. 6	First atomic bomb dropped on Hiroshima.
8	Russia declared war on Japan.
9	Atomic bomb dropped on Nagasaki.
9–12	Russians invaded Manchuria and North Korea.
14	Japan surrendered.

4 The United Nations and Human Rights Declarations

The League of Nations had been discredited by the outbreak of the Second World War. It was agreed among the Allies that a new world organisation must be set up which would, hopefully, avoid the mistakes and weaknesses of its predecessor. The new organisation – the United Nations – was determined to have particularly clear declarations on Human Rights.

Representatives of what would later come to be called the Third World had tried to lobby the statesmen at Paris in 1919 but with little success. They had rather more success in influencing the United Nations and their input grew as former colonies became independent and themselves members of the United Nations. In time the 'Afro-Asian bloc' became a formidable group, although the structure of the United Nations Organisation, as set up in 1945, left key institutions, notably the Security Council, largely in the hands of the old Great Powers.

Origins

1941 Atlantic Charter. The British Prime Minister, Winston Churchill, met the American President, Franklin D. Roosevelt, on a warship in mid-Atlantic in August 1941 (before the United States had entered the war) to formulate aims for peace after the war had been won. The eight aims of the Atlantic Charter drew on Roosevelt's earlier 'Four Freedoms' speech – freedom of speech and expression, freedom of worship, freedom from want, and freedom from fear. They included self-determination.

1942 (1 January) Representatives of 26 Allied nations, describing themselves as the 'United Nations', signed a joint declaration, endorsing the Atlantic Charter and agreeing to support a common war effort against the Axis Powers. They included most of the exiled European governments and the Free French.

1943 Moscow. The foreign ministers of the United States, Britain and the USSR discussed a possible charter for a future United Nations.

1944   (21 August–7 October) Dumbarton Oaks conference. Representatives of the United States, Britain, the USSR and China met at Dumbarton Oaks, near Washington DC, to draft proposals for the new organisation.

1945   (February) Yalta Conference. The 'Big Three' – Roosevelt, Churchill and the Soviet leader, Joseph Stalin – agreed that a conference should convene in San Francisco to fine-tune the Dumbarton Oaks proposals.

(25 April–26 June) San Francisco Conference. Some 50 nations were represented and on 26 June 1945 they all signed the Charter of the new United Nations. President Roosevelt, one of the main architects of the new organisation, had died suddenly on 12 April. Germany surrendered on 7 May but the war with Japan was still continuing when the conference dispersed.

(24 October) The United Nations opened in a temporary home in New York. It then had 57 members:

Argentina	Ethiopia	Paraguay
Australia	France	Peru
Belgium	Greece	Philippines
Bolivia	Guatemala	Poland
Brazil	Haiti	Saudi Arabia
Byelorussian SSR	Honduras	Syria
Canada	India	Turkey
Chile	Iran	Ukrainian SSR
China	Iraq	Union of South Africa
Columbia	Lebanon	Union of Soviet
Costa Rica	Liberia	Socialist Republics
Cuba	Luxembourg	United Kingdom
Czechoslovakia	Mexico	United States
Denmark	Netherlands	Uruguay
Dominican Republic	New Zealand	Venezuela
Ecuador	Nicaragua	Yugoslavia
Egypt	Norway	
El Salvador	Panama	

One of the weaknesses of the League of Nations had been the absence of major Powers, especially the United States and, at various times, the USSR and the ex-enemy nations, notably Germany. The United Nations was more inclusive, although it too, at first, excluded the ex-enemy nations, including Germany, Japan and Italy.

The Structure of the United Nations (as relevant to colonial issues)

The General Assembly

All member states are represented and each has one vote. Although the Assembly meets regularly only once a year, it can be convened for special sessions.

The Security Council

This consists of eleven members: five permanent members – China, France, United Kingdom, USSR (now the Russian Federation) and the USA – and six non-permanent members, each elected for two-year terms. All members have only one vote but each of the permanent members has a veto on any decision.

Trusteeship Council

This replaced the League of Nations Mandate Commission. During the discussions at San Francisco and elsewhere, some countries had argued for the extension to all dependent territories of an international trusteeship system and a recognition of their right to evolve speedily to full independence. This had been opposed by Britain, France and even the United States, on the grounds that it did not take account of the very diverse conditions of colonial territories in terms of size, resources, current state of development etc. Instead it was agreed on 18 June 1944 that a distinction should be maintained between 'trust territories' and 'non-self-governing territories'. Trust territories were defined as the former League of Nations mandated territories, colonial territories which colonial Powers wished to assimilate to that status and territories taken from enemy powers as the result of the Second World War. All other colonies were re-defined as non-self-governing territories. Chapters XII and XIII of the UN Charter dealt with trust territories; Chapter XI with non-self-governing territories.

The Trusteeship Council was to consist of all members administering trust territories, all permanent members of the Security Council not included in the first category, and other members elected by the General Assembly. The Council had to be equally divided between members who administered trust territories and others who did not. The Trusteeship Council, on behalf of the General Assembly, was to receive reports from the administering authority, receive petitions if requested to do so, and arrange periodic visits to the trust territories.

Before the system could become operative, the administering Power had to conclude an agreement, acceptable to the United Nations. On

13 December 1946 the General Assembly approved eight such agreements, all relating to former mandate territories: Cameroons (part) and Togoland (part) – France; Cameroons (part), Togoland (part) and Tanganyika – Britain; Ruanda-Urundi – Belgium; New Guinea – Australia; and Western Samoa – New Zealand. The following year the United States submitted an agreement relating to the Marshall, Mariana and Caroline Islands, which had been Japanese mandates. These agreements covered virtually all the League of Nations Class B and Class C mandates. The conspicuous exception was South West Africa. South Africa refused to recognise the United Nations Trusteeship Council as the legitimate successor of the League of Nations Mandate Commission and declined to continue to submit reports or otherwise acknowledge its jurisdiction.

Human Rights (and Similar) Declarations (of relevance to colonial issues)

United Nations Charter

Chapter XI Declaration Regarding Non-Self-Governing Territories.

Article 73

> Members of the United Nations which have or assume responsibilities for the administration of territories whose peoples have not yet attained a full measure of self-government recognize the principle that the interests of the inhabitants of these territories are paramount, and accept as a sacred trust the obligation to promote to the utmost, within the system of international peace and security established by the present Charter, the well-being of the inhabitants of these territories, and to this end:
> (a) to ensure, with due respect for the culture of the peoples concerned, their political, economic, social, and educational advancement, their just treatment, and their protection against abuses;
> (b) to develop self-government, to take due account of the political aspirations of the people, and to assist them in the progressive development of their free political institutions, according to the particular circumstances of each territory, and its peoples and their varying stages of advancement . . .

[It will be seen that this involved a distinct commitment to evolution to self-government, an element which had been missing from most of the 'mandates', and never previously expressed concerning colonies otherwise acquired, but it left the timing very largely to the discretion of the colonial Power.]

Chapter XII International Trusteeship System

Article 76

> The basic objectives of the trusteeship system ... shall be:
> (b) to promote the political, economic, social, and educational advancement of the inhabitants of the trust territories, and their progressive development towards self-government or independence as may be appropriate to the particular circumstances of each territory and its peoples and the freely expressed wishes of the people concerned, and as may be provided by the terms of each trusteeship agreement;
> (c) to encourage respect for human rights and for fundamental freedoms for all without distinction as to race, sex, language, or religion, and to encourage recognition of the interdependence of the peoples of the world ...

Universal Declaration of Human Rights, 1948

[Adopted by General Assembly of United Nations, 10 December 1948]

Article 1

> All human beings are born free and equal in dignity and rights. They are endowed with reason and conscience and should act towards one another in a spirit of brotherhood.

Article 2

> Everyone is entitled to all the rights and freedoms set forth in this Declaration, without distinction of any kind, such as race, colour, sex, language, religion, political or other opinion, national or social origin, property, birth or other status.
> Furthermore, no distinction shall be made on the basis of the political, jurisdictional or international status of the country or territory to which a person belongs, whether it be independent, trust, non-self-governing or under any other limitation of sovereignty.

Article 4

> No one shall be held in slavery or servitude: slavery and the slave trade shall be prohibited in all their forms.

Article 6

> Everyone has the right to recognition everywhere as a person before the law.

Article 21

> 1. Everyone has the right to take part in the government of his country, directly or through freely chosen representatives.

2. Everyone has the right of equal access to public service in his country.

3. The will of the people shall be the basis of the authority of government; this will shall be expressed in periodic and genuine elections which shall be by universal and equal suffrage and shall be held by secret vote or by equivalent free voting procedures.

Declaration on the Granting of Independence to Colonial Countries and Peoples, 1960

[Adopted by the General Assembly of the United Nations on 14 December 1960: 89 states voted in favour; 9 abstained. The 9 who abstained were Australia, Belgium, Dominican Republic, France, Portugal, Spain, Union of South Africa, United Kingdom and United States.]

The General Assembly declares that:

1. The subjection of peoples to alien subjugation, domination and exploitation constitutes a denial of fundamental human rights, is contrary to the Charter of the United Nations and is an impediment to the promotion of World peace and co-operation.

2. All peoples have the right to self-determination; by virtue of that right they freely determine their political status and freely pursue their economic, social and cultural development.

3. Inadequacy of political, economic, social or educational preparedness should never serve as a pretext for delaying independence.

4. All armed action or repressive measures of all kinds directed against dependent peoples shall cease in order to enable them to exercise peacefully and freely their right to complete independence, and the integrity of their national territory shall be respected.

5. Immediate steps shall be taken, in Trust and Non-Self-Governing Territories or all other territories which have not yet attained independence, to transfer all powers to the people of those territories, without any conditions or reservations, in accordance with their freely expressed will and desire, without any distinction as to race, creed or colour, in order to enable them to enjoy complete independence and freedom.

6. Any attempt aimed at the partial or total disruption of the national unity and the territorial integrity of a country is incompatible with the purposes and principles of the Charter of the United Nations.

7. All States shall observe faithfully and strictly the provisions of the Charter of the United Nations, the Universal Declaration of

Human Rights and the present Declaration on the basis of equality, non-interference in the internal affairs if all States, and respect for the sovereign rights of all peoples and their territorial integrity.

International Covenant on Civil and Political Rights, 1966

[Adopted by the General Assembly of the United Nations on 16 December 1966. It came into force on 23 March 1976, by which time 95 states had adhered to it.]

The States Parties to the present Covenant agree upon the following articles:

Part I
Article 1

1. All peoples have the right to self-determination. By virtue of that right they freely determine their political status and freely pursue their economic, social and cultural development.

2. All peoples may, for their own ends, freely dispose of their natural wealth and resources without prejudice to any obligation arising out of international economic co-operation, based upon the principle of mutual benefit, and international law. In no case may a people be deprived of its own means of subsistence.

3. The States Parties to the present Covenant, including those having responsibility for the administration of Non-Self-Governing and Trust Territories, shall promote the realization of the right of self-determination, and shall respect that right, in conformity with the provisions of the Charter of the United Nations.

International Convention on the Suppression and Punishment of the Crime of Apartheid, 1973

[Adopted by the General Assembly of the United Nations on 30 November 1973: 91 states voted in favour, 4 against and 26 abstained. Portugal, South Africa, the United Kingdom and the United States voted against. The Convention came into force on 18 July 1976, by which time 88 states had adhered to it.]

The States Parties to the present Convention have agreed as follows:
Article I

1. The States Parties to the present convention declare that *apartheid* is a crime against humanity . . .

2. The States Parties to this Convention declare criminal those organizations, institutions and individuals committing the crime of *apartheid*.

Article II

For the purposes of the present Convention, the term 'the crime of *apartheid*' . . . shall include similar policies and practices of racial segregation and discrimination . . . practised in southern Africa.

[There follow detailed descriptions of the discriminatory policies of *apartheid*, including exclusion from political life.]

Convention Concerning Indigenous and Tribal Peoples in Independent Countries, 1989

[This was adopted by the General Conference of the International Labour Organisation in June 1989. Even decolonisation did not solve all problems, as this document illustrates.]

Article 1

1. This Convention applies to:

(a) tribal peoples in independent countries whose social, cultural and economic conditions distinguish them from other sections of the national community, and whose status is regulated wholly or partially by their own customs or traditions or by special laws or regulations;

(b) peoples in independent countries who are regarded as indigenous on account of their descent from populations which inhabited the country, or a geographical region to which the country belongs, at the time of conquest or colonisation or the establishment of the present state boundaries and who, irrespective of their legal status, retain some or all of their own social, economic, cultural and political institutions.

Article 3

1. Indigenous and tribal peoples shall enjoy the full measure of human rights and fundamental freedoms without hindrance or discrimination . . .

Article 14

1. The rights of ownership and possession of the people concerned over the lands which they traditionally occupy shall be recognised . . .

Text of documents above taken from either L.M. Goodrich, Edvard Hambro and Anne Patricia Simons, *Charter of the United Nations: Commentary and Documents* (3rd edn, 1969), or Ian Brownlie (ed.) *Basic Documents on Human Rights* (3rd edn, 1994).

SECTION TWO

Metropolitan Politics

Great Britain

Ministries

Ministries		Prime Minister (with date of appointment)
1916–22	Wartime coalition	David Lloyd George (6 Dec. 1916)
1922–24	Conservative	A. Bonar-Law (23 Oct. 1922) Stanley Baldwin (22 May 1923)
1924	Labour	J. Ramsay MacDonald (22 Jan. 1924)
1924–29	Conservative	Stanley Baldwin (4 Nov. 1924)
1929–31	Labour	J. Ramsay MacDonald (5 June 1929)
1931–35	'National' (coalition)	J. Ramsay MacDonald (24 Aug. 1931)
1935–40	'National' (predominantly Conservative)	Stanley Baldwin (7 June 1935) Neville Chamberlain (28 May 1937)
1940–45	Wartime coalition	Winston Churchill (10 May 1940)
1945	'Caretaker' government	Winston Churchill (23 May 1945)
1945–51	Labour	Clement Attlee (26 July 1945)
1951–55	Conservative	Sir Winston Churchill (26 Oct. 1951)
1955–64	Conservative	Sir Anthony Eden (6 April 1955) Harold Macmillan (10 Jan. 1957) Sir Alec Douglas-Home (19 Oct. 1963)
1964–70	Labour	Harold Wilson (16 Oct. 1964)
1970–74	Conservative	Edward Heath (19 June 1970)

	Ministries	Prime Minister (with date of appointment)
1974–79	Labour	Harold Wilson (4 March 1974) James Callaghan (5 April 1976)
1979–97	Conservative	Margaret Thatcher (4 May 1979) John Major (28 Nov. 1991)
1997–	Labour	Tony Blair (2 May 1997)

Ministers with Special Responsibilities for Empire

Secretaries of State for India

Austen Chamberlain (Dec. 1916)
Edwin Montagu (July 1917)
Viscount Peel (Mar. 1922)
Lord Olivier (Jan. 1924)
Earl of Birkenhead (Nov. 1924)

Viscount Peel (Oct. 1928)
Wedgewood Benn (June 1929)
Sir Samuel Hoare (Aug. 1931)
Marquess of Zetland (June 1935)

Secretaries of State for India and Burma (from 1937)

Leo Amery (May 1940)
Lord Pethick-Lawrence (Aug. 1945)

Earl of Listowel (Apr. 1947)
(Office abolished 4 Jan. 1948)

Colonial Secretaries

William Long (Dec. 1916)
Viscount Milner (Jan. 1919)
Winston Churchill (Feb. 1921)
Duke of Devonshire (Oct. 1922)
J. Thomas (Jan. 1924)
Leo Amery (Nov. 1924)
Lord Passfield (June 1929)
J. Thomas (Aug. 1931)
Sir P. Cunliffe-Lister (Nov. 1931)
Malcolm MacDonald (June 1935)
J. Thomas (Nov. 1935)
W. Ormsby-Gore (May 1936)
Malcolm MacDonald (May 1938)
Lord Lloyd (May 1940)

Lord Moyne (Feb. 1941)
Viscount Cranborne (Feb. 1942)
Oliver Stanley (Nov. 1942)
G. Hall (Aug. 1945)
Arthur Creech Jones (Oct. 1946)
James Griffiths (Feb. 1950)
Oliver Lyttelton (Oct. 1951)
A. Lennox-Boyd (July 1954)
Iain Macleod (Oct. 1959)
Reginald Maudling (Oct. 1961)
Duncan Sandys (July 1962)
Anthony Greenwood (Oct. 1964)
Earl of Longford (Dec. 1965)
Frank Lee (Apr. 1966)

(The Colonial Office and the Commonwealth Relations Office merged to form the Commonwealth Office on 1 August 1966. The Colonial Office was abolished in January 1967)

Dominion Secretaries

(Office created 11 June 1925)	Sir T. Inskip (Viscount Caldecote)
Leo Amery (June 1925)	(Jan. 1939)
Lord Passfield (June 1929)	Anthony Eden (Sept. 1939)
J. Thomas (June 1930)	Viscount Caldecote (May 1940)
Malcolm MacDonald (Nov. 1935)	Viscount Cranborne (Oct. 1940)
Lord Stanley (May 1938)	Clement Attlee (Feb. 1942)
Malcolm MacDonald (Oct. 1938)	Viscount Cranborne (Sept. 1943)

(Became Commonwealth Relations Office on 7 July 1945)

Viscount Addison (July 1945)	Viscount Swinton (Nov. 1952)
P. Noel Walker (Oct. 1947)	Earl of Home (Apr. 1955)
Patrick Gordon-Walker (Feb. 1950)	Duncan Sandys (July 1960)
Lord Ismay (Oct. 1951)	Arthur Bottomley (Oct. 1964)
Marquess of Salisbury (Mar. 1952)	

(Merged with the Colonial Office to form the Commonwealth Office on 1 August 1966)

Herbert Bowden (Aug. 1966)	Michael Stewart (Mar. 1968)
George Thomson (Aug. 1967)	

(Merged with the Foreign Office to form the Foreign and Commonwealth Office in October 1968)

Sir Alec Douglas-Home (June 1970)	Sir Geoffrey Howe (June 1983)
James Callaghan (Mar. 1974)	John Major (June 1989)
Anthony Crosland (Apr. 1976)	Douglas Hurd (Oct. 1989)
David Owen (Feb. 1977)	Malcolm Rifkind (July 1995)
Lord Carrington (May 1979)	Robin Cook (May 1997)
Francis Pym (Apr. 1982)	

France

Third Republic

Presidents

Raymond Poincaré (1913–20)	Gaston Doumergue (1924–31)
Paul Deschanel (1920)	Paul Doumer (1931–32)
Alexandre Millerand (1920–24)	Albert Lebrun (1932–40)

Selected Prime Ministers

G. Clemenceau (1917–20)	R. Poincaré (1922–24)
A. Briand (1921–22)	E. Herriot (1924–25)

A. Briand (1925–26)

E. Herriot (1926)

R. Poincaré (1926–28)

A. Briand (1929)

P. Laval (1931–32)

E. Herriot (1932)

E. Daladier (1933)

E. Daladier (1934)

P. Laval (1935–36)

A. Sarraut (1936)

L. Blum (1936–37)

C. Chautemps (1937–38)

L. Blum (March–April 1938)

E. Daladier (1938–40)

P. Reynaud (March–June 1940)

P. Pétain (1940)

End of the Third Republic

On 16 June 1940 President Lebrun appointed Marshall Pétain, a hero of the First World War, as Prime Minister. On 22 June Pétain saw no alternative to concluding an armistice with Germany. The German army was to occupy northern France for the duration of the war (which it was anticipated would continue only until Britain too sued for peace – the British surrender was expected to quickly follow that of France). In the meantime, a French provisional government was set up in the provincial town of Vichy, which was to administer the rest of France.

The key figures in the Vichy administration were Marshal Pétain, who became head of the executive (11 July 1940), Admiral Jean François Darlan (successor-designate to Pétain, and Minister of National and Empire Defence) and Pierre Laval (Prime Minister and Minister for Foreign Affairs).

On 23 June 1940 a French officer, General de Gaulle, declaring that the French government had surrendered before all means of resistance had been exhausted, announced the formation of a Provisional National Committee, 'to defend that part of the French Empire which has not yet been conquered by Germany and to free that part of France still under the yoke of the invader'. De Gaulle's movement was usually known as the 'Free French', although its name was officially changed to 'La France Combattante' ('Fighting France') on 14 July 1942.

On 26 August 1943 the United Nations recognised de Gaulle's Committee of Liberation as the body representing France. Paris was liberated on 23 August 1944. De Gaulle formed a provisional administration which on 13 October 1944 was recognised by the United Nations as the government of France.

Fourth Republic

A Constituent Assembly was elected in October 1945 but its draft constitution was rejected by a national referendum in May 1946. A second Constituent Assembly was elected in June 1946 and its draft constitution was finally approved by a national referendum on 13 October 1946. The new Fourth Republic had a President (indirectly elected) and a two-chamber Legislature, the National Assembly being chosen by direct elections and the Council of the Republic by indirect elections. The President had strictly limited powers.

General de Gaulle had resigned office in January 1946. The Fourth Republic was never stable. Most ministries were coalitions and between the liberation of Paris and the end of the Fourth Republic in September 1958, there were 26 cabinets with an average life of just over five months.

Presidents

Vincent Auriol (1947–53)   René Coty (1953–59)

Prime Ministers

F. Gouin (1946)	R. Pleven (1951–52)
G. Bidault (1946)	E. Fauré (1952)
L. Blum (1946–47)	A. Pinay (1952–53)
P. Ramadier (1947)	R. Mayer (1953)
R. Schuman (1947–48)	J. Laniel (1953–54)
A. Marie (1948)	P. Mendès-France (1954–55)
R. Schuman (1948)	E. Fauré (1955–56)
H. Queuille (1948–49)	G. Mollet (1956–57)
G. Bidault (1949–50)	M. Bourges-Manoury (1957)
H. Queuille (1950)	F. Gaillard (1957–58)
R. Pleven (1950–51)	P. Pflimin (1958)
H. Queuille (1951)	C. de Gaulle (1958)

Fifth Republic

The Fourth Republic fell, partly as a result of its inherent weaknesses in domestic affairs, partly as the result of insurrections in Algeria and Corsica. The loyalty of the armed forces could no longer be relied upon and in May 1958 President Coty invited General de Gaulle to take office as Prime Minister with powers to govern by decree for six months, during which time a new constitution would be drawn up and submitted to a national referendum.

The constitution of the Fifth Republic was ratified by a national referendum on 28 September 1958. The referendum was held in France's overseas departments and territories as well as in metropolitan France. The constitution came into force on 4 October 1958. The office of President was greatly strengthened, especially against the Parliament, which now consisted of the National Assembly and a Senate. On 21 December 1958 General de Gaulle was elected President by an overwhelming majority.

Presidents

General Charles de Gaulle (1959–69)
Georges Pompidou (1969–74)
Valéry Giscard d'Éstaing (1974–81)

François Mitterand (1981–95)
Jacques Chirac (1995–)

Prime Ministers

M. Debré (1959–62)
G. Pompidou (1962–68)
M. Couve de Murville (1968–69)
J. Chaban-Delmas (1969–72)
P. Messmer (1972–74)
J. Chirac (1974–76)
R. Barré (1976–81)
P. Mauroy (1981–84)

L. Fabius (1984–86)
J. Chirac (1986–88)
M. Rocard (1988–91)
E. Cresson (1991–92)
P. Bérégovey (1992)
E. Balladur (1993–95)
A. Juppé (1995–97)

The Netherlands

The Netherlands were overrun by the Germans in May 1940. Queen Wilhemina escaped to London and a government in exile was set up. The Netherlands were not finally liberated until May 1945. The government then returned to The Hague.

Heads of State

Queen Wilhelmina (1890–1948)
Queen Juliana (1948–80)

Queen Beatrix (1980–)

Prime Ministers

R. de Beerenbrouck (1918–25)
H. Colijn (1925–26)
D. de Geer (1926–29)
R. de Beerenbrouck (1929–33)
H. Colijn (1933–39)
D. de Geer (1939–40)
P. Gerbrandy (1941–45)
W. Schermerhorn (1945–46)
L. Beel (1946–48)
W. Drees (1948–58)
L. Beel (1958–59)

J. de Quay (1959–63)
V. Marijnen (1963–65)
J. Cals (1965–66)
J. Zijlstra (1966–67)
P. de Jong (1967–71)
B. Biesheuvel (1971–73)
J. den Uyl (1973–77)
A. van Agt (1977–82)
R. Lubbers (1982–94)
W. Kok (1994–)

Portugal

Presidents

A. Carmona (1926–51)
A. Salazar (1951)
F. Lopez (1951–58)
A. Tomás (1958–74)
A. de Spinola (1974)

F. Gomes (1974–76)
A. Eanes (1976–86)
M. Soares (1986–96)
J. Sampãio (1996–)

Prime Ministers

A. Salazar (1932–68)
M. Caetano (1968–74)
A. Carlos (1974)
V. Gonçalves (1974–75)
P. de Azevedo (1975–76)
M. Soares (1976–78)
N. da Costa (1978)
C. Pinto (1978–79)

M. Pintassilgo (1979)
F. Carneiro (1979–80)
D. do Amarel (1980)
P. Balsemao (1980–82)
M. Soares (1983–85)
A. Silva (1985–95)
A. Guterres (1995–)

Spain

Heads of State

General F. Franco Bahamonde (1939–75)
King Juan Carlos I (1975–)

Prime Ministers

General F. Franco Bahamonde
    (1939–73)
Adm L. Carrero Blanco (1973–74)
C. Arias Navarro (1974–75)

A. Suarez Gonzalez (1975–81)
L. Calvo Sotelo (1981–82)
F. González Márquez (1982–96)
J.M.A. Lopez (1996–)

Belgium

Heads of State

King Albert I (1909–34)   King Leopold III (1934–51)
(Leopold remained in Belgium during the German occupation and was
unacceptable to the Belgian people after the Liberation.)
Regent Prince Charles (1944–50)   King Albert II (1993–)
King Baudouin (1951–93)

Prime Ministers

P. Spaak (1938–39)
H. Pierlot (1939–45)
A. van Acker (1945–46)
P-H. Spaak (1946)
A. van Acker (1946)
C. Huysman (1946–47)
P-H. Spaak (1947–49)
G. Eyskens (1949–50)
J. Duvieusart (1950)
J. Pholien (1950–52)
J. van Houte (1952–54)
A. van Acker (1954–58)

G. Eyskens (1958–61)
T. Lefevre (1961–65)
P. Harmel (1965–66)
P. Vanden Boeynants (1966–68)
G. Eyskens (1968–72)
E. Leburton (1973–74)
L. Tindemans (1974–78)
P. Vanden Boeynants (1978)
W. Martens (1979–81)
M. Eyskens (1981)
W. Martens (1981–92)
J-L. Dehaene (1992–)

SECTION THREE

The Chronology of Decolonisation

1 Changing Perceptions of Empire

In the late nineteenth century thinking had been influenced by Social Darwinian theories and by the perception that most of the world was falling under the rule of a handful of technologically advanced nations. It was expected that the whole world would remain under their rule for the foreseeable future. Hopefully, that rule would be benevolent and prepare the 'backward' races of the world for self-government at some, more or less remote, date in the future.

The First World War began to raise questions. Europe, supposedly the most advanced civilisation, had seriously damaged both its material prosperity and its moral authority by falling into a devastating 'total' war. The war became an ideological one in which the belligerents, particularly Britain and France, bid for the support of neutral America and its high-principled President, Woodrow Wilson, by formulating war aims based on international justice and progress. Wilson himself codified these as his Fourteen Points and Four Principles. The latter included self-determination. The Allies meant this to apply to the successor states of the Austro-Hungarian empire and, eventually, the successor states of the Ottoman empire. They did not mean it to apply to their own empires, but their colonial subjects saw no reason why it should not. Representatives of the Indian National Congress, the [South] African National Congress and individuals like Ho Chi Minh of Indo-China went to Paris to lobby the statesmen at the Peace Conference in 1919. Dr W.E.B. Dubois and Blaise Diagne organised a meeting of the Pan-African Conference there. They met with, at best, polite platitudes.

Nevertheless, attitudes were changing. The League of Nations Mandate System imposed specific obligations on Mandatory Powers. The acquisition of new colonies was now unacceptable. The Japanese intervention in Manchuria in 1931 and the Italian invasion of Abyssinia in 1935 would have been regarded as unexceptional in the nineteenth century. Both were condemned, although not effectively prevented, by the League of Nations in the 1930s.

During the inter-war period both Britain and France began to plan the future of their empires. Their plans differed widely in accordance with their different concepts of empire. The French looked forward to continued centralisation but greater equality. The British anticipated greater devolution and assumption of responsibility for local affairs.

The Second World war provided the catalyst for much more rapid change than had been envisaged in the inter-war period. Italy, as a defeated Power, lost her empire in circumstances similar to those in which Germany had forfeited hers at the end of the First World war. Despite being on the winning side in 1945, both Britain and France had been greatly weakened by the war. France, like Belgium and the Netherlands, had suffered humiliating defeat and occupation by the Germans in 1940. Britain, although never defeated, had experienced severe military reverses and had emerged with a devastated economy and heavily dependent on assistance from the United States, which was historically unsympathetic to the whole concept of the British empire. Spain and Portugal, both authoritarian Powers at this time, had remained neutral during the war and were slow to see the need to initiate any changes in their empires.

The war had been a global one and colonies had been involved at many different levels. Some had been occupied by the enemy. Some had provided troops, who saw something of the world and were inclined to demand their rights on their return home. At the same time educated elites were emerging in many colonies, who would demand swift progress to independence, often in conflict with traditional forces in their own societies, as well as with the colonising Power.

2 The British Empire

The British empire, the largest of the European empires, dissolved more peacefully than most. In very few places were there battles between colonised and colonisers (Kenya and Cyprus were two exceptions) and the end of empire had a minimal effect on the course of politics at home.

Britain had lost her first empire when she accepted the independence of the United States in 1783 and the British always retained a sense that empires were temporary. Colonies would 'grow to maturity' and seek independence. If the process was well managed they would remain trading partners and potential allies. Decolonisation was, therefore, about the management of the process. From the time of Edmund Burke (1729–97), the British had formulated high ideals of 'trusteeship', which alone justified holding an empire. Britain seldom lived up to those ideals but they provided a framework of reference. Even in the heyday of jingoistic imperialism in the late nineteenth century, they were repeated in the much-misunderstood poetry of Rudyard Kipling.

The Structure of the British Empire

In the colonies of settlement, such as those of North America, British emigrants believed that they took their rights as Englishmen with them. These included the right not to be deprived of their property, even for purposes of taxation, without their own consent. This necessitated the setting up of some kind of representative system, which became the distinctive hallmark of British colonies, from a very early date. Over time these representative assemblies acquired legislative powers and eventually the power to control the executive in the colony (known in the British system as 'responsible government'). From more or less complete control of domestic legislation, they progressed after the First World War to control of foreign policy as well. Canada generally pioneered the way, closely followed by Australia, New Zealand and South Africa (regarded until after the Second World War as essentially a white colony of settlement like the others). The stage of near-total independence but retaining links, sentimental and otherwise, with Britain was known as 'Dominion status' (defined by the Balfour Report on Inter-imperial Relations of 1926 and the Statute of Westminster of 1931). It was the status to which India aspired between the Wars and many African colonies in the years immediately after the Second World War. Between the wars Britain and the Dominions collectively made up the Commonwealth, as distinct from the 'dependent empire'. The 'dependent empire' (India was a special case) was generally made up of Crown Colonies and Protectorates but by the Second World War these were in very different states of constitutional evolution.

Crown Colonies

In a classical example, power would initially be invested entirely in the Governor, appointed from London, but he would normally be assisted by an Executive Council, made up of officials. As the colony evolved, a Legislative Council would usually be created to assist in preparing legislation. The Legislative Council might be made up entirely of officials but it usually also included nominated or elected members. The latter could be elected by direct or indirect methods and, at least at first, often represented defined interest groups. British colonial constitutions were, virtually without exception, 'colour blind', that is the right to vote or sit as a representative did not depend on an individual's race, but property (or less often educational) qualifications were drafted in such a way as to give a heavy weighting in favour of Europeans.

As in the colonies of settlement, these Legislative Councils (or Assemblies) evolved into miniature Parliaments and the constitutional maturity of a colony can often be judged by the proportions of official, 'non-official' nominated and 'non-official' elected members.

The British government defended its right to choose the members of the Executive Council more jealously than those of the Legislative Council. Although Executive Councils would in most cases evolve into Ministries or Cabinets, few non-officials and few non-Europeans had been admitted to them before the Second World War in most colonies.

Protectorates

Although the position of a Protectorate was different in international law from that of a Crown Colony, in practice its administration often differed little. In theory, in a Protectorate (or Protected State) the Protecting Power controlled foreign relations, and usually defence and trade, but left the indigenous authorities to control the domestic administration. In practice European powers tended to intervene when they chose, but in the British case this was tempered by their liking for 'Indirect Rule'.

Indirect Rule

This went back ideologically to Edmund Burke's believe in the organic nature of society and the foolishness of believing that it could be changed according to theories and blueprints. Britain had no right to interfere with the Indian way of doing things. The Indians knew what suited them best. The British were never great centralisers. Even in the United Kingdom the Scots kept their own legal system. The 'man on the spot' was likely to know best. The British happily devolved authority. Lord Lugard perfected the idea of 'Indirect Rule', first in East Africa and then in Nigeria, relying heavily on African (usually traditional) authorities. Devolution made the transfer of power easier but, because of its dependence on traditional authorities, did not always provide the best training for independence.

Asia

India

India was the prototype for the evolution of the rest of the British empire, as Canada had been for the colonies of settlement.

1858   (2 August) Government of India Act. Jurisdiction over 'British India' (the Presidencies of Bengal, Madras and Bombay) passed from the dual government of the East India Company and the British Crown, wholly to that of the British Crown. All Indians within British India became 'subjects' of Queen Victoria. About half of India remained under the rule of the 'Native Princes', assisted (and sometimes coerced) by British 'Advisers'.

(1 November) Queen Victoria's Proclamation. This promised 'so far as may be, our subjects, of whatever race or creed, [shall] be freely and impartially admitted to offices in our service, the duties of which they may be qualified, by their education, ability, and integrity, duly to discharge ... and ... in framing and administering the law, due regard [shall] be paid to the ancient rights, usages, and customs of India'.[1] This equality remained the ideal, but in reality it was habitually broken in favour of the Europeans.

1885   (December) The Indian National Congress held its first meeting in Bombay. It was initially a very moderate body, made up almost

[1] C.H. Philips, *Select Documents on the History of India and Pakistan* Vol. 4, 1962, p. 11.

entirely of professional men, lawyers, teachers and journalists. Because they represented the western-educated classes, the differential up-take of that education by Hindus and Muslims meant that Muslims, who made up rather more than one-fifth of the population of India, were always under-represented in the Congress.

1899–1905 Viceroyalty of Lord Curzon. Curzon's authoritarian style of government acted as a catalyst. The Congress began to divide between the 'Moderates', exemplified by G.K. Gokhale, who had absorbed and largely adopted western-style liberalism, and the 'Extremists', led by B.G. Tilak, who wished to reaffirm traditional Hindu values (even including child marriage and opposition to small-pox vaccination) and were prepared to resort to political violence.

1906 (30 December) Foundation of the Muslim League. Muslims from all over India, nervous of being dominated by the majority Hindu community, met in Dacca to found a political association which, while professing goodwill towards all men, would defend their interests.

1909 (25 May) Indian Councils Act (popularly known as the Morley–Minto Reforms, from John Morley, the Secretary of State for India, and Lord Minto, the Viceroy). This built on the earlier Indian Councils Acts of 1861 and 1891 to introduce a small measure of representative government into India. This added some elected members to the Legislative Councils (previously composed entirely of nominated members) of various Provinces. Morley had reluctantly agreed to Muslim demands that they should have separate electorates lest they be always outvoted by the Hindus.

1917 (20 August) Montagu Declaration. Many Indians had been pleased by the 1909 reforms and by the visit of King George V and Queen Mary in 1911. Relations improved and India supported Britain in the First World War. Indian troops served in several theatres, including France. The Secretary of State for India, Edwin Montagu, promised 'the increasing association of Indians in every branch of the administration and the gradual development of self-governing institutions with a view to the progressive realisation of responsible government in India as an integral part of the British Empire'. Politically active Indians interpreted this to mean speedy progress to Dominion status after the war. They underestimated the potential for delay in a later sentence, 'The British Government and the [British-controlled] Government of India, on whom the responsibility lies for the welfare and advancement of the Indian peoples, must be the judges of the time and measure of each advance'.[2]

1919   (February) Rowlatt Bills. These measures, named after the legal member of the Viceroy's Executive Council, were intended to replace the Defence of India Act, which lapsed at the end of the war. They were rather draconian measures to repress disorder. Although they were never enforced, their passage aroused suspicions.

(10 April) Amritsar massacre. This was even more fatal to understanding. There had been disorder in the Punjab and some isolated attacks on Europeans. The British commander, General Dyer, forbade public gatherings. Nevertheless, a crowd assembled in the Jallianwala Bagh in Amritsar. On Dyer's orders, troops opened fire. At least 379 people died. Dyer was condemned by an Anglo-India committee of enquiry, presided over by a Scottish judge, Lord Hunter, for not giving sufficient warning and continuing to fire for too long. The fact that some sections of the British public defended Dyer further alienated Indian opinion. The Indian National Congress held its own enquiry and condemned Dyer unreservedly.

(23 December) Government of India Act (sometimes called the Montagu–Chelmsford Reforms, Lord Chelmsford being the Viceroy). The central government was to consist of the Viceroy (Governor-General) and two chambers, the Council of State and the Legislative Assembly. Although 100 of the 140 members of the Legislative Assembly were to be elected, the franchise remained narrow and executive authority remained in the Viceroy's hands. At the provincial level, in the eight 'Governor's' Provinces, at least 70 per cent of each Legislative Council was to be elected.

Matters dealt with by the Provincial Governments were divided into two categories. 'Transferred subjects', such as education, public health, public works, and some aspects of agriculture and industrial development, became the responsibility of the provincial legislature. 'Reserved subjects', such as the police, justice,

---

[2] Philips, *Select Documents*, pp. 264–5.

famine relief, irrigation and the land revenue administration, were reserved for the Governor. This division became known as 'Dyarchy'. Indian nationalists were bitterly disappointed by the Act.

1919–39 The emergence of new leaders – M.K. Gandhi and J. Nehru. Gokhale died in 1915 and Tilak in 1920. Neither Gandhi nor Nehru was originally anti-British. Both were affected by the Amritsar massacre. In 1919 Gandhi began to organise a civil disobedience campaign – *satyagraha* – against the Rowlatt measures. It was Gandhi who transformed the Congress into a mass movement and from Gandhi the aristocratic Nehru learned how to lead the Indian masses.

1920 (December) Indian National Congress meeting at Nagpur. Some 14,000 delegates attended and its social composition had changed. An alarmed official wrote that it had been swamped by 'a mass of semi-educated persons swept up from all parts of India'.[3] The whole organisation was overhauled and the 300 members of the All-India Congress Committee became the effective steering group. The meeting adopted Gandhi's resolution, 'The object of the Indian National Congress is the attainment of *Swarajya* [self-government] by the people of India by all legitimate and peaceful means'.[4]

1922 (18 March) Gandhi imprisoned. After Gandhi's latest non-cooperation campaign had degenerated into serious violence, culminating in the murder of 22 Indian police constables at Chauri Chauri in the United Provinces, he was arrested and sentenced to six years in gaol (of which he actually served two). The trial saw a remarkable exchange between accused and judge. Gandhi said, 'I am here . . . to invite and submit cheerfully to the highest penalty that can be inflicted upon me for what in law is a deliberate crime and what appears to me to be the highest duty of a citizen'. The judge, Mr C.N. Broomfield, replied, 'It would be impossible to ignore the fact that, in the eyes of millions of your countrymen, you are a great patriot and leader. Even those who differ from you in politics look upon you as a man of high ideals and of noble and even saintly life. I have to

---

[3] Quoted J. Brown, *Gandhi's Rise to Power: Indian Politics, 1915–1922*, 1972, p. 293.
[4] Philips, *Select Documents*, p. 216.

deal with you in one character only [that of law-breaker] ... I do not presume to judge or criticise you in any other character.'[5]

1927–29 Simon Commission. The 1919 Government of India Act was due to be reviewed after ten years and a Commission of British MPs (including the future Prime Minister, Clement Attlee) was appointed under the chairmanship of Sir John Simon. The Commission recommended that Dyarchy should be ended in the Provinces and all subjects (apart from some emergency powers) transferred to the Indian ministers. The franchise should be widened and communal electorates phased out, although they would be retained for the time being, partly to give representation to the Untouchables. The Commission recognised that future developments must allow for the reunion of British India and the Princely States, and proposed the beginning of a federal system, with a Federal Assembly composed of representatives elected on the basis of population from both British India and the Princely States.

1929 (31 October) Irwin Declaration. The Viceroy, Lord Irwin, issued a statement, with the full support of the new Labour government in London, that the 'natural issue' of India's progress was Dominion status and that a round table conference of British and Indian representatives should meet to work out the way forward. This was meant as an answer to Indian anger that no Indian had sat on the Simon Commission.

1930 (March–April) Gandhi's march to Dandi. In the meantime Gandhi had been organising his campaign from his *ashram* at Ahmedabad, living a simple life, advocating *swadeshi* (boycotting foreign goods, but see Glossary for full definition) and *khadi* (the wearing of home-spun and -woven cloth), and fighting for the rights of the Untouchables. He led a 240-mile march to Dandi on the coast to pick up untaxed, and therefore illegal, sea salt.

1930–32 Round Table Conferences. These met in three sessions but their authority was undermined by the fact that only at the second session in 1931 were all the main Indian leaders there together, and by the fundamental divergences of view between the Indian National Congress and other groupings. The Congress

---

[5] Philips, *Select Documents*, pp. 223–4.

claimed to speak for the whole of India and protested that the British recognition of other groups was a crude attempt to divide and rule. The Congress position was not accepted by the Muslim League, now led by M.A. Jinnah, who had left the Congress in 1920 and who insisted that the Congress was a Hindu organisation and that the Muslims had the right to speak for themselves. It was also not accepted by the Untouchables, led by Dr Ambedkar, who protested that the Congress spoke only for the caste Hindus. Both the Muslims and the Untouchables demanded the continuation of communal electorates.

1935   (2 August) Government of India Act. Because of the failure of the Round Table Conferences to produce a firm agreement, the Bill was drawn up by the India Office in London, where Sir Samuel Hoare was now Secretary of State. Its passage into legislation was deliberately delayed by its opponents, Lord Salisbury in the House of Lords and Winston Churchill in the Commons. The franchise was widened but communal electorates retained. Dyarchy was abolished in the Provinces. In each of the (now eleven) Provinces, the ministries were to be wholly responsible to the elected legislatures (although the Governor retained some emergency powers). There was now to be Dyarchy at the centre with most subjects being transferred, but foreign policy and defence reserved. The worst stumbling block continued to be the attempt to secure a federal solution since there was little trust between the Congress and the Princes. It was provided that the clauses relating to the central government should not become operative until 50 per cent of the Princes had accepted it. They had not done so when the Second World War broke out and important parts of the 1935 Act never came into force.

1937   Provincial elections. These went ahead and the Congress won absolute majorities in Madras, the United Provinces, Bihar, the Central Provinces and Orissa, and a near-absolute majority in Bombay. It was the strongest party in Assam and the North-West Frontier Provinces. But in Bengal it polled only 24 per cent; in Sind, 13 per cent; and in the Punjab, 10 per cent. The latter three had large Muslim populations. But, overall, the elections confirmed the Congress in its belief that it spoke for the whole of India. The Muslim League was very disappointed by its performance and was initially anxious to seek a reconciliation with the Congress. The Congress was unresponsive and the final breakdown of relations, which led to partition in 1947, can probably be dated from this point. The Congress had originally intended to contest the elections to show its strength and then refuse to take any further part in government, but the magnitude of its victory and the possibility of achieving real reforms persuaded it to take office in seven Provinces.

1939   (3 September) Outbreak of Second World War. Indian leaders expressed anger that Britain had taken them into the war without their consent. The Congress ministries in the Provinces resigned the following month.

(10 October) All-India Congress Committee Resolution. 'India must be declared an independent nation, and present application must be given to this status to the largest possible extent.' India's future constitution must be determined by an Indian constituent assembly.

1940   (24 March) Resolution of the Muslim League at Lahore. The Muslim League rejected the scheme for federation embodied in the 1935 Government of India Act and demanded the setting up of 'independent states' in those north-western and north-eastern parts of India where there was a Muslim majority.[6]

(8 August) British concessions. The Viceroy, Lord Linlithgow, invited a number of Indians to join his Executive Council and promised the establishment of a constitution-making body after the war. Congress rejected this as inadequate and launched a new civil disobedience campaign. Although by 1941 the Executive Council had an 8:3 Indian majority, the Indians on the Council did not represent the political parties and Congress was still dissatisfied. Matters were further complicated by Muslim demands for equal representation on the Council.

1941   (8 December) Japan entered the Second World War.

1942   (4 February) Fall of Singapore.

(30 March) The Cripps Offer. Sir Stafford Cripps, a staunchly left-wing politician, known for his sympathy with the cause of Indian independence, was sent to India to propose a compromise. He offered more Indian participation in the government immediately. More important were the promises for the future. As soon as the war ended the Indians should elect a constituent assembly and Britain would undertake to accept its conclusions,

[6] Philips, *Select Documents*, pp. 354–5.

even if they included secession from the Commonwealth. But Cripps was compelled to insist on guarantees for racial and religious minorities and, more particularly, that each Province should be free to decide whether or not to join the Indian Union. Negotiations went on for seventeen days but broke down in the end. Communal problems were still the main difficulty. Congress feared that the Muslims might take the Punjab, or even Bengal, out of the Union, even though those states had large Hindu minorities. Instead Congress demanded an immediate transfer of power to a cabinet, nominated by the political parties. Cripps replied that this would be unrepresentative and repeated that constitutional reform must await the end of the war. This remained the British position until 1945.

(20 May) The Japanese arrived on the frontiers of India. Although the fall of Singapore was arguably the greatest blow of the war to British prestige, Indians generally showed no inclination to ally themselves with Japan. Only a few joined the Japanese-inspired National Liberation Army. But the Indian political leaders were stiffened in their resolve to reject what they regarded as inadequate British offers.

(8 August) 'Quit India' resolution. The All-India Congress Committee demanded that the British should withdraw from India immediately. A provisional government would be formed by agreement between the political parties. India would join the United Nations and continue the struggle against the Axis Powers. This government would 'evolve a scheme' for a constituent assembly, which would draw up a constitution. Congress believed that this constitution should be a federal one but with 'the largest measure of autonomy' for the federating units. If this was rejected, they would sanction 'the starting of a mass struggle on non-violent lines on the widest possible scale' and ask Gandhi to lead it.[7]

(9 August) Arrest of Congress leaders, including Gandhi. The All-India Congress Committee was declared disbanded. Some sporadic acts of rebellion followed but not the mass struggle promised by the Congress resolution. Although the Muslim League also rejected the Cripps offer, its tone was softer and it continued to cooperate with the British, while it consolidated its hold on its heartland. Muslim ministries were formed in Assam, Sind, Bengal and the North-West Frontier Province.

---

[7] Philips, *Select Documents*, p. 342.

1944   (September) Negotiations between Jinnah and Gandhi. Gandhi insisted that India was indivisible but offered practical concessions. Plebiscites should be held in Muslim areas in the northwest and north-east. If the vote went in favour, they should become autonomous, although still linked to India for purposes of foreign policy, defence and trade. Jinnah was not now prepared to accept anything less than independence for six Provinces, including Bengal.

1945   (May–July) End of the war in Europe and the election of a Labour government in Britain. The Labour Party, led by Clement Attlee, had long sympathised with the Indian desire for independence but was still concerned about safeguarding the rights of minority communities. Britain was no longer fighting for her life but her economy was wrecked and she was heavily dependent on the support of the United States, which had little sympathy for the British position in India.

(June) Simla Conference. The Viceroy, Lord Wavell, on whose initiative the conference had been called, presided over the meeting of the leaders of Congress and the League (including Gandhi, Nehru and Jinnah), representatives of the Untouchables (now officially called the 'Scheduled Castes') and various other politicians, including the premiers, or ex-premiers, of the Provinces. The Conference again ran aground on the differences between the Congress and the League.

1946   (May) Cabinet Mission. Three cabinet ministers, Lord Pethick Lawrence (the Secretary of State for India), A.V. Alexander (First Lord of the Admiralty) and Sir Stafford Cripps, were sent out to seek an agreed basis for negotiations with the Indian leaders. Part of their task was to convince the Indians that Britain's withdrawal was now imminent. They met with Congress and League leaders, first in New Delhi and then in Simla.

They reported[8] that they had seriously considered the possibility of partition because they understood Muslim anxiety but they concluded that the 'setting up of a sovereign state of Pakistan on the lines claimed by the Muslim League would not solve the communal minority problem'. The population of the northwest and the north-east would be approximately 40 per cent non-Muslim and 20 million Muslims would remain dispersed throughout the rest of India. A smaller Pakistan, confined to

---

[8] *India, Statement by the Cabinet Mission and His Excellency, the Viceroy,* Cmd 6821, 1946.

the Muslim-majority areas, also seemed impractical and the Mission declared itself opposed to the partition of the Punjab or Bengal, which would be contrary to the wishes of a large proportion of their inhabitants. Partition would also be unworkable from the point of view of defence, administration and the economy; the transport, telegraph and postal systems had all been established on the basis of a united India. The Princely States would find it difficult to associate themselves with a divided India. 'Finally . . . the two halves of the proposed Pakistan are separated by 700 miles and the communication between them both in war and peace would be dependent on the goodwill of Hindustan (India without Pakistan).'

Instead they proposed a form of federation:

(i) There should be a Union of India, embracing both British India and the States, which should deal with the following subjects: foreign affairs, defence, and communications; and should have the powers necessary to raise the finances required for the above subjects.

(ii) The Union should have an executive and a legislature . . . [Any question 'raising a major communal issue' was subject to a complex voting procedure.]

(iii) All subjects other than the Union subjects and all residuary powers should be vested in the Provinces.

(iv) Provinces should be free to form groups with executives and legislatures, and each group should determine the provincial subjects to be taken in common.

Provision was made for any Province to ask for a revision of the constitution after ten years. Briefly, it looked as if agreement could be reached but the Congress leaders took fright at the fourth proposal, which they feared would allow the establishment of Pakistan by another route. Jinnah then also withdrew his consent.

(8 August) Congress leaders accepted Wavell's invitation to join an interim government, to which representatives of the Muslim League were added in September.

(16 August) Direct Action Day. Jinnah declared 16 August 'Direct Action Day'. He insisted subsequently that he intended only rallies and demonstrations to show the support the League enjoyed, but demonstrations slid into violence in Bengal. Some 4,000 people died, mainly in Calcutta.

(9 December) Constituent Assembly (elected on the old franchise because it was thought that it would take too long to bring

in a new one) met. Muslims refused to take their seats. Nehru said Congress would withdraw from government unless the Muslim League ministers were dismissed. Wavell told Attlee that Britain must either resign herself to staying and administering India for another fifteen years or name a firm date for withdrawal and, if necessary, transfer power to the only functioning authorities, the Provinces. Attlee rejected this advice and resolved to replace Wavell by Lord Mountbatten, who had the prestige of having been the Allied Commander-in-Chief in South East Asia in the last stages of the war. (Mountbatten later gave him similar advice.)

1947   (20 February) Attlee announced in the Commons that the British would definitely leave India by June 1948.

(23 March) Mountbatten succeeded Wavell as Viceroy.

(20 April) Nehru said publicly, 'The Muslim League can have Pakistan . . . but on condition they do not take away other parts of India [primarily West Bengal and East Punjab], which do not wish to join Pakistan'.[9]

(2 May) Mountbatten sent his plan for the transfer of power to London. Power would be transferred to the Constituent Assembly in respect of Madras, Bombay, Orissa, the United Provinces, the Central Provinces and Bihar, which would form the Indian Union. Assam, Bengal, Punjab, Sind, Baluchistan and the North West Frontier Province would have the choice of joining the Indian Union or of forming one or more independent states. The non-Muslims of Bengal and the Punjab would have the additional option of demanding a partition so that the Hindu-majority areas could join the Indian Union.

(10 May) Nehru expressed his disapproval of Mountbatten's plan.

(11 May) V.P. Menon suggested amendments which would reduce the number of possible states to two, India and Pakistan. This Nehru accepted.

(18–31 May) Mountbatten discussed the amended plan with the British government in London.

(2 June) Representatives of Congress, the League and the Sikhs met in Delhi and accepted the amended partition plan.

(3 June) Attlee announced the plan in the Commons. Mountbatten announced that the withdrawal date would be brought forward to August 1947.

---

[9] Quoted in V.P. Menon, *The Transfer of Power in India*, 1957, p. 354.

(20–23 June) The Legislative Assemblies of Bengal and Punjab opted for partition.

(26 June–17 July) Sind, Baluchistan, Sylhet and the North West Frontier Province opted to join Pakistan.

(4 July) Attlee introduced the Indian Independence Bill into the Commons.

(18 July) The measure received the Royal Assent. The Act provided that two independent Dominions (the term was still used) should be set up to be known as India and Pakistan respectively. Pakistan was to include East Bengal, West Punjab, Sind, Baluchistan and the North West Frontier Province. The rest of 'British' India was to constitute the Dominion of India. The lines of demarcation in Bengal and the Punjab were to be drawn up by Boundary Commissions, appointed by the Governor-General (the title to which the Viceroy had now reverted). The position of the Princely States was still unclear.

(25 July) Conference of the Princes. Mountbatten presided but all the preliminary work had been carried out by the Congress, primarily by V.P. Menon. Only three Princely States had not signed the Instrument of Accession to India by 15 August. The three exceptions were Hyderabad, Junagadh and Kashmir. In the first two, the population was over 80 per cent Hindu but the rulers were Muslims. The Nawab of Junagadh tried to affiliate his state to Pakistan but was overthrown. The Nyzam of Hyderabad tried to remain independent but the state was occupied by the Indian army in September 1948. In Kashmir, 80 per cent of the population was Muslim but the ruler was Hindu. Kashmir was the occasion for several subsequent wars between India and Pakistan.

(13 August) Radcliffe Award completed. The task of determining the boundaries had been entrusted to Sir Cyril Radcliffe. Two commissions (each consisting of two Hindus and two Muslims) were appointed to demarcate the boundaries in Bengal and the Punjab respectively. They failed to agree and Radcliffe made the final decision himself. Knowing that it would dissatisfy both sides and not wishing to mar the celebrations of 14/15 August, Mountbatten did not announce the details until 17 August.

(14 August) The Dominion of Pakistan was inaugurated in Mountbatten's presence in Karachi. Jinnah became Governor-General. Liaquat Ali Khan became Prime Minister.

(midnight 14/15 August) The Dominion of India was inaugurated in Mountbatten's presence in Delhi. Nehru uttered the historic words, 'Long years ago we made a tryst with destiny, and now the time comes when we shall redeem our pledge, not wholly or in full measure, but substantially. At the stroke of the midnight hour, when the world sleeps, India will awake to life and freedom.'[10] The British Raj came to an end. Mountbatten was sworn in as the first Governor-General of the new Dominion. Nehru became Prime Minister.

Events after independence

1947   (autumn) Serious disorders followed independence, mainly in Bengal and the Punjab. Up to 250,000 people died. About one million non-Muslims fled from Pakistan and a comparable number of Muslims fled to Pakistan. The violence was compounded by natural disasters, including floods. The Sikhs began to demand a separate state.

1948   (30 January) Mahatma Gandhi, who had tried to conciliate the two sides, was assassinated by a Hindu fanatic.
First Indo-Pakistan war arising from clashes in Kashmir. The United Nations established a truce line, leaving approximately one-third of Kashmir in the possession of Pakistan.

1950   India and Pakistan both opted to become republics. Changes in the definition of the role of the Crown at the 1950 Commonwealth Conference enabled them to remain members of the Commonwealth.

1961   (December) Indian forces occupied Goa (still a Portuguese colony). Subsequently declared to be Indian territory.

1971   Establishment of Bangladesh. On 26 March, Sheikh Mujibur Rahman, leader of the Awami League which had won the elections, proclaimed East Pakistan an independent republic under the name of Bangladesh. The revolt was initially put down by West Pakistani forces but India became involved as the result of the influx of refugees as guerrilla war continued. On 3 December the Pakistani air force launched a surprise attack on Indian airfields. On 4 December Indian troops invaded East Pakistan. Pakistani forces in East Pakistan surrendered on 16 December and Pakistan recognised the existence of Bangladesh.

[10] J. Nehru, *Independence and After* (Delhi, 1949), pp. 3–4.

1972   Pakistan left the Commonwealth. Bangladesh admitted.

1989   Pakistan rejoined the Commonwealth.

Burma

Burma was always regarded as an outwork of the British empire in India. Already a fragmented country, with rival groups contending for power, it was conquered in three wars, those of 1824–26, 1852 and 1885. Sporadic resistance continued throughout the British period. Until 1937 it was governed as a province of British India. Apart from its strategic importance when the French established themselves in Indo-China, it was an important source of food, mainly rice, for India. The Japanese conquest of Burma caused a great famine in Bengal in 1944.

1937   Burma was given responsible government in domestic matters. The Governor still had 'reserved' powers over defence and foreign policy. The Lower House was all elected, although there was now a Senate, half of whose members were nominated. Burmese held all government portfolios and officials ceased to sit in Parliament.

1937–42   Burmese ministries were formed, although politics were confused, with many competing parties.

1941–44   Second World War. Unlike Indian political leaders, some Burmese politicians were inclined to make common cause with the Japanese against the British. In 1941 '30 comrades', including the future leader, Aung San, left to receive military training from the Japanese. Aung San founded the Burma National Army and fought with the Japanese in 1942.

1943   (August) Japan declared Burma to be an independent country. Ba Maw, who had been Prime Minister, 1937–39, became head of state.

1944   Aung San made secret overtures to the British. He considered himself a Burmese patriot and was prepared to play each side off against the other.

1945   (March) Aung San assisted General Slim in the re-capture of Rangoon.

1945–46   Ba Maw fled to Japan but returned to active participation in Burmese politics the next year.

1945   Britain agreeable to Burmese independence. If Britain was leaving India, there was no point in retaining Burma. The Attlee government promised a Constituent Assembly, and complete independence for Burma by 1949 at the latest.

1946   (September) Aung San became Prime Minister, as leader of an all-party Anti-Fascist People's Freedom League.

1947   (January) Aung San visited London and reached agreement with Attlee.
  (April) Aung San won big election victory.
  (19 July) Aung San and 6 other cabinet ministers were assassinated by a political rival. (The perpetrator, Saw, was tried and executed in May 1948.) Aung San was succeeded by his former foreign secretary, Thakin Nu.
  (17 October) Anglo-Burmese Treaty signed in London.

1948   (4 January) Union of Burma came into existence. Unusually for an ex-British colony, Burma opted not to join the Commonwealth.

Ceylon (Sri Lanka)

Britain acquired the Dutch bases in Ceylon during the Napoleonic Wars, when Holland was a satellite of France. She retained them at the end of the war in 1814–15 because of their strategic importance in relation to British India. Britain extended her rule to the interior (Kandy) between 1803 and 1818.

Although Ceylon had a majority community (Sinhalese) and a minority community (Tamils), it seemed to present a smaller and more manageable problem than the sub-continent of India. Between the Wars Britain was proud of its achievements in Ceylon, which it came to regard as a model for the constitutional development of a 'tropical' colony.

1883   Creation of a Legislative Council. This was to consist of 9 'official' (i.e. civil servant) members and 6 'appointed' members. The latter, representing business interests, could be either Europeans or 'natives'. The Governor retained his Executive Council, composed entirely of officials.

1910   Introduction of elective element into Legislative Council: 4 of the 21 members were to be elected (2 European, 2 non-European).

1919   Foundation of Ceylon National Congress. This included both Sinhalese and Tamils, but in 1921, fearing Sinhalese domination, the Tamils withdrew.

1920   Extension of Legislative Council: 16 of the 37 members were now elected; 11 on a territorial basis; 5 by the 'communities' (i.e. the Europeans, the 'burghers' (men of mixed Dutch and Singalese descent), the chamber of commerce and the association of producers). Four non-officials (2 Sinhalese, 1 Tamil and 1 European) were also added to the Executive Council.

1927–28   Donoughmore Commission examined the constitutional position and the reasons for some deadlocks in administration.

1931   Donoughmore Constitution. The Legislative and Executive Councils were replaced by a Council of State. This consisted of 60 members: 8 appointed (4 European, 4 'native') and 52 elected on a territorial basis. Elections were by universal suffrage but with a five-year residence qualification. Ceylon now had an elected majority in its Parliament. It also had a considerable measure of 'responsible government'. Certain subjects (i.e. defence, foreign affairs, justice and finance) were 'reserved' and the Governor retained some powers of legislation and the right of veto, but other matters were transferred to 'executive committees' (virtually ministries) responsible to the Council of State. This was the kind of leisurely progression to representative and then to responsible government which Britain considered ideal for her colonies. It was less rudely interrupted in Ceylon by the events of the Second World War than in most Asian colonies.

1944–45   Further enquiries into the possibilities of constitutional advance were made by the Soulbury Commission. This resulted in a new constitution in 1946.

1946   (May) Ceylon now had complete internal self-government, although defence and foreign policy were still 'reserved'. The committees of the Donoughmore Constitution were replaced by a Cabinet, headed by a Prime Minister. Pressure for further advance to full independence continued.

1947   Ceylon Independence Act.

1948   (4 February) Ceylon became independent but remained within the Commonwealth.

Events after independence

1972   Ceylon adopted new constitution and new name as the Republic of Sri Lanka.

Malaysia and Borneo

Malaysia was particularly important in Britain's post-war economy because of its rubber and tin exports, which underpinned the whole Sterling Area. The states which made up Malaysia had been acquired piecemeal in various ways during the nineteenth century.

Acquisition

1819   Sir Stamford Raffles acquired the island of Singapore from the Sultan of Johore.

1826   Singapore, Penang and Malacca made up the Straits Settlements under the jurisdiction of the East India Company.

1842   Sir James Brooks was installed as the Rajah of Sarawak.

1846   The island of Labuan was ceded to Britain by the Sultan of Brunei. (Added to the Straits Settlements in 1907.)

1867   The Straits Settlements were transferred to the jurisdiction of the Colonial Office.

1874–96   The Federated Malay States (Perak, Selangor, Negri Sembilan and Pahang), although remaining Princely States, not formally British colonies, fell under British control and British residents 'assisted' their rulers.

1881   The British North Borneo company acquired the administration of North Borneo.

1906   Brunei became a British Protectorate.

1909   Five more states (Kedah, Kelantan, Trengganu, Johore and Perlis), sometimes called the 'Unfederated States', passed from the jurisdiction of Thailand to that of Britain.

Until 1942   The British Governor of the Straits Settlements, based at Singapore, was also High Commissioner for the Malay States and responsible for the outlying British possessions, the Brunei Protectorate, North Borneo and Sarawak.

Developments during and after the Second World War

1942–45   Under Japanese occupation.

Malaya

1945–46   Discussions for a new post-war settlement. Unlike other countries in Asia, Britain had no immediate plans to decolonise the area (because of its economic importance) but did wish to rationalise the structure. Acute problems arose from the developing ethnic mix. The Malays were now outnumbered by the Chinese and Indians, who had come to work on the rubber plantations or in the production of tin. A 1941 census gave the figures as Malays, 41 per cent; Chinese, 43 per cent; and Indians, 14 per cent.

1946   (January) Britain asked the Sultans of the individual states to surrender the old treaties and accept a new centralised government under a British Governor. The Sultans initially agreed. But it was also proposed to extend citizenship to the Indian and Chinese populations and this was unacceptable to the Malays.

(March) A nationalist movement, the United Malays National Organisation (UMNO), was formed.

(May) Britain reopened negotiations with the Sultans.

1948   A new scheme was agreed. The sovereignty of the Sultans was restored and the 1946 citizenship proposals scrapped. A new federal form of government was accepted and the Federation of Malaya came into existence.

1948–60   Malayan Emergency. Communist guerrillas, who received assistance from neighbouring communist China, began a campaign. On 6 October 1951 the British High Commissioner, Sir Henry Gurney, was murdered. In January 1952 General Gerald Templer was appointed to direct military operations and Britain committed 20 battalions to the struggle. By 1954 the guerrillas had essentially been defeated and Malaya was subsequently held up as a model. In fact circumstances had been unusual. The Malay population in general did not sympathise with the guerrillas, and the Briggs Plan, put into operation in 1950 to move the Chinese rural population into 'protected villages' where they could neither supply nor be intimidated by the guerrillas, was effective.

1952   UMNO and the Malaya Chinese Association came together to form the Alliance Party to cooperate on constitutional demands.

1955   The Alliance Party (which now also included the Malayan Indian Congress) won all but one of the elected seats in the Legislative Council and asked for independence within four years.

1956   A constitutional conference in London fixed independence for August 1957. The Alliance leaders were essentially conservative politically and Britain promised to assist an independent Malaya in both internal and external security. The Malayan leaders agreed to keep their country within the Sterling Area.

1957   (31 August) The Federation of Malaya became an independent country within the Commonwealth.

Singapore

1946   Singapore became a separate colony.

1948   A new (and conservative) constitution was agreed. The active politicians were a wealthy minority, represented by the Progressive Party.

1954   The Labour Front and the People's Action Party were formed.

1955   The Rendel constitution increased the elected element. The Labour Front won the elections.

1956   Constitutional talks with Britain broke down because of Britain's determination to retain Singapore as a naval base.

1957   It was agreed in further talks that Singapore should have full internal self-government while Britain retained control of foreign policy and defence.

1958   A new constitution set up the State of Singapore. A People's Action Party government was formed, which hoped for union with the Malay Federation.

1961   Duncan Sandys, the Commonwealth Relations Secretary, and Lord Mountbatten, the Chief of the Defence Staff, visited Singapore and Malaya for talks.

    (August) Singapore and Malaya agreed on a merger, subject to the inclusion of the Borneo states (to act as a counter-weight to the large Chinese population in Singapore).

    (November) London Conference. Britain agreed to back the creation of a Malaysian Federation, subject to the continued use of Singapore as a naval base. Objections from the Philippines and Indonesia, which had rival claims in the area, led to a United Nations enquiry which, however, reported in favour of the Malaysian plan.

1963   (16 September) The Malaysian Federation came into being. The Federation included Sabah (former British North Borneo) and Sarawak.

1965   (9 August) Singapore left the Federation.

Borneo

1946   Sarawak and North Borneo became Crown Colonies.

1963   (16 September) Sarawak and North Borneo (Sabah) joined the Malaysian Federation.

Brunei

1946   Brunei reverted to protected status.

1957   The Sultan granted a written constitution (for the first time), which included a Council of Ministers and a Legislative Council.

1984   Brunei became independent but remained within the Commonwealth.

Africa

The British empire in Africa had mostly been built up during the period of the Scramble for Africa in the late nineteenth century, although Britain had had stations on the West Coast dating back to the seventeenth century, and she had retained Cape Colony after capturing it from the

Dutch during the Napoleonic Wars. Many areas were acquired as Protectorates and therefore, at least in their early years, came under the Foreign, not the Colonial, Office. In many parts of Africa British rule lasted less than 70 years. An individual could have seen the British come when he was a boy and leave when he was an old man. British influence was often more superficial in Africa than in India. Unlike the French, they did not try to 'assimilate' their subjects but preferred 'Indirect Rule', leaving the traditional authorities and culture intact, while controlling external relations, defence and, to some extent, trade.

In time this created friction between the traditional authorities and the new rising class of modern nationalists. The latter were the products of western education. Christian missionaries established schools widely in British Africa and most of the first generation of nationalists received their first education in mission schools. Until after the Second World War, although there were teachers' training colleges at Achimota on the Gold Coast, Fourah Bay in Sierra Leone and Makerere in Uganda, there were no universities in British Africa. Ambitious young men went to London or the United States. This had the advantage of allowing potential leaders from the different colonies to meet each other and contributed importantly to the later development of pan-African ideals. It also allowed Africans, from West Africa in particular, to meet black Americans and the American connection was important in raising black, and subsequently national, consciousness. The key names in this cross-fertilisation were Edward W. Blyden and Marcus Garvey, both West Indians by birth, and the American academic, W.E.B. Dubois.

The decolonisation of British Africa took place over a remarkably short time-span. Leaving aside the abnormal case of Zimbabwe (Southern Rhodesia), it was accomplished between the independence of Ghana (the former Gold Coast) in 1957 and the independence of Swaziland in 1968. The British government had not expected such rapid decolonisation. Until about 1960 the received wisdom was that Africa was extremely backward both economically and culturally and would be far behind Asia in becoming independent. Views on African culture changed with greater knowledge. The economic problems were real, although some states discovered great natural resources, for example oil and gas in Nigeria. The problems were compounded by the fact that many of the international boundaries drawn up during the Scramble period were totally artificial. It is surprising that so many independent states have grown up within their colonial boundaries, with comparatively few border disputes. It is, perhaps, less surprising that the 'Westminster model', that is parliamentary democracy, which the British hoped would be the main legacy of their empire, has seldom survived in Africa.

From the British point of view, there were great differences between the decolonisation of colonies where there was no significant settler element, which, once the decision had been taken, was relatively straight-forward, and those where there was a substantial European population, as in Kenya and Southern Rhodesia.

i. West Africa

Ghana (Gold Coast)

The Gold Coast, under its new name of Ghana, was the first British colony in tropical Africa to gain its independence. It was regarded as being of a manageable size, without irreconcilable differences between its diverse peoples, and with a sound economy. In 1945 its principal exports were gold, cocoa, manganese ore and diamonds, but cocoa was considered the mainstay of the economy. After the Second World War, the Gold Coast was the world's chief supplier. Cocoa was grown almost entirely by small proprietors. Despite a few experiments, there had been no development of the kind of plantation economy which had been established in parts of East Africa. Unhappily, just before independence, the cocoa crop became prey to a serious fungal disease, which posed a threat to the whole economy.

Acquisition

One of the British trading posts on the coast of West Africa, Cape Coast Castle, dating from the seventeenth century, became the nucleus of the Gold Coast Colony. In 1872 the British bought out the remaining Dutch stations in the area. British trading relations with the Fanti people on the coast involved them in conflict with the rival (and powerful) Ashanti Confederation. Britain fought wars with the Ashanti in 1823, 1826, 1874, 1896 and 1900–01. Political reorganisation of the area tended to follow these wars.

1874   Formal establishment of the Gold Coast Colony. This covered only a narrow, although well-populated, strip of territory on the coast.

1896   Lands of the Ashanti Confederation brought under a British Protectorate.

1901   Northern Territories brought under British protection.

1919   Parts of Togoland added as mandated territory.

Early political developments

The Gold Coast was always at the forefront of political developments in British tropical Africa.

1850   A Legislative Council (all Europeans) was created to assist the Governor at Cape Coast Castle.

1888   First two Africans nominated to seats on the Legislative Council.

1894   Municipal councils set up in Accra, Cape Coast and Sekondi, with some elected element.

1897   Aborigines' Rights Protection Society established among group of chiefs.

1918   Gold Coast lawyer, J.E. Casely Hayford, founded the National Congress of British West Africa.

1925   Reorganisation of the Legislative Council. This now consisted of 15 official and 14 elected members. Of the latter, 5 were Europeans and 9 Africans; 6 of the Africans were elected by the Provincial Councils (in practice by the traditional chiefs) and 3 by the municipal electorates of the principal coastal towns, Accra, Cape Coast and Sekondi.

1920s   The Gold Coast was in the forefront of asking for more constitutional advance throughout British West Africa, in particular demanding elected majorities in all Legislative Councils, the admission of Africans to the Governor's Executive Council, and African control of taxation.

1930s   Britain came to realise that development was necessary, and in 1939 sent out Lord Hailey. His report, *Native Administration and Political Development in British Tropical Africa*, was to be very influential.

Developments during and after the Second World War

1942   Two Africans nominated to the Executive Council.

1943   The Colonial Secretary, Oliver Stanley, visited the Gold Coast for consultations with the Governor and local representatives.

1944   The Governor, Sir Alan Burns, called a conference which formulated proposals, which became the basis of the 1946 constitution.

1946   Burns Constitution. This covered the whole country: the old colony, the Ashanti lands and the Northern Territories. A third African was added to the Executive Council but this remained essentially an official body and no member of the Legislative Council had an automatic right to sit on it. There was an important change on the Legislative Council, which now consisted of 18 elected, 6 nominated and 6 official members. For the first time a British colony in Africa had an elected African majority. The new constitution was expected to be followed by a period of consolidation.

1947   J.B. Danquah formed his United Gold Coast Convention (UGCC) to work for further advance. Danquah was a lawyer and the UGCC originally consisted of moderate professional and business men, who hoped to see a smooth transition of power to African hands, with no change to the basic structures of Gold Coast society. Danquah asked Kwame Nkrumah, who was then in London, to return to the Gold Coast to help organise the party, without realising that Nkrumah's views were much more radical and revolutionary than those of the UGCC.

1947–48   Nkrumah returned and organised the party.

1948   (February) Serious riots occurred in Accra, which spread to other towns. Although these originated in returning ex-servicemen's economic grievances, Nkrumah was suspected of fomenting trouble. The British government appointed Aiken Watson K.C., a British lawyer, to enquire into the riots. His committee reported in June that the Burns constitution was already out of date.

1949   Coussey Committee. The British government set up a committee with an all-African membership, including J.B. Danquah, under an African judge, Mr Justice Coussey, to advise on a new constitution. It reported in October 1949.

    Nkrumah, who had been released from prison but not invited to serve on the Coussey Committee, broke with the UGCC and founded his own party, the Convention People's Party (CPP). He launched a newspaper, the *Accra Evening News*. He had taken most of the 'Youth' section of the UGCC with him and set out to organise trade union support. He relied now on mass support and a campaign of 'positive action', based on the Gandhian model of strikes, boycotts and non cooperation. He denounced the Coussey proposals as totally inadequate.

1950   (January) Nkrumah was arrested and subsequently sentenced to three years' imprisonment on various charges of sedition. But the imprisonment was not rigorous and he continued to smuggle his orders out of gaol.

1951   (February) Elections were held under the Coussey constitution, which relied on a complicated mixture of direct and indirect elections to balance various forces. The CPP emerged as the strongest single party but without an overall majority in the Legislative Assembly. The Governor, Sir Charles Arden-Clark, immediately released Nkrumah from prison and made him Leader of Government Business (in effect Prime Minister). Nkrumah spent two years consolidating his position and reorganising local government to diminish the power of the chiefs.

1952   The British government declared its willingness to consider any proposals for constitutional advance.

1953   (June) Nkrumah's government, after wide consultations, issued a White Paper, asking for the Africanisation of the government, direct elections and the grant of Dominion status.

1954   (April) A Commission, presided over by Mr Justice Van Lare, drafted a new constitution, subsequently accepted by the British government. This gave the Gold Coast almost complete internal self-government. The size of the Legislature was increased and it was chosen by direct elections. The Executive Council became a Cabinet, selected by the Prime Minister.

Elections. The CPP was fighting a loose coalition of the remnants of the UGCC (now named the Ghana Congress Party) and various northern parties. There were still strong differences between the traditional authorities, represented by the chiefs, and the new nationalists, which coincided to some extent with regional differences between the coastal region and the more conservative interior. The CPP won 72 out of the 104 seats.

1955   Those who opposed the CPP organised. These included the Northern People's Party (NPP), which supported the traditional chiefs, the National Liberation Movement (NLM), centred in Ashanti, and the Moslem Association Party (MAP), which represented the Muslims, mainly in Accra and Kumasi. (Muslims constituted about 10 per cent of the population, compared with 30 per cent Christian and 60 per cent others.)

1956   The British Colonial Secretary, Alan Lennox-Boyd, insisted on new elections but promised that if a 'reasonable majority' in the new assembly voted for independence, he would set a date.

Elections. The CPP won 72 seats, the NPP 15, and the NLM 12. The CPP had won 8 seats in Ashanti. But some doubted whether the result was as decisive as it appeared. There was a low poll and the CPP had a smaller margin in the popular vote (400,000:300,000) than on seats won.

The assembly passed a motion in favour of independence by 72 votes to nil, the opposition having boycotted the vote. Lennox-Boyd, as he had promised, named the date.

1957   (6 March) The Gold Coast became an independent state within the Commonwealth, with the name of Ghana. By taking the name of an ancient West African empire, from which they claimed their people descended, the Ghanaians set a precedent, followed by many others, in trying to reconnect themselves to their past before the colonial era.

Events after independence

1960   Ghana became a republic, with Nkrumah as President.

1960s   Ghana progressively became a one-party state and Nkrumah assumed dictatorial powers. Political leaders were imprisoned, including J.B. Danquah, who died in prison.

1966   (February) The army and police staged a successful coup when Nkrumah was visiting Peking. Thereafter Ghana alternated between military government and short-lived attempts to restore civilian government – setting a pattern for many other ex-colonies.

Nigeria

Nigeria was the largest British colony in tropical Africa, acquired piecemeal and with no natural unity.

Acquisition

Mid-nineteenth century   In the 1840s a group of British philanthropists
tried to develop the palm oil trade in the Niger delta to replace
the now illegal slave trade. Although the 'Niger Experiment'
failed after many of the pioneers succumbed to malaria, a
flourishing trade in palm oil did develop.

1861   Lagos annexed during the final struggle to stamp out the embers
of the slave trade.

1885   At the end of the Berlin West Africa Conference, Britain proclaimed a Protectorate over the 'Oil Rivers', that is the rivers of
the Niger Delta, in order to protect the area from French and
German encroachment.

1886–89   A Chartered Company, the Royal Niger Company, acquired
jurisdiction over a large area of the middle Niger and its tributar-
ies in the course of contests with the French, who were expanding their control from their colony of Senegal. The Royal Niger
Company surrendered its administrative and political functions
to the British government in 1899 and reverted to being a trading
company.

1919   The German Cameroons, a mandated territory, was added to
Nigeria for administrative purposes.

Nigeria in the colonial period
Regionalism. Besides Lagos, Nigeria consisted of three distinct regions:

(i) The West, inhabited by the Yoruba people with long trading
connections with Europeans.
(ii) The East, inhabited by the Ibo people, where the nature of the
terrain compelled the inhabitants to live in isolated villages.
(iii) The North, inhabited by the Hausa and Fulani peoples. Open
savannah-type country, unlike the forests further south. The
people were mainly Muslims and had well-organised legal and
political systems.

Religion. The Muslims of the North were suspicious of Christian missionaries and education. The people of the South, who had been mainly
animist, welcomed the missionaries, and mission schools were vital in

providing education. As in India, this differential uptake of western-style education stored up problems for the future.

Economy. Between the wars Nigeria was not rich. It was primarily an agricultural country but palm oil was less important than it had been and there was no flourishing cash crop comparable to cocoa in Ghana. It had little spare money for education and other services. Only in the 1960s did it become apparent that it had vast reserves of oil and natural gas.

Early political developments

Nigeria was technically divided between the Colony, a strip of land on either side of Lagos, and the Protectorate, which covered the rest, but this was not the most important division in the administration of Nigeria. After the Royal Niger Company surrendered its political rights in 1899, Nigeria had been divided for administrative convenience into the North and the South.

Lord Lugard, who was High Commissioner for Northern Nigeria in 1900–06 and Governor of the whole of Nigeria in 1912–19, perfected his ideas of 'Indirect Rule' there. It worked smoothly in the well-organised North, where there was a clearly defined chain of command, but much less satisfactorily in the more-fragmented Ibo East, where Lugard had to create artifical 'warrant chiefs'. But strengthening traditional authorities, particularly in the North, and incorporating them in the system created further strains when modern politics began to develop.

1913   'Nigerian Council' set up to cover the Protectorates, both North and South. It had 36 members, 24 official, 6 unofficial Europeans and 6 unofficial Africans, all representing specified interests. It was never popular and the 1922 constitution swept away both the Nigerian Council and other previous constitutional arrangements, including the Legislative Council in the Colony proper, which at the time of the First World War had 6 official and 4 unofficial members, 2 of them Africans.

1922   New constitution coverering the Colony and the southern half of the Protectorate. The Legislative Council of 46 included 15 nominated and 4 elected members. The northern half of the Protectorate reverted to the 'Indirect Rule' it had had before 1913.

1939   The Southern Province was divided into Eastern and Western regions. The constitutional arrangements of the inter-war period thus tended to confirm the existing divisions.

African reactions

1920   Nigerians were present at the Accra meeting of the National Congress of West Africa and they too put forward demands, e.g. that at least half of the members of the Legislative Council should be elected.

1922   Herbert Macaulay founded the Nigerian National Democratic Party to fight elections under the new constitution. The lack of an expanding middle class, and the regional divisions, including the deeply conservative forces in the North, meant that conditions were less favourable in Nigeria than in the Gold Coast for constitutional development, but between the wars one major figure emerged: Nmande Azikiwe.

1937   Azikiwe set up a chain of popular newspapers, including the *West African Pilot.*

1942   Azikiwe set up the National Council of Nigeria and the Cameroons (NCNC), the first national party in Nigeria, intended to embrace all tribal groupings.

1944   NCNC merged with the Nigerian Democratic Party, although retaining the acronym NCNC.

1946   Richards constitution. One of the new post-war constitutions, generally called by the name of the then Governor, Sir Arthur Richards. The central government now included a Legislative Council, responsible for the whole country, with 16 official and 28 non-official members; of the latter 24 were nominated and 4 elected. The country was divided into three regions, North, East and West, each of which had its own House of Assembly. The Regional Assemblies were chosen by a complicated procedure, which gave the chiefs and traditional authorities a great deal of power. The Assemblies themselves were only advisory. The Governor retained legislative powers. The Nigerian constitution was thus very conservative, much more so than that of the Gold Coast. Protests were organised by Azikiwe, who visited London and the United States.

1950   Ibadan Conference, mainly African in composition, discussed constitutional development but regional difficulties became very apparent.

1951   Macpherson constitution, named for the Governor, Sir John Macpherson. Although this represented a step towards responsible government and was an advance on the Richards constitution, it was still essentially conservative and regional. The Legislative Council was renamed the House of Representatives and acquired wider legislative powers. Elections continued to be indirect and determined by a regional distribution of seats. The Governor's Executive Council was replaced by a Council of Ministers, made up of 6 official members and 12 African members, drawn from the House of Representatives.

Early 1950s   Three parties emerged, each regionally based: Azikiwe's NCNC, which tried to be an all-Nigeria party but which was strongest in the Eastern Region; Chief Awolowo's Action Group in the Western Region; and the Northern People's Congress, in the Northern Region, led by Ahmadu Bello, Sardauna of Sokoto, assisted by Abubakar Tafawa Balewa.

1953–54   Constitutional conferences in London and Lagos.

1954   New constitution, federal in form. Federal elections. Azikiwe, Awolowo and the Sardauna chose to stand in their own regions, rather than for the Federal House of Representatives. Balewa, previously unknown outside the Northern Region, became a significant figure in the capital, Lagos.

1957   The House of Representatives, inspired by the example of the Gold Coast, passed a resolution asking for independence by 1959. Balewa became Prime Minister with a genuinely federal coalition cabinet.

1957–58   Further constitutional conferences in London. Independence fixed for 1960.

1959   (December) Federal elections. Azikiwe and Awolowo stood for Federal House. Seats were allocated on a regional basis, in proportion to population: North, 174 seats; West, 62; East, 73; South Cameroons, 8; and Lagos, 3. (The Eastern and Western Regions disputed the population figures on which this allocation was based.) As a result of the elections, the Northern People's Congress won 142 seats and its small ally, the Northern Elements Progressive Union, won 8, while the NCNC won 89 and the

Action Group won 73. After complicated political manoeuvrings, the NCNC formed a coalition with the two Northern parties, under Abubakar as Prime Minister. Awolowo led the opposition. Azikiwe did not take a ministry but became Governor-General on independence.

1960   (1 October) Nigeria became an independent state within the Commonwealth.

Events after independence

1961   After a plebiscite the southern part of the Cameroons joined the Republic of Cameroon (the former French mandated territory); the northern part joined Nigeria.

1963   Nigeria became a republic with Azikiwe as President.

1964   Federal elections brought tensions between the Northern and Eastern Regions to a head.

1966   (January) Military coup in which Balewa, Ahmadu Bello and Akintola were assassinated. Ibo General Ironsi became President.
       (July) Ironsi assassinated in Northern-led coup and replaced by General Gowon. Massacre of Ibos in the Northern Region.

1967   (May) Colonel Ojukwu, the military governor of the Eastern Region, declared it an independent republic under the name of Biafra.
       (July) Nigerian civil war began.

1970   The Biafran army surrendered and 'Biafra' was dissolved. Nigeria was reconstituted.

Sierra Leone

Acquisition

1788   Captain John Taylor established a station for freed slaves (antedating by some 30 years the better-known American experiment in Liberia).

1807   The peninsula of Sierra Leone (a small area of some 250 square miles) was ceded to Britain and became the 'Colony'. Its capital,

Freetown, was an important naval harbour and the Governor of Sierra Leone was at one time (1866–74) responsible for all the British stations on the West African coast.

1896   The much larger hinterland (some 28,000 square miles) was acquired as a Protectorate during the Scramble period.

Early political developments

Sierra Leone enjoyed a modest prosperity, founded on coal and diamonds, but there were always tensions between the more developed, but very conservative, Colony and the Protectorate.

1863   Nominated Legislative Council established in the Colony.

1924   The Colony now elected members of the Legislative Council. The Protectorate now had nominated members.

1930s/1940s   Fourah Bay College, one of the few post-secondary colleges in British Africa, provided an important training ground for early nationalists.

Attainment of independence

1948   Unofficial majority in the Legislative Council but members representing the Protectorate were still nominated, not elected.

1951   New constitution: 7 members of the Legislative Council were to be directly elected from the Colony and 14 indirectly from the Protectorate. The Executive Council was to have equal numbers of official and unofficial members.
      Milton Margai formed the first political party, the Sierra Leone People's Party (SLPP), which aimed to unite the interests of the Colony and the Protectorate.

1957   The Legislative Council was enlarged and became the House of Representatives. The SLPP, which had the support of Protectorate chiefs, won the elections.

1957–59   New parties emerged, among them the United Progressive Party (which won 9 of the 39 seats in contention in 1957), the more radical People's National Party (led by Albert Margai and Siaka Stevens) and the All People's Congress (established a little later by Wallace Johnson and Siaka Stevens).

1958   Milton Margai became Prime Minister with a Cabinet of nine African ministers.

1960   SLPP and other groups formed a common front to ask for independence. Constitutional conference in London agreed on independence date.

1961   (27 April) Sierra Leone became an independent nation within the Commonwealth.

1971   Sierra Leone became a republic.

The Gambia

The Gambia was the oldest British trading base in West Africa, but in the nineteenth century it had become so hemmed in by French territory that its viability was called into question and there were several abortive attempts to exchange it.

Acquisition

1588   Elizabeth I granted a Charter to British merchants to trade on the Gambia River.

1783   The French acknowledged British rights.

1816   The British established a garrison on the island of Banjul (Bathurst) to put down the slave trade.

1889   Boundaries established by agreement with France.

Political developments

Despite its small size, there were divisions, which paralleled those in Sierra Leone, between the coastal area round the capital, Bathurst, and the hinterland, still ruled by the chiefs. There was some agitation for political advance immediately after the Second World War but the general opinion was that the Gambia was too small ever to be viable as an independent nation.

1947   New constitution. Bathurst elected members to the Legislative Council. Other 'unofficial' members were nominated. Unofficial members, both elected and nominated, were eligible to serve on the Executive Council.

1954   Unofficial members had 7:5 majority on the Executive Council. Unofficial members also had a majority on the Legislative Council. Of the 14 elected members, 4 were elected by universal suffrage in Bathurst, the other 10 by indirect elections from the rest of the Gambia.

1955   New political parties formed to fight for universal suffrage throughout the country: the United Party, led by Pierre N'Jie and based in Bathurst, and the People's Progressive Party (PPP), led by David Jawara, which drew its support more from the Protectorate.

1960   Franchise extended to all adults and Legislative Council enlarged. PPP won election.

1962   Gambia gained internal self-government.

1964   Constitutional conference to prepare for independence.

1965   (18 February) Became independent nation within the Commonwealth.

1970   Became a republic.

ii. East Africa

British 'East Africa' is conventionally taken to mean what became Kenya, Uganda, Tanganyika and the Sultanate of Zanzibar. Generally British connections with East Africa developed later than those with West Africa. They were bound up with the British empire in India from both a commercial and a defence point of view. The British Consulate at Zanzibar, the great entrepôt, originally came under the government of India. After the opening of the Suez Canal in 1869 a new dimension was added to strategic concerns.

Nevertheless, the decolonisation of the British colonies in East Africa followed a similar course to that in West Africa, except in Kenya, where there was the complication of a settler population.

Kenya

Here there were minority European and Asian populations as well as the much larger African population. The figures on the eve of independence were (1959): African, 6,500,000; Arab and Asian, 200,000; European, 65,000. The African population was divided into a number of tribes of whom the Kikuyu, farming peoples living round what became the capital, Nairobi, and the Masai, pastoralists and nomads, whose chief wealth was in their herds of cattle, were particularly important. For a time the British Colonial Office tried to promote the idea of 'partnership' between the races, that is, cooperation between the communities, disregarding the great disparity in numbers but also see below for the trenchant comments of the Devonshire White Paper.

Acquisition

1886   Anglo-German Agreement left what became Kenya in the British sphere of influence.

1888   Imperial British East Africa Company (IBEAC) chartered with a view to opening up the region.

1895   Imperial British East Africa Company, which was always under-capitalised, surrendered its Charter.
       (June) British Protectorate (East African Protectorate) proclaimed over most of what became Kenya, including the coastal strip, which had previously been under the jurisdiction of the Sultan of Zanzibar.

1902   (April) Plans were mooted for a merger between the East African Protectorate and the neighbouring Uganda Protectorate, to facilitate railway development. These came to nothing but the Eastern Province of the Uganda Protectorate was transferred to the East African Protectorate and had the accidental result of concentrating all the land considered suitable for European settlement in the East African Protectorate.

Early developments

Propagandists for development had seen Kenya as a possible area for European settlements from the 1880s and even called it 'the new Australia'. Their proposals were based on the idea that the area was underpopulated, which arose partly from a lack of understanding of the requirements of nomadic peoples, partly from a failure to realise that the population was abnormally low at the time because of a series of natural disasters, including smallpox and rindepest. The British government initially doubted its right to sell lands in a Protectorate, as distinct from a colony.

1895–1901   The building of the railway from Mombasa to Lake Victoria. This crossed the Protectorate. The indentured Indian labourers, who came to build it, mostly returned home at the end of their contract, but the enterprising traders who came with them did not and remained to provide an energetic, but sometimes resented, commercial class.

1899   The British government concluded that it did have the right to sell land in a Protectorate.

1901   Land Department created. Europeans could buy 160 acres at an advantageous price and, once they had developed it, a further 480 acres on similar terms.

1901–4   Sir Charles Elliott, the High Commissioner, favoured European settlement. A steady stream began to arrive and set up large European-style farms, mainly producing coffee, tea and cotton. Some came from existing colonies, including South Africa during and after the Boer War, and they came with already clearly formed views on their political rights.

1903   Colonists' Association formed by European settlers to demand a say in the government.

1906   In response to this pressure the East African Protectorate was transferred to the jurisdiction of the Colonial Office (although technically remaining a Protectorate) and its government assimilated to that of a Crown Colony, with a Governor assisted by Executive and Legislative Councils. The Legislative Council included unofficial, although not elected, members.

1911   A number of colonists' associations came together to form the Convention of Associations, popularly referred to as the 'Settlers' Parliament'. This became very active after the First World War, demanding progress to Dominion status but on a whites-only franchise.

Developments between the Wars

1919   The Indian community too began to ask for representation.

1919–22   Representatives of the various communities, including Lord Delamere, the settlers' leader, went to London for discussions with the Colonial and India Offices. Various proposals were put forward which met with strong opposition from the settlers.

1920   Kikuyu Association formed: the first African pressure group, but composed of older men and chiefs and very moderate in its demands.

1921   Young Kikuyu Association (later Kikuyu Central Association) formed by younger, more radical men, often mission-educated, who wanted faster progress. Its main weakness was that it attracted little support outside the Kikuyu.

1923   Devonshire White Paper. The Duke of Devonshire, the Colonial Secretary in Bonar Law's Conservative administration, issued a key White Paper, stating bluntly that responsible government was 'out of the question' for the foreseeable future because 'primarily Kenya is an African territory, and His Majesty's Government think it necessary definitely to record their considered opinion that the interests of the African natives must be paramount, and that if and when those interests and the interests of the immigrant races should conflict, the former should prevail'. This was a trust they could neither delegate nor share. This was a position from which the British government never retreated, although the later 1920s and 1930s saw enquiries into the possibilities of economic advance and 'partnership'.

1924–25   East African Commission under W.A. Ormsby-Gore. Reported in favour of dual development for both Europeans and Africans, which had echoes of Lord Lugard's ideas of the 'Dual Mandate'.

1927–28   Hilton Young Commission made similar recommendations and raised the additional possibility of an East African Federation of British territories to further economic development.

1927   The Legislative Council was reconstituted with 20 official, 11 elected European, 5 elected Indian and 1 elected Arab members. There was to be one nominated member to speak for African interests there.

1928   The Hilton Young Commission led to some outspoken missionary support for African interests and also to increased African interest in politics.

Jomo Kenyatta became the General Secretary of the Kikuyu Central Association but went to London the following year and did not return until 1946.

Second World War

Kenya was regarded as being in a frontline position because of the proximity of the Italian colonies. The authorities had also been disturbed by a serious dock strike in Mombasa in 1939. They clamped down on dissent (the Kikuyu Central Association was banned) and the settlers once again began to hope for backing in their ambitions.

Developments after the Second World War

There was an increase in British emigration, including some who disliked the advent of a Labour government in Britain in 1945 and whose attitudes did not bode well for interracial cooperation. Although there were hard-working planters and farmers among them, the European population before 1939 had already earned an unenviable reputation for hedonism and irresponsibilty, portrayed in James Fox's *White Mischief* (1982). They tended to resist all advances in African representation.

1944   Eliud Mathu, a Balliol-educated African, was appointed to the Legislative Council. With others he formed the Kenya African Union, to work for African self-government (but with guarantees for minorities) and the righting of land grievances.

1946   Dissatisfaction began to become more militant. Kenyatta returned to Kenya, after attending the Pan-African Conference in Manchester. Believing that political organisations were still too narrowly Kikuyu in membership, he tried to broaden their base by working with Oginga Odinga from Luo tribe.

1948   The Legislative Council now had an unofficial majority but the Africans had only 4 nominated members.

1952   The African membership of the Legislative Council (increased to 6) was now elected on an indirect system.
        Eliud Mathu was the first African appointed to the Executive Council (opposed by settlers).

1950–55   Mau Mau emergency. This was a terrorist campaign, virtually confined to the Kikuyu. Some 32 white civilians were killed, but most of the violence was directed towards Africans who would not join the campaign (1,819 African civilians were killed).

Kenyatta was suspected of involvement and sentenced to seven years' detention. British troops were sent to restore order. The need for British intervention finally ended settler claims to be a Dominion – they had demonstrated that alone they could not control the country.

1956   Suez crisis. The British, expelled from Egypt, briefly thought of setting up bases in Kenya, but this was dropped with the abandonment of the 'East of Suez' policy.

1957–59   The British government strove to reconcile conflicting interests, including those among the Africans themselves, by still advocating the 'partnership' ideal. A few Europeans, e.g. Michael Blundell and his United Country Party, hoped for this, but the majority of the settlers did not want to share power at all, while the Africans were now not prepared to settle for anything less than 'one person, one vote'. With Kenyatta still in detention, new leaders emerged, notably Tom Mboya. Mboya, a Luo, had made his name as a trade union leader.

Two political parties now emerged. One, the Kenya African National Union (KANU), developed from the Kenya African Union and was mostly supported by the Kikuyu and Luo. It demanded the return of the so-called White Highlands, where European land ownership was concentrated, and wanted a centralised form of government. Second, the Kenya African Democratic Union (KADU) was supported by the Masai and other pastoral and nomadic peoples and wanted a more federal form of government.

1959   Harold Macmillan was re-elected as British Prime Minister and appointed Iain Macleod as his Colonial Secretary. Both men wanted to free Britain from her remaining, often embarrassing, entanglements in Africa. Their determination was increased by events such as the Hola Camp massacre of that year.

Many Kikuyu men had been detained in camps for 'rehabilitation'. A hard core refused to renounce Mau Mau and 1,000 of these, detained in Hola camp, were told that they must work to grow their own food. When some refused, they were beaten by the guards (themselves Africans) and 11 died.

1960   Conference, representing all the main Kenyan groups, held at Lancaster House in London. This agreed in principle to an African majority on the Legislative Council.

1961   Kenyatta freed from detention.

1962   Second Lancaster House Conference. Kenyatta attended. Events in the neighbouring Congo after independence alarmed the settlers and some left. The new Colonial Secretary, Reginald Maudling, tried to find a solution which would satisfy Europeans, Asians and KADU, as well as KANU. This led (1963) to the appointment of Malcolm MacDonald (the son of Ramsay MacDonald, the first Labour Prime Minister), who had already established a reputation as a trouble-shooter, as Governor.

1963   (May) Elections resulted in a clear victory for KANU.
          (June) Kenyatta became Prime Minister on a programme of 'Uhuru' (Freedom) and 'Harambee' (Cooperation). Despite earlier fears, two-thirds of settlers decided to stay on.
          (12 December) Kenya became independent.

After independence

1964   (December) Kenya became a republic, with Kenyatta as President.

1970s   Kenya expelled Asians, although less brutally than neighbouring Uganda, and making a distinction between those who had, or had not, taken out Kenyan citizenship.

Uganda
The British were attracted to Uganda, partly because of concern for the head waters of the Nile, which had implications for the security of Egypt and the Suez Canal, but also because it was believed to be populous with good trading possibilities. It proved to be a turbulent area, on which colonisation imposed further problems.

The area which became the British Protectorate of Uganda included four African kingdoms, Buganda, Bunyoro, Toro and Ankole. Buganda, ruled by its Kabaka, was the largest and most powerful. (The 1948 census showed that Buganda had 1,296,000 out of a total Ugandan population of 5,342,900.) After the Second World War, the determination of Buganda's ruling classes to go their own way, maintain their traditional position and retain their dominance clashed sharply with the British intention of decolonising Uganda as a single unit with the usual Westminster model and a wide franchise.

Religion was a further complication. In the late nineteenth century, Islamic and Christian missionaries arrived at about the same time from the coast. France patronised the Catholic missions and Britain patronised the Protestant missions. Uganda was the scene of some massacres in the nineteenth century. In the end each of the main groups, Catholic, Protestant and Muslim, made about one million converts and religion was often the basis for political parties in the twentieth century.

In the late nineteenth century the main contest for the region was between Britain and Germany, after the German Chancellor, Otto von Bismarck, confirmed some treaties which a German explorer, Karl Peters, had concluded in the region which later became Tanganyika.

Acquisition

1886   Anglo-German Agreement left Uganda in the British sphere of influence.

1888   Imperial British East Africa Company (IBEAC) chartered to administer the region.

1890   Frederick Lugard employed by the IBEAC. Experimented with forms of Indirect Rule.

1892   The British government gave backing to the building of a railway from Mombasa to Lake Victoria, which was carried out from 1895 to 1901. One result of this was to introduce an Asian (mainly Indian) community into East Africa. (The 1948 census showed Uganda to have an Asian population of 47,400, compared with an African population of 5,286,000 and a European one of 6,600.) The Asians became very successful in commerce and strains developed with the African population.

1894   Formal Protectorate proclaimed over Uganda.

1895   Imperial British East Africa Company surrendered its Charter.

1900   Uganda Agreement gave Buganda a privileged position, guaranteed land in African hands and recognised the Kabaka as the ruler 'under Her Majesty's protection'.

1905   Uganda transferred from the jurisdiction of the Foreign Office to that of the Colonial Office.

1904 onwards   Britain actively supported the development of cotton-growing in Uganda and some plantation farming began, but in 1923 the Colonial Office under the Duke of Devonshire signalled

a clear preference for small proprietors. Uganda developed a
type of peasant economy, similar to that of the Gold Coast, not
a plantation economy like Kenya or Rhodesia.

Early political developments

1921 The British established a Legislative Council for the whole of
Uganda.

1920s Older Bagandans believed themselves to be in treaty relations
with the British, rather than under British rule. They resented
interference with the Great Lukiko, the Bugandan Assembly.

1926 The British forced the resignation of Kagwa, the Katikivo (Chief
Minister), who had been in office since 1889. In the short run
this made the British popular with the younger men, who wanted
change.

1920s/1930s Suggestions for a federation of Kenya, Uganda and Tanganyika (see Hilton Young Commission etc. under Kenya) came to
nothing but aroused fears that Uganda would be placed under
white domination in a larger unit.

1939–45 Second World War. Uganda seemed prosperous and peaceful.
Was now exporting both cotton and coffee and, because there
were few European residents, the wealth was in African hands.
The country was loosely administered in a decentralised system.
In Buganda, the Kabaka, assisted by the Lukiko, ruled with little
British interference.

Developments after the Second World War

Late 1940s Strains began to show but conflicts were at first between
feudal authorities and peasantry, rather than between nationalists and colonial power. Bataka, essentially a peasant party, was
founded. Joined with African Farmers Union to organise strikes
and demonstrations against the land rights of both chiefs and
Christian missions.

1950 Legislative Council consisted of 8 Africans, 4 Europeans and
4 Indians.

1951   Buganda asked to be transferred to the Foreign Office from the Colonial Office and allowed to resume its special status as a 'Protected State', but this was denied. The young Kabaka, Mutesa II, was compelled to agree that 36 of the Lukiko's 89 members should be elected but the concession was accompanied by repression. Strong feeling was aroused in Buganda by proposals to merge Buganda in a larger Uganda and also by renewed discussions of an East African Federation.

1952   Uganda National Congress founded, representing the 'have nots', but mainly Ganda in membership. Weakened by action of Bagandans in rallying to the support of the Kabaka in 1953.

1953   (November) The British Governor, Sir Andrew Cohen, deposed Mutesa and deported him to London.

1954   Sir Keith Hancock sent on a special mission to report on situation.
   Namirembe conference led to dropping of the idea of an East African Federation and, with it, the idea of a 'partnership' of the races, African, European and Indian, in East Africa. It was clearly affirmed that Uganda was an 'African' country.

1955   Kabaka restored. Buganda was given almost complete self-government.
   Progressive Party, mainly Protestant in membership, founded.

1956   Democratic Party initiated by Catholic bishops, who feared 'communist' tendencies of the Uganda National Congress.

1958   First direct elections to the Legislative Council. The Lukiko instructed Bagandans to boycott the elections.
   Uganda People's Union founded with the aim of combatting Buganda separatism.

1959–60   Boycott of Asian traders in Buganda.

1961   Milton Obote, who had emerged as an important figure and led the non-Gandan wing of the Uganda National Congress, brought about an amalgamation with the Uganda People's Union to form the Uganda People's Congress. He also negotiated a compromise, which gave Buganda considerable autonomy and allowed the Lukiko to select Baganda representatives in the National Assembly.

1962   Obote won the election and became Uganda's first Prime Minister. (9 October) Uganda became an independent country within the Commonwealth.

Events after independence

1963   Uganda became a republic and the Kabaka became the President. Relations between Buganda and the rest of the country deteriorated.

1966   Milton Obote engineered a coup against the Kabaka, who fled to England. The man who led the troops against the Kabaka's palace was Idi Amin.

1971   While Obote was abroad, Idi Amin, now Army Commander, proclaimed himself Head of State. His regime was marked by savage repression and much bloodshed. In 1972 he forcibly expelled all Asians from residence in Uganda.

1978   Uganda invaded Tanzania in a border dispute.

1979   Tanzanian forces invaded Uganda and assisted the Uganda Liberation Front to overthrow Amin.

Tanganyika
The population was approximately 10 million. There was a small Asian population, engaged as in Uganda and Kenya mainly in commercial enterprises. Despite the presence of some Germans (and Greeks), there was never any substantial European settlement. The struggles tended to be, not ethnic ones, but between traditional vested interests and the 'new men'. Britain initially organised the territory like any Crown Colony but with a heavy dependence on 'Indirect Rule', through the existing chiefs.

Acquisition

1886   Anglo-German Agreement left Tanganyika (German East Africa) in the German sphere.

1914–18   First World War saw some fighting in the area between German and British empire (mainly South African) troops.

1920   Former German East Africa became British mandated territory. It was a Class B Mandate, that is, Britain was obligated to establish good government and report to League of Nations but not to prepare the country for speedy independence.

Early developments

1926   The Legislative Council had 13 official and 7 unofficial members, comprising 5 Europeans and 2 Asians. African membership was considered a matter for the future.

1919–39   Most agriculture was at subsistence level, although cotton and sisal growing were already established. To these were added tea and sugar plantations. These were European enterprises and the Europeans also wanted to keep coffee-growing a European enterprise, but Sir Horace Byatt, Governor (1920–24) backed the African coffee-growers, the Chagga, already established near Mount Kilimanjaro. There was little political activity.

Developments after the Second World War

1946   The United Nations Trusteeship Council assumed the rights of the League of Nations Mandate Commission. Its authority was recognised by the British and it made clear its preference for early independence in Tanganyika.

1952   Julius Nyerere, who was to establish himself as the most important leader, returned to Tanganyika from his studies in Edinburgh.

1954   Nyerere founded the Tanganyika African National Union (TANU), which came completely to dominate Tanganyikan politics.

1955   The British introduced a new constitution. This was based on equal representation for Europeans, Asians and Africans. Most members of the Legislative Council were nominated by the Governor, after consulting the different communities. Each community also had two unofficial members on the Executive Committee. Those appointed were usually the traditional chiefs or their supporters.

   (March) Nyerere protested to the United Nations and asked for a guarantee of independence within 25 years and a declaration that Tanganyika was primarily an African country.

1956   With official encouragement a rival multiracial party, the United Tanganyika Party, was set up to work for 'partnership'. It attracted only a fraction of the support which was flowing to TANU.

1958   Sir Richard Turnbull was appointed Governor. His predecessor, Sir Edward Twining, had worked closely with the Colonial Secretary, Alan Lennox-Boyd, to press for partnership. Turnbull, like Iain Macleod, who became Colonial Secretary in 1959, was convinced that Tanganyika was an African country and must soon become independent on that basis. Turnbull worked closely with Nyerere.

1958–59   TANU decisively won elections.

1961   (March) Constitutional conference in Dar-es-Salaam.
(9 December) Tanganyika became independent.

Events after independence

1962   (December) Tanganyika became a republic, although remaining within the Commonwealth, with Nyerere as Executive President.

1964   (April) Tanganyika and Zanzibar united to form Tanzania. Nyere became President of the United Republic.

Zanzibar
Zanzibar comprised the islands of Zanzibar, Pemba and Latham. In pre-colonial times the Sultan of Zanzibar ruled a strip of coast on the mainland and had more shadowy claims to areas further inland. Arab influence was very strong. Zanzibar was part of the great Indian Ocean trading nexus and had an unenviable reputation for slaving. The British Consulate originally came under the government of India. Sir John Kirk was the great British Consul-General of the nineteenth century. Germany too had trading interests there from the 1840s.

Acquisition

1890   Heligoland Agreement. In return for the cession to Germany of the island of Heligoland (which had been in British possession since the Napoleonic Wars) Germany recognised British claims to Zanzibar, including the coastal strip. Zanzibar became a British Protectorate. The British envisaged controlling only foreign relations and otherwise leaving the Sultan's authority intact.

1891   The British Agent, Gerald Portal, under pressure from the anti-slavery lobby at home, carried out a virtual coup d'état and replaced all the senior officials (almost all Arabs) by Europeans.

Early developments

The coastal strip was leased to Britain and Britain considered linking Zanzibar with Kenya. The Governor of Kenya became the High Commissioner for Zanzibar but this arrangement was dropped in 1925 because of its unpopularity in Zanzibar. The Hilton Young Commission (1927–28) included Zanzibar in its consideration of an East African Federation.

Developments after the Second World War

For a time Zanzibar continued peaceful but subsequently became very turbulent. Its small population (300,000) was split between Arabs, Asians and Africans. Although technically the British 'advised' the Sultan, various trappings of British colonial administration had appeared, including Executive and Legislative Councils. In 1948 Africans were added to Arabs, Asians and Europeans on the latter.

1954 onwards   Arabs took the lead in asking for constitutional advance but disliked the 1956 constitution.

1956   A new constitution made provision for some elected members of the Legislative Council. The franchise was restricted to males who met property and educational tests.

Formation of political parties. The Arabs formed the Zanzibar Nationalist Party (ZNP), a radical party with links with Egyptian nationalists and suspected by the British of being communist. The Africans formed the Afro-Shirazi Party (ASP), which was initially much weaker in organisation.

1957   Elections demonstrated how politics were dominated by ethnic loyalties, and communal disturbances and bloodshed resulted.

1961   (January) Elections resulted in political deadlock.

(June) New elections led to serious rioting and loss of life. The political deadlock continued, although this time the ZNP was able to form a government with the help of the small Zanzibar and Pemba Peoples' Party.

1962   Constitutional conference in London to agree on new constitution and independence.

1962–63 Deadlock between the ZNP and ASP continued. The ASP wanted elections before independence, the ZNP did not.

1963 The imminence of Kenyan independence demanded action. In February the Colonial Secretary, Duncan Sandys, visited Zanzibar and reached agreement with the Sultan that the coastal strip (still leased to Britain) should be transferred to Kenya.

(June) Zanzibar gained internal self-government.

(December) Zanzibar became independent.

Events after independence

1964 (12 January) The Sultan was deposed and the Afro-Shirazi Party proclaimed a republic. They appealed to Eastern bloc countries and China for help and began to confiscate large estates and businesses. At the time this seemed a possible prelude to army mutinies all over East Africa and British forces were despatched.

(April) Zanzibar united with Tanganyika to form Tanzania, with Julius Nyerere as President of the United Republic. This was intended to curb Zanzibar, which it was feared might disrupt the whole development of East Africa, although under the agreement Zanzibar retained a considerable degree of autonomy, still managing its own education, agriculture, health and community development.

iii. South Central Africa

This was the slightly clumsy name given in colonial times to the British colonies of Northern and Southern Rhodesia and Nyasaland (later Zambia, Zimbabwe and Malawi). Southern Rhodesia (after 1964 usually called simply 'Rhodesia') provided Britain with its severest test in the whole decolonisation process in Africa.

Southern Rhodesia (Zimbabwe)

Rhodesia, both North and South, was essentially the creation of one man, Cecil John Rhodes, millionaire, Prime Minister of Cape Colony and ardent advocate of the expansion of the British empire. He was hoping both for riches from the supposed gold deposits and for a tilting of the balance of power in southern Africa from the Boers to the British. The gold proved to be illusory and Southern Rhodesia was opened up to agriculture instead, but settlement had always been part of Rhodes's plan. In 1959, when the rest of Africa was on the verge of decolonisation, the balance of population in Southern Rhodesia was estimated at

2,500,000 Africans, 215,000 Europeans, and 15,000 others (mainly Arabs and Indians). The Europeans were a minority but a large minority who had no intention of surrendering the degree of self-government they had already obtained. Rhodesia proved a much more intractable problem than Kenya, not only because the European population was bigger, but also because, whereas Kenya had been governed as a normal colony and the Colonial Office view that it was primarily an African territory was bound ultimately to prevail, Southern Rhodesia had enjoyed a long period of 'Company' rule, which culminated in 1923 in the premature grant of something very like Dominion status while it still had, for all practical purposes, a white franchise.

Lying just north of the Transvaal and west of the Portuguese colony of Mozambique, Southern Rhodesia was inhabited by the Shona peoples (Mashona), the majority population, who were farmers, and the Matabele (Ndebele), who were an offshoot of the Zulus and who had conquered part of the area a generation before the Europeans arrived.

Acquisition

1888   Rudd Concession. Lobengula, the King of the Matabele, thinking to rid himself of competing concession hunters, granted C.D. Rudd (Rhodes's emissary) exclusive mineral rights in his dominions and some ill-defined rights to administer and defend his concession.

1889   Rhodes secured a Charter for his British South Africa Company, which allowed it to administer the area.

1890   Rhodes sent his 'Pioneers' into Mashonaland and later into Matabeleland.

1891   The Charter was extended to what became Northern Rhodesia. Agreements with Portugal and Germany defined various boundaries in southern Africa.

1893   War with the Matabele.

1896   War with the Mashona.

Early developments

1898   The settlers, who were not entirely happy with Company rule, persuaded the British government to set up a Legislative Council.

1902   Rhodes died.

1907   Elected members gained majority on Legislative Council. The franchise was 'colour blind', i.e. did not depend on race, but included a property qualification which excluded the great majority of Africans, as well as the poorer whites.

1911   Settlers numbered about 23,000, compared with (estimated) one million Africans.

Developments after the First World War
It was recognised that Company rule was becoming an anachronism. Rhodesians had a choice of joining the Union of South Africa or developing independently.

1922   A referendum of the electorate showed a big majority for independent development.

1923   The Company relinquished its political functions. Southern Rhodesia became a 'self-governing colony'. The meaning of the term was unclear. It seems to have been meant to stop short of Dominion status but the Prime Minister of Southern Rhodesia attended Commonwealth Conferences and was treated like a Dominion premier. Southern Rhodesia was to have a Legislative Assembly of 30. The franchise now depended on a mixture of property and educational qualifications but there was no overt colour bar. The country had responsible internal government, although Britain had the right to veto legislation which discriminated between Europeans and Africans, but this was allowed to fall into disuse.

1919–39   Southern Rhodesia was economically prosperous and administration came to seem more important than politics. Godfrey Huggins became Prime Minister in 1933 and remained in office until 1953. There was some talk of a federation of the Rhodesias and Nyasaland but no progress was made. Land might have been seen as a potential problem. An 1898 Order in Council creating 'Native Reserves' had introduced some measure of demarcation. The 1930 Land Apportionment Act increased the size of the Reserves but made it more difficult for Africans to buy land outside them.

1934   Southern Rhodesian African National Congress founded.

Developments after the Second World War

There was a considerable increase in the white population. Some came from Britain because they disliked the policies of the new Labour government, but others came from South Africa because they disliked the hard-line *apartheid* policies applied after 1948.

Southern Rhodesia in this period had a much more liberal attitude to race than South Africa. Many looked on it as a hopeful example of 'partnership' in action, notably in the multiracial university in the capital, Salisbury. But African majority rule seemed a prospect only for the distant future.

African protests began to grow as in other parts of Africa. Returning ex-servicemen were impatient for improvements. The new white immigrants were, in some instances, taking jobs from Africans. There was some fear of the spread of hard-line policies from South Africa. But, generally, protests were still mild.

The Central African Federation

As seen from London, the main attraction of a federation of the Rhodesias and Nyasaland was economic. Southern Rhodesia was a prosperous agricultural area, exporting tobacco and other cash crops grown on European farms. Northern Rhodesia was an industrial and mining area. Nyasaland had a ready supply of well-educated African labour. It was also hoped that a federation would create a strong state, able to balance South Africa, whose relations with Britain were becoming increasingly strained.

1950   Plan for a Central African Federation drawn up in a conference at the Colonial Office, presided over by Sir Andrew Cohen, who was committed to the idea.

1951   James Griffiths, who favoured the idea, succeeded Arthur Creech-Jones, who had opposed it, as Colonial Secretary. The different status of Southern Rhodesia was tacitly admitted by the fact that Patrick Gordon Walker, the Commonwealth Secretary, visited it, while James Griffiths, the Colonial Secretary, went to Northern Rhodesia and Nyasaland.

Victoria Falls Conference between representatives of the three territories and the British government. Britain remained non-committal in the face of divided opinions in Africa. The whites in Northern Rhodesia and Nyasaland were broadly in favour; the whites in Southern Rhodesia, fearing to lose their quasi-Dominion status, doubtful; and the Africans almost unanimously against an arrangement likely to prolong white domination.

(October) Conservative election victory brought Oliver Lyttelton, who wanted the federation, to the Colonial Office.

1953   London Conference to draw up constitution. Africans refused to attend from Northern Rhodesia and Nyasaland. Only white delegates were invited from Southern Rhodesia.

(April) The Southern Rhodesian electorate (almost all white) approved the constitution.

(July) The constitution was approved by the British Parliament, although most Labour MPs now opposed it on the grounds that it was clearly not desired by the majority population.

(September) The Federation came into effect. There was a Federal Assembly of 35, of whom 26 were elected. Each territory was to keep its existing franchise. Southern Rhodesia had raised its property qualification in 1951 with the intention of reducing the number of African electors. Nyasaland had no franchise and the scheme devised (and finally operated in 1956) was heavily weighted in favour of the Europeans. The other 9 members of the Assembly, who were to represent African interests, were chosen by a complicated mixture of elections and consultations. Godfrey Huggins became Federal Prime Minister (7 September).

First federal elections held. The Federal Party won 24 of the 26 seats.

1953–63   Federation existed. It was a time of economic prosperity when, for example, the Kariba Dam was built on the Zambezi to provide the largest hydro-electric scheme in Africa. Politically, the scene was less rosy. African opposition increased.

1960   It had been agreed that the Federation would be reviewed after ten years and the Conservative government sent out Walter Monckton to report. The Monckton Commission reported in September that African representation should be rapidly increased and that each territory should have the right to secede.

1960–62   Negotiations continued, with Duncan Sandys, the Commonwealth Secretary, taking responsibility for Southern Rhodesia, and Iain Macleod and Reginald Maudling, successively Colonial Secretaries, taking responsibility for the other two territories. In 1962 R.A. Butler was given overall responsibility for Central

African affairs. In the end it was agreed that the Federation should be dissolved.

1963   (December) Dissolution of Central African Federation.

Towards Southern Rhodesia's Unilateral Declaration of Independence
After the dissolution of the Federation Northern Rhodesia and Nyasaland quickly became independent. Britain was not prepared to give independence to Southern Rhodesia until the African majority had a voice in proportion to their population. Most white Rhodesians felt betrayed, believing they had given up virtual independence (Dominion status) in order to enter the Federation at Britain's invitation. Even during Federation there had been attempts to safeguard the continuation of white supremacy while preserving the appearance of partnership.

1955   New constitution. This provided for two electoral rolls. The property and educational qualifications for the 'ordinary' or upper roll were much higher than for the 'special' or lower roll. The number of voters on the lower roll was never to exceed one-fifth of that on the upper. It was anticipated that few Africans would qualify for the upper roll.

1958   Garfield Todd, a man with a missionary background and a reputation for comparative liberality, who had succeeded Godfrey Huggins as Prime Minister in 1953, was replaced by the more right-wing Sir Edgar Whitehead.

1960   Law and Order Maintenance Act, which seemed to echo South African legislation, led to the resignation of the Chief Justice, Sir Robert Tredgold.

1961   New constitution agreed at a conference presided over by Duncan Sandys. There was to be a Bill of Rights for Africans and Africans were guaranteed 15 seats out of 65 in the Legislative Assembly. Joshua Nkomo, on behalf of the National Democratic Party, at first accepted, then rejected the constitution.

1962   Africans boycotted elections, which were won by Winston Field and the right-wing Rhodesian Front.

1963   New groupings of African parties. In 1960 the National Democratic Party, with Joshua Nkomo as its President, had replaced the moribund Southern Rhodesian African National Congress. When this was banned in December 1961 by Whitehead's government, Nkomo founded a new party, the Zimbabwe People's Union (ZAPU). But in 1963 Nkomo and another veteran African leader, Rev Ndabaningi Sithole, split and Sithole, together with Robert Mugabe, founded the Zimbabwe African National Union (ZANU).

1965   Elections, at which the Rhodesian Front, now led by Ian Smith, gained an increased majority.

(11 November) Southern Rhodesia unilaterally declared its independence. The reasons for the precipitate action have been disputed. White opinion was alarmed by events in the Congo and still felt betrayed by the winding up of the Federation. They felt they could no longer rely on Britain and must act for themselves. Economically, Rhodesia was still prosperous and it has been suggested that they thought that quite soon enough Africans would qualify for the franchise to create an African majority by legal process. The Declaration attracted strong international condemnation but Rhodesia was protected by the fact that it was a land-locked state and two of its neighbours, South Africa and the Portuguese in Mozambique, were sympathetic. London judged a military operation against Rhodesia impractical and opted for economic sanctions.

1966   (January) The British Prime Minister, Harold Wilson, told a meeting of Commonwealth Prime Ministers in Lagos that sanctions would work 'in weeks rather than months'. But neither South Africa nor Mozambique really cooperated in sanctions and even the African so-called 'frontline' states, such as Zambia, had such close economic ties with Rhodesia that they were at first half-hearted.

(December) Harold Wilson met Ian Smith aboard HMS *Tiger* off Gibraltar but failed to reach an agreement.

1968   (October) Wilson met Smith on HMS *Fearless*. This time Wilson offered substantial concessions but the Rhodesians were suspicious and ultimately refused them.

1966–79   African nationalists waged increasingly bitter guerrilla warfare against the Smith regime. They eventually found bases in neighbouring countries. ZIPRA, the military wing of Nkomo's ZAPU which mainly recruited from the Matabele, operated from Zambia, and ZANLA, the military wing of Mugabe's ZANU, recruited from the Shona, operated from Mozambique. On 9 October 1976 they united to form the Patriotic Front.

1974–75   Portugal's empire collapsed. South Africa was under increasing international pressure and Rhodesia's position began to become untenable.

1978   Smith bypassed Nkomo and Mugabe to reach an 'internal settlement' with Sithole and Bishop Abel Muzorewa, who had led a pressure group seeking a negotiated settlement since 1971. A new constitution gave a black majority in Parliament but control of the army, police, judiciary and civil service was to remain in white hands for the foreseeable future.

1979   Conservative victory in British general election. The Prime Minister, Margaret Thatcher, would have recognised the Muzorewa government but the Foreign Secretary, Lord Carrington, would not and asked for negotiations.

(September) Carrington persuaded Smith, Muzorewa, Nkomo and Mugabe to come to a conference at Lancaster House. Mugabe unexpectedly agreed to a proposal to reserve a certain number of seats in the Parliament for the white population (numbering about 250,000, compared with 7 million Africans). In return Smith agreed that Rhodesia should return temporarily to colonial status while elections were held, monitored by a small force from other Commonwealth countries.

1980   Elections. Of the 100 seats in the Assembly, 20 were reserved for Europeans. Of the other 80 Mugabe's ZANU won 57; Nkomo's ZAPU, 20; and Muzorewa, 3. The British government feared Mugabe as a communist and had hoped for a ZAPU–Muzorewa coalition. In reality it was more alarming that voting had split along tribal lines.

(17 April) Rhodesia became independent as the Republic of Zimbabwe, adopting the name of an ancient African empire.

Northern Rhodesia (Zambia)

Northern Rhodesia shared a common origin with Southern Rhodesia. Both were part of Cecil Rhodes's Charterland and originally administered by the British South African Company. But Northern Rhodesia was much less of a problem to decolonise than Southern Rhodesia, partly because the European population was much smaller (73,000 in 1959, compared with Southern Rhodesia's 215,000) but also because it was of a different nature. Most Europeans in Northern Rhodesia were not settlers and farmers but engineers, technicians and others engaged in support services for the mining and industries of the Copper Belt, who expected to move on eventually.

Early developments

1924   After the British South Africa Company surrendered its political functions, Northern Rhodesia became a Protectorate with Crown Colony style government of a Governor, assisted by Executive and Legislative Councils. In practice, there was some degree of Indirect Rule. Although elected members (white) were added to the Legislative Council in 1926, it had an official majority until 1945 and made no serious claim to be the germ of a Parliament.

In some ways Northern Rhodesia was less developed than the South but the discovery of important copper deposits in the 1920s transformed the economy. European workers jealously guarded their positions and did not want to see Africans admitted to highly skilled occupations.

Developments after the Second World War

1946   Formation of Federation of African Welfare Societies (Friendly Societies). (African organisations at first took the form of trade unions – friendly societies – rather than overt political parties.)

1948   This became the Northern Rhodesian African National Congress, of which Harry Nkumbula became President in 1951.

1949   Kenneth Kaunda, who was to be Zambia's most important leader, offered his services to Nkumbula.

1952   (October) African Mineworkers' Union led a well-disciplined three weeks' strike in the Copper Belt for increased wages.

Central African Federation
(For main outline of events see under Southern Rhodesia.)

In Northern, as in Southern, Rhodesia, the Africans opposed the idea of the Federation but they were better organised in the North. They also began to struggle against the exclusion of Africans from skilled jobs. Kaunda and Nkumbula were eventually both arrested and gaoled.

1958   The younger men of the Northern Rhodesian African National Congress opposed Nkumbula for not being radical enough. Kaunda and others left to form the Zambian National Congress (later, in 1960, the United National Independence Party).

1961   A new constitution was agreed. For a long time Africans were kept out of the franchise on the grounds that they were 'protected persons', not British subjects. The 1961 constitution, brokered by the British Colonial Secretaries, Iain Macleod and Reginald Maudling, attempted to put complicated machinery in place for 'partnership' between the races.

1962   (October) Elections. The complications of the electoral system had left a deadlocked situation but Kaunda and Nkumbula eventually agreed to form a coalition.

1963   (31 December) Central African Federation dissolved.

1964   (January) New elections. Kaunda's United National Independence Party won a clear majority; 10 seats were reserved for Europeans and were all won by supporters of John Roberts's National Progress Party, who opposed Kaunda.

(24 October) Northern Rhodesia became independent as Zambia. Kaunda became President.

Nyasaland (Malawi)

Although it was to become the third member of the Central Africa Federation, it had a quite different history from that of the Rhodesias. European influence penetrated into the area in the form of Scottish Presbyterian missionaries, who established an excellent education system, which in the colonial period allowed young men from Nyasaland to establish themselves all over Southern Africa as clerks. (In the 1930s, 90 per cent of the boys and 75 per cent of the girls between the ages of five and fifteen attended school.) There was never any question that it was an African country and European numbers, even in the 1950s, never rose above 8,000–9,000. There was also a small Asian community: 12,000 in 1959, compared with nearly 3 million Africans. The main problem was that it was initially regarded as too small and poor in resources to become a viable state. It developed two cash crops, tea and tobacco, but both on a small scale.

Early developments

1891   Became a British Protectorate.

1907   Crown Colony type government established, with Governor assisted by Executive and Legislative Councils. A good deal of Indirect Rule.

1932   Indirectly elected representatives of various groups introduced into the Legislative Council.

1944   Nyasaland African National Congress established.

Central African Federation
(For main outline of events see under Southern Rhodesia.)

The Africans objected to the Federation and organised some protests through the Nyasaland African National Congress. The chiefs also opposed it. There was some violence, economic rather than political in origin, in 1952.

1955   New constitution which provided that 6 of the 22 members of the Legislative Council should be directly elected by Europeans and Asians, but that the 5 African members should be indirectly elected by the Provincial Councils. Africans objected to the discrimination.

1958   (July) Dr Hastings Banda returned to Nyasaland and became President of the Congress.

1959   State of Emergency declared, following some disorders and rumours of a plot to massacre all Europeans. Congress was banned and Banda arrested. A British judge, Mr Justice (later Lord) Devlin, was sent out to investigate. He submitted a trenchant report that there had never been a 'massacre plot' and that Nyasaland was beginning to resemble a police state. Although the Colonial Secretary, Alan Lennox-Boyd, initially rejected the findings, they probably influenced the Prime Minister, Harold Macmillan, in his decision to extricate Britain from Africa.

1960   (April) Banda released from gaol.
        (August) New constitution, which ensured African majority.

1961   (August) Elections. Malawi Congress Party secured 23 seats against 5 for the United Federal Party of Roy Welensky, now the Federal Prime Minister.

1962   (December) R.A. Butler, the minister in charge of Central African affairs, granted Nyasaland the right to secede from the Federation.

1963   (31 December) Central African Federation dissolved.

1964   (February) Nyasaland granted internal self-government.
      (6 July) Nyasaland became independent as the Republic of Malawi.

iv. The High Commission Territories

The three High Commission territories, Basutoland (Lesotho), Bechuana-land (Botswana) and Swaziland, were the relics of conflicts in Southern Africa in the nineteenth century. It was at one time assumed that they would be incorporated into Cape Colony or the Transvaal but the Anglo-Boer War of 1899–1902 intervened. The Union of South Africa Act of 1909 also envisaged ultimate incorporation but the chiefs in all three territories protested and the British government promised that sovereignty would not be transferred against the wishes of their inhabitants. The *apartheid* regime in South Africa after 1948 and South Africa leaving the Commonwealth in 1961 put such a transfer out of the question and the three territories were decolonised rather hastily in the 1960s according to what had, by then, become the normal process.

Basutoland (Lesotho)

1830s   The Basotho clans, led by Moshoeshoe I, clashed with the Boers.

1842   First sought the protection of the British Crown.

1868   (March) Basothos taken under British protection, jurisdiction exercised by the British High Commissioner in South Africa.

1871   Jurisdiction transferred to Cape Colony.

1884   (March) Taken under direct British rule as Basutoland.

1910   Advisory Basuto Council, with most members nominated by the Paramount Chief, established.

1945   Elected members introduced.

1952   Basutoland Congress Party (BCP) founded by Dr Ntsu Molkhehle. Basuto National party (BNP) founded by Chief Lebua Jonathan.

1960   A Legislature (Basutoland National Council) and an Executive Council established.

1964   Constitutional conference in London.

1965   New constitution. Moshoeshoe II, Paramount Chief since 1960, recognised as King. Bi-cameral legislature established, with a nominated Senate and an elected Assembly.
        (April) Internal self-government. Elections narrowly won by BNP. Passed independence motion.

1966   (March) Issued White Paper with detailed suggestions for independence.
        (June) Constitutional conference in London.
        (4 October) Became independent state within the Commonwealth.

Bechuanaland (Botswana)
Inhabited mainly by Sotho peoples (Botswana) and some associated groups, who felt threatened by both the Boers and the Matabele.

1880s   Ruler, Khama III, asked for British protection.

1885   Bechuanaland was declared to be under British protection. The territory south of the Molopo River was constituted a colony, the rest remained a Protectorate.

1891   Order in Council provided form of government under British High Commissioner in South Africa.

1960   A new constitution established a Legislature with an elected majority.

1963   Link with High Commissioner in South Africa broken. Resident Commissioner fulfilled functions as Governor.

1965 Internal self-government came into operation.

1966 (30 September) Became independent state within the Commonwealth.

Swaziland

1890–94 British government and the Transvaal (Boer Republic) exercised condominium.

1894 Transferred to jurisdiction of Transvaal.

1899–1902 Anglo-Boer War. Transvaal lost control.

1909 Union of South Africa Act envisaged possible restoration of Transvaal rule but not implemented.

1910 Remained under British control when Transvaal became a province of the Union of South Africa.

1963 New constitution established Legislative Council with elected majority.

1964 First elections. Council made proposals for independence.

1966 Internal self-government.

1968 (6 September) Became an independent state within the Commonwealth.

v. South Africa and Namibia

Although most of the story of South Africa lies outside the scope of this study, it is so closely linked with African decolonisation, especially in Namibia, that some mention must be made of it.

1899–1902 Anglo-Boer War.

1910 Union of South Africa established, consisting of four provinces, the Cape, Natal, the Transvaal and the Orange Free State.

1920 South Africa became the League of Nations Mandatory Power for the former German South West Africa. Between the wars South Africa fulfilled its obligations of supplying reports to the League.

1945   South Africa refused to accept the United Nations Trusteeship Council as the legal successor of the League's Mandate Commission and subsequently (1949) ceased to supply reports. It also made some moves to incorporate South West Africa, for political and other purposes, into its own territory.

1948   The National Party, under Daniel Malan, won the elections and proceded to institute the policy of *apartheid*. All residents of South Africa were defined as white, coloured (i.e. of mixed race), black or Asian. All non-whites were subject to discriminatory legislation.

           Apartheid was technically a domestic matter and the United Nations had no right to intervene or even comment, but South Africa's irregular position in South West Africa opened the way for discussions in the United Nations. After 1949 South West Africa was brought before the United Nations and the International Court of Justice on a number of occasions but with inconclusive results.

1959   South West Africa National Union (SWANU) founded.

1960   South West African People's Organisation (SWAPO) founded.

           Sharpeville shootings: 69 demonstrators were killed by the police. South Africa government 'banned' (declared illegal) both the African National Congress (ANC) and the Pan Africanist Congress (PAC). (Unsuccessful) demands for economic sanctions were made at the United Nations.

1961   South Africa became a republic after a referendum of an almost entirely white electorate and allowed its membership of the Commonwealth to lapse.

           ANC began an 'armed struggle'. Nelson Mandela was imprisoned. ANC leaders took refuge in Zambia, PAC leaders in Lesotho and, later, Tanzania.

1966   (27 October) The United Nations General Assembly formally terminated South Africa's mandate and declared South West Africa to be the direct responsibility of the United Nations.

1969   The Security Council endorsed the General Assembly's resolution.

1971   The International Court of Justice upheld the legality of these decisions.

1970s   With the collapse of the Portuguese empire, ANC and PAC stepped up guerrilla activity from outside South Africa. South African security forces raided neighbouring (so-called frontline) states. SWAPO guerrillas became active in South West Africa.

1976   (30 January) The Security Council called on South Africa to transfer power to the people of Namibia and allow free elections under United Nations supervision.

1977   'Contact Group' of Britain, France, the United States, Canada and West Germany set up to negotiate directly with South Africa about the future of Namibia. The death in police custody of Steve Biko, whose Black Consciousness ideals had been influential beyond South Africa, led to further international condemnation of South Africa.

1978   (25 April) South Africa accepted the proposals for elections in Namibia as a preliminary to independence.
    (4 May) South African forces raided SWAPO bases in Angola. Further negotiations were delayed indefinitely by an intensification of fighting.

1980s   Economic sanctions were applied by the United States and most Commonwealth and European Community countries, but resisted by the Thatcher government in Britain. South African forces seemed to be fighting a losing (or at least too costly) battle against SWAPO, which now had Angolan and Cuban support.

1988   The United States mediated direct talks between South Africa, Angola and Cuba.
    (December) Agreement by which South Africa would accept UN plan for Namibia if Cuban forces withdrew from Angola.

1989   (April) 'Transition process' began, observed by United Nations and Commonwealth.
    (November) Election of Constituent Assembly, which drafted an independence constitution. Though SWAPO did well, more moderate parties also made a good showing. This may have encouraged the South African government (now under pressure from business interests, as well as world public opinion) to relax its policies and seek compromises.

1990   (21 March) Namibia became independent and joined the Commonwealth as its 50th member. De Klerk's government began to dismantle *apartheid*. The ANC and PAC were 'unbanned' and Nelson Mandela released.

1993   (June) Agreement reached between South African government, ANC and other parties.
         (December) Parliament completed new constitution.

1994   (April) Democratic elections in South Africa resulted in an overwhelming victory for the ANC.
         (1 June) South Africa rejoined the Commonwealth.

The Caribbean

The West Indies had been regarded as a rich prize by the European Powers in the eighteenth century and many islands had changed hands several times between the British, French and Spanish.

All the inhabitants of the British West Indies were, for practical purposes, the descendants of immigrants. By the twentieth century the population was very heterogenous. There had been a small number of white settlers, some of whom had arrived involuntarily as transported criminals or political prisoners. There was also a rather larger Asian population, most of whose ancestors had arrived as indentured labourers, usually in the nineteenth century. The majority were, however, the descendants of African slaves from various parts of West Africa. Britain (and the United States) had outlawed the slave trade in 1807. Slavery itself had been outlawed throughout the British empire by Act of Parliament in 1833 and this had marked an important turning point in the history of the West Indies.

There had been a considerable 'planter' influence in the eighteenth and nineteenth centuries and constitutional developments in some of the British islands had followed the same course as those on mainland America. Barbados and Jamaica, for example, acquired Legislative Assemblies in the seventeenth century. That of Barbados survived into the twentieth century but the Jamaican Assembly voted for its own abolition after the panic caused by the 1865 rebellion. St Kitts, Nevis, Antigua, the Virgin Islands and Montserrat were the subjects of various constitutional experiments during the Victorian period. The result was a patchwork of constitutional arrangements, but, generally speaking, the electorates were small and the franchise narrow.

The West Indies, which had been so rich in the eighteenth century, were economically in decline by the late nineteenth century. A new crisis developed after the fall of the world price of sugar in 1929. After the Second World War they were regarded as a problem area. The received wisdom was that a country needed a certain size and degree of prosperity to be viable as a nation state. The West Indian islands seemed to fail on both counts. Various experiments of federation were suggested, or tried, without much success.

Pre-1945 developments
The West Indies produced some remarkable thinkers, among them Edward Blyden and Marcus Garvey, who developed ideas of negritude and made the growth of black consciousness and black nationalism possible. Their main influence tended to be in Africa rather than in the West Indies, although Garvey was regarded as a hero there in the 1930s.

The serious economic depression of the inter-war period encouraged the development of trade unions and produce associations. (Some had been founded earlier, e.g. the Working Men's Association in Port of Spain, Trinidad, in 1907.)

1929–31 Establishment of Banana Producers' Association (Jamaica), Nutmeg Growers' Association (Grenada), Co-operative Citrus Growers' Association (Trinidad), Citrus Growers' Association (Jamaica), Lime Growers' Association (Tobago) and others covering rice, cotton and coconut producers. These could develop political programmes.

1935 Sugar workers struck in St Kitts and Barbados. Strikes also occurred in Trinidad oil fields.

1938 Serious disorders in British Guiana and Jamaica. Royal Commission established to consider depression in West Indies.

1940 The West Indies benefited considerably from the Colonial Development and Welfare Act (and also those of 1945 and 1949). Up to 1950, of £76,400,000 grants made to the empire as a whole, the West Indies received £18,700,000.

1939–45 The Second World War brought some recovery of prosperity but 65 new trade unions were founded and new leaders emerged. The most important of these were W.A. (Sir Alexander) Bustamente (Jamaica), N.W. Manley (Jamaica), Grantley Adams (Barbados), Bradshaw (St Kitts) and Bird (Antigua). They began to ask for the end of Crown Colony government, new constitutions and responsible government.

Jamaica

Jamaica was generally in the forefront of reforms.

1866   Old Legislative Assembly voted for its own abolition. Jamaica reverted to Crown Colony status.

1888   Elected members reintroduced into Legislative Council.

1944   New constitution. House of Representatives to be elected by full adult suffrage.

1953   Responsible government in internal matters, although Britain retained control of defence and foreign policy. W.A. Bustamente became Chief Minister.

Attempts to set up federation

Federations had been proposed before in 1876, 1921 and 1936 and one had been established in the Leeward Islands in 1871.

1938   Labour congress meeting in British Guiana urged federation.

1947   Conference met at Montego Bay and set up Standing 'Closer Association' Committee.

1953   The Committee's report was submitted to a conference meeting in London. It was accepted (subject to some modifications) and submitted to the individual governments. British Guiana and British Honduras were unwilling to join, but Jamaica (led by Norman Manley) and the other islands accepted it.

1956   Conference in London agreed on the setting up of a federation.

1957   Federation of the British West Indies set up.

1958   Federal elections. The Federalist Party, which was supported by Grantley Adams, Norman Manley and Dr Eric Williams, (the Prime Ministers of Barbados, Jamaica and Trinidad respectively) won a small majority. Grantley Adams became Federal Prime Minister. But the larger islands always had reservations about the Federation.

1961   Jamaicans voted in a referendum to leave.

1962   (May) Federation dissolved by an Act of the British Parliament.

1962–65   Smaller islands negotiated, generally unsuccessfully, for more limited federations.

Achievement of independence by individual islands

1953–58   Trinidad, Barbados, British Guiana and British Honduras achieved responsible government in internal matters similar to that won by Jamaica in 1953.

1962   (6 August) Jamaica became independent state within the Commonwealth.

(13 August) Trinidad and Tobago became an independent state within the Commonwealth.

1966   (November) Barbados became an independent state within the Commonwealth. Antigua (with Barbuda and Redonde), St Kitts-Nevis-Anguilla, Dominica, Grenada, St Lucia and St Vincent became 'Associated States' with Britain. All had full internal self-government, but Britain remained responsible for foreign policy and defence. A relic of the Federation remained in that they all shared one Supreme Court. (A more limited form of self-government was granted to Montserrat and the Virgin Islands.)

British Honduras (Belize)

1638   British settlement. The boundaries and even the existence of the colony were always a matter of dispute with the Spanish empire. The colonists evolved what the *Commonwealth Yearbook, 1993–4* described as a 'primitive form of democracy by Public Meeting'.[11]

1862   Became a British colony under the name of British Honduras.

1871   Informal constitutional arrangements were replaced by nominated Legislative Council.

1939   Guatemala revived Spanish claims and denounced the 1859 treaty settling boundaries.

1954   Legislative Assembly with elected majority. People's United Party formed.

---

[11] *Commonwealth Yearbook*, 1993–4, p. 140.

1960   Constitutional conference in London.

1961   People's United Party won all 18 elected seats in the Legislative Assembly.

1964   Full internal self-government.

1964–80   Guatemala pressed territorial claims. British troops sent. Commonwealth supported Belize's claims before United Nations.

1973   (1 June) Name changed officially to Belize.

1980   United Nations resolution called for independence on basis of territorial integrity by the end of 1981.

1981   (March) 'Heads of Agreement' signed to resolve territorial dispute but treaty not signed.
          (21 September) Belize became an independent state within the Commonwealth.

1991   (September) Guatemala recognised Belize's independence in return for concessions on the use of ports.

British Guiana (Guyana)

1961   Full internal self-government. Elections. Won by Dr Jagan's People's Progressive Party.

1962   Riots in capital, Georgetown. Constitutional conference in London failed to find solution.

1963   General strike. State of emergency declared and British troops sent.

1964   Crisis repeated. In December new elections were held. The resulting coalition government asked for independence.

1966   (May) Became independent under name of Guyana.

Bahamas (700 islands, not strictly within the Caribbean)

1629   Claimed by Britain.

1783–89   Influx of American Loyalists after the War of Independence.

1841   Legislative Council established.

1848   Turks and Caicos islands separated from Bahamas.

1950s   New prosperity arising from growing tourist trade.

1964   New constitution of a nominated Senate, a House of Assembly, elected by universal suffrage, and a cabinet system of government.

1967   Election. Progressive Liberal Party (PLP) and Labour Party formed coalition, after tying with 18 seats each. United Bahamian Party (UBP) became official opposition.

1968   (April) Fresh elections. PLP won.
     (September) Constitutional conference.

1969   (May) New constitutional arrangements, short of full independence. Governor retained special powers over external affairs and defence and, to some extent, internal security.

1972   (March) Independence proposals presented to Assembly.
     (September) PLP, fighting on an independence programme, won election.
     (December) Constitutional conference in London agreed new constitution.

1973   (10 July) Bahamas became independent within the Commonwealth.

Bermuda

1609   British settlement.

1684   British Crown took over government.

1964   New constitution. The Governor retained responsibility for external affairs, defence, internal security and police.

1995   (August) Bermudans rejected proposals for independence in a referendum by 16,369 to 5,714.

The Middle East

Egypt

Acquisition

1869   Suez Canal, built largely by French capital and technical expertise but Egyptian labour, opened.

1875   Britain acquired large financial stake in Suez Canal Company.

1882   Britain occupied Egypt (still nominally part of the Turkish empire), mainly to safeguard the Canal, which was a vital artery of British trade, as well as providing an essential link with her Indian empire. Her, legally irregular, position in Egypt was a diplomatic embarrassment to Britain until the First World War.

1888   International Convention guaranteeing freedom of passage through the Suez Canal to ships of all nations.

1914   (3 November) Turkey declared war on Britain.
         (18 December) Egypt declared to be a British Protectorate.

Early developments

1922   (28 February) The British Protectorate over Egypt was terminated and Egypt declared a sovereign, independent state, but substantial rights were reserved to Britain, pending further agreements regarding (a) the security of the British empire in Egypt (that is, communications), (b) the defence of Egypt against all foreign aggression or interference, direct or indirect, (c) the protection of foreign interests and minorities in Egypt, and (d) the Sudan. British troops remained in Egypt, as well as in the Sudan.

1923   Western-style constitution adopted, with a two-chamber legislature: the Chamber of Deputies entirely elected, the Senate partly elected, partly nominated by the King (Fuad). The Wafd Party, led first by Saad Zaghul and then by Mustafa al-Nahas, emerged as the most important political group. But after 1928, it was challenged by the Muslim Brotherhood, a fundamentalist organisation.

1924   (19 November) The murder, in a Cairo street, of Sir Lee Stack, the Sirdar (Commander-in-Chief) of the Egyptian army and the

Governor-General of the Sudan, led to a crisis in Anglo-Egyptian relations. Egyptian troops were withdrawn from the Sudan and cooperation between the British and Saad Zaghul ended.

1936   (28 April) Death of Fuad and succession of Farouk. (Regency until July 1937.)

(26 August) Anglo-Egyptian Treaty. This provided for the gradual withdrawal of the British troops in Egypt to the Canal Zone and the Sinai peninsula. But Britain reserved the right of reoccupation, together with the use of Egyptian ports, airfields and roads, in the event of war. The treaty was to be reviewed in 20 years.

1939   (September) The outbreak of the Second World War led to a complicated legal position in the Middle East. The areas of the former Ottoman empire under British and French control (which for this purpose included Egypt) were not themselves belligerents but they were within the war zone and fighting took place. Egypt remained the main British base and command centre for Middle Eastern operations.

1942   (4 February) The British compelled Farouk to accept Nahas Pasha, the Wafd leader, as Prime Minister, because he was prepared to cooperate with the Allies when other Egyptian groups had Italian or Fascist sympathies. Nahas Pasha was dismissed by Farouk in 1944.

1945   (March) Egypt was one of the leading Powers in setting up the Arab League, which also included Lebanon, Iraq, Syria, Transjordan, Yemen and Saudi Arabia, to work together to further Arab interests.

Developments after the Second World War

1945   Negotiations began on the revision of the 1936 treaty. Difficulties arose about British rights to send troops back into Egypt in the event of an international crisis (increasingly important as the Cold War developed) and Egyptian claims over the Sudan.

1946   (February–March) Serious rioting.

(October) Sidky–Bevin Agreement. All British forces would be withdrawn from the Cairo and Alexandria areas by 31 March 1947 and from the whole country by September 1949. The understanding again broke down over the Sudan. Sidky resigned as

Egyptian Prime Minister and was succeeded by Nokrashy Pasha. The Agreement was never ratified. In partial compliance, British troops were withdrawn to the Canal Zone.

1947   (August) Egypt referred the Sudan question to the United Nations Security Council but with no immediate result.

1948 (May)–1949 (January) Nokrashy's government became reluctantly involved in the armed struggle to prevent the establishment of the state of Israel in the former British-mandated territory of Palestine. The Egyptians felt humiliated by the poor showing of their army. Nokrashy declared the Muslim Brotherhood, which had taken advantage of the situation, dissolved in November 1948. Nokrashy himself was assassinated on 28 December 1948. Farouk's prestige was also irreparably damaged and young army officers ('Free Officers') began to plot.

1951   (October) Nahas Pasha, again Prime Minister, unilaterally denounced the 1936 Treaty, declared Farouk King of the Sudan, as well as Egypt, and began a campaign of harassment against the British troops still in the Canal Zone.

1952   (25 January) Battle between British forces and Egyptian police at Ismailia resulted in 50 dead and many injured. The next day (Black Saturday), there were serious riots in Cairo. Although British property (including the famous Shepheard's Hotel) was particularly targeted, attacks were also launched against other European-owned businesses.

(22/23 July) 'Free Officers' staged coup. Farouk abdicated on 26 July and was allowed to go into exile. The moving spirit of the Free Officers was Gamal Abdul Nasser, then a colonel, but since January 1952 their President had been the more senior General Mohammed Neguib. Neguib now headed the Revolutionary Command Council.

(August) The new Egyptian government agreed to separate the question of the Sudan from that of the presence of British forces in the Canal Zone (mistakenly believing that, given a free choice, the Sudanese would opt for union with Egypt).

1953   (18 June) Egypt proclaimed a republic, with Neguib as President and Nasser as his deputy.

1954   (19 October) Anglo-Egyptian Agreement signed. Britain would withdraw all her armed forces from the Canal Zone within 20 months. The Canal base would be maintained by civilians and could be reactivated in the event of an attack on Turkey or one of the Middle Eastern Arab states. (The British Prime Minister, Anthony Eden, had been contending for this since early 1953 as part of Britain's Cold War strategy.) Britain and Egypt agreed to uphold the 1888 Convention, guaranteeing freedom of navigation in the Suez Canal. The agreement was denounced by right-wing Conservatives in Britain (the Suez Group) and by the Muslim Brotherhood in Egypt.

(14 November) Nasser forced Neguib out of office and became Head of State in his place.

1956   (31 March) Three months earlier than provided for in the agreement, the last British troops left Egypt.

Suez crisis

1956   (26 July) Nasser announced the nationalisation of the Suez Canal. Nasser had staked his reputation on the economic regeneration of Egypt, for which he believed the building of the Aswan High Dam to be essential, and on Egypt's military strength in the continuing conflict between Israel and the Arab powers. As the Western powers, particularly the United States, continued to supply arms to Israel, Nasser turned to the Eastern bloc. America then became unwilling to lend money for the Aswan project. Since Nasser promised to continue to observe the 1888 Convention, the consensus of world opinion was that there was nothing illegal in Nasser's nationalisation proposals. But both Eden's government in London and Mollet's government in Paris determined to stop them if they could. Eden was influenced by his belief that Nasser was, if not another Hitler, at least a Mussolini, who wished to dominate the Arab world. Initially, the Americans too were unsympathetic to Nasser's actions.

(summer) There were various attempts to find an acceptable international solution: on 16–23 August a meeting of 'maritime nations' in London suggested an International Suez Canal Board to run the Canal; on 12/13 September Britain and France agreed to a proposal, put forward by the American Secretary of State, John Foster Dulles, for a Canal Users' Association. But Britain and France were dissatisfied because these schemes seemed to have no teeth and they feared Nasser would reject or evade them.

In parallel with these international negotiations, Britain, France and Israel drew up military contingency plans, at first separately, then in conjunction.

(30 July) Harold Macmillan, then British Chancellor of the Exchequer, told Robert Murphy, the American Deputy Under Secretary, that Britain and France were prepared to participate in a military operation.

(1 August) Dulles told Selwyn Lloyd, the British Foreign Secretary, and Christian Pineau, the French Foreign Minister, that Washington did not rule out the use of force but it would have to be backed by world opinion.

(1 September) Moshe Dayan, the Israeli Minister of Defence, was told of Anglo-French military plans.

(20 September – 1 October) Macmillan visited Washington and formed the opinion that Dulles and the American President, Dwight Eisenhower, would not oppose British use of force.

(28 September) Israeli Prime Minister, David Ben-Gurion, sent a high-powered delegation to Paris for discussions. These concluded that it would be better to act before the American Presidential elections on 5 November.

(12 October) Conferences started in Paris between French and Israelis to plan joint intervention, on the assumption that Britain and America would both remain neutral, although British military participation was regarded as highly desirable to take out the Egyptian air force at an early stage.

(14 October) Pineau's deputy and a member of the French General Staff met Eden at Chequers to propose a plan by which Israel would attack Egypt across Sinai. Britain and France would then intervene, ostensibly to separate the combatants and leave a force to guard the Canal.

(16 October) Eden and Selwyn Lloyd flew to Paris to discuss this with Mollet and Pineau.

(18 October) British Cabinet agreed that Britain and France should intervene to protect the Canal in the event of an Israeli attack.

(22–24 October) Conference at Sèvres between British, French and Israelis to discuss operational plans.

(22–24 October) International situation complicated by Hungarian rising against Soviet occupying forces.

(29 October) Israelis launched attack across the Suez Canal and, by 3 November, had virtually occupied the whole of Sinai.

(30 October) Mollet and Pineau flew to London for consultations and an Anglo-French ultimatum to both combatants was issued, to expire at dawn on 31 October.

(31 October) Britain and France attacked Egyptian airfields.

(4 November) Egyptians sank ships to block the Suez Canal.

(5 November) British and French paratroopers dropped at Port Said and Port Fuad, with intention of advancing to occupy the Canal.

British public opinion was deeply divided. Denunciations began in the House of Commons on 31 October, led by Hugh Gaitskill, the widely respected leader of the Labour Party. The Commonwealth generally had not been consulted and had no detailed knowledge of the planned operation. Australia and New Zealand supported the Anglo-French action. Canada tried to mediate. Many other member states denounced the action. At the United Nations, the Security Council first met on the afternoon of 31 October. Dag Hammarskjold, the Secretary General, demanded action. Britain and France used their vetoes, although the United States too denounced the operation. The Yugoslav delegate invoked (2 November) the 'Uniting for Peace' procedure, first used at the time of the Korean War, which circumvented the veto by transferring the discussion to the General Assembly.

(6 November) Eisenhower re-elected as President of the United States.

(7 November) Britain and France agreed to a cease-fire, before completing their objective of occupying the length of the Canal. Although the Soviet Union had hinted at the possibility of world war, or at least of pouring Russian 'volunteers' into the Middle East if Britain and France did not desist, the most effective pressure seems to have been exerted by the United States' readiness to enforce economic sanctions, including blocking Britain's drawing rights on the International Monetary Fund. The fear of a 'run on sterling' was decisive with the Chancellor of the Exchequer, Harold Macmillan, and, once he had withdrawn his support, Eden's position became untenable. Eden's health collapsed in the middle of the crisis, as did that of Dulles.

(15 November) United Nations forces arrived in the Canal Zone to replace the Anglo-French force and remain in position to separate the Egyptians and Israelis. Although primarily

observers, this was one of the earliest successful deployments of a United Nations force in a peace-keeping operation.

(22 December) Britain and France completed their withdrawal.

1957   (9 January) Eden resigned as British Prime Minister and was succeeded by Harold Macmillan.

Consequences of the Suez crisis

The United States was compelled to assume a more active role in the Middle East in the Cold War situation. For both Britain and France the humiliation of the failed Suez intervention was important in their final disillusionment with their imperial role.

For France it followed the disaster of Dien Bien Phu and coincided with the Algerian war. In 1956 the *loi cadre* was passed. Two years later the Fourth Republic fell and de Gaulle ended the Algerian war and negotiated a new relationship between France and her colonies in the French Community.

In Britain, the lessons were absorbed only slowly. The right-wing opposition to the dismantling of empire, which had manifested itself, for example, in the Suez group, was seriously discredited but lived on to fight other battles. The Suez crisis did not lead directly to the independence of Ghana the following year or to the decolonisation of the rest of Africa during the next decade – many of the crucial decisions had already been taken – but it did mean that there was little groundswell of opposition to accepting what was now seen as inevitable by the public generally: a contraction of Britain's world role and, in particular, a reduction of her responsibilities 'East of Suez', although that policy was not formally abandoned until 1968.

Anglo-Egyptian Sudan

Theoretically part of the Ottoman empire, Ottoman influence in this region of the Upper Nile was slight by the nineteenth century. Large parts were conquered by Mehemet Ali, the Pasha (Governor) of Egypt (1805–48), in pursuit of his own ambitions. The Egyptians, under British pressure, tried to suppress the slave trade and a British hero, General Charles Gordon, was Governor of the Sudan as an Egyptian employee, 1877–80. In 1880 a new leader, Mahomed Ali, proclaimed himself Mahdi (Messiah) in Kordofan and declared a holy war against the infidels. The decision was taken to evacuate most of the Sudan but the bungled evacuation led to the death of Charles Gordon at Khartoum in January 1885. 'Avenge Gordon' was a potent cry in the era of the new imperialism and General (later Field Marshal) Kitchener reconquered the Sudan in 1896–98. The fiction was maintained that the Sudan was the joint responsibility

of Britain and Egypt (although Britain was very much the senior part-
ner) and this was embodied in the Condominium Agreement of 1899.
The same year its western boundaries were agreed with France, following
the Fashoda crisis of the autumn of 1898. The future of the Sudan was a
major stumbling block in the resolution of Anglo-Egyptian differences
after 1945.

The Condominium

1924   After the murder of Sir Lee Stack, the Governor of the Sudan,
in Cairo on 19 November, Britain insisted on the evacuation of
the Egyptian army from the Sudan. Britain now effectively administered the Sudan alone and created a new Sudanese army.

1937   Foundation of Graduates' General Congress, a cultural organisation but one which gave rise to political parties with conflicting aims. The Ashiqqa wanted union with Egypt but the Umma
and the Ansar (which regarded itself as the heir of the Mahdists)
wanted independence for the Sudan.

1944   Advisory Council established with 24 Sudanese and 4 foreign
members. Its members were drawn from the Arab and Muslim
North and this tended to underline the division from the Black
Christian or Pagan South, where Indirect Rule was still firmly
established.

1945   (September) As part of the revision of the 1936 Anglo-Egyptian
Treaty, the Egyptians demanded the transfer of the Sudan to
their control and (in January 1947) took the matter to the
United Nations, which did not pronounce a judgment.

1947   Economic prosperity had grown under British rule and a strong
trade union movement had developed, led by the railway workers.
The Sudan Workers' Trade Union Federation called a successful
general strike.

1948   A new consitution was adopted (first discussed at a conference
in April 1946). The Legislative Assembly had 75 members, most
of whom were elected by male voters with certain property qualifications but 13 were chosen by chiefs and councils in the South
and 10 nominated by the Governor-General. Some 7 members
of the Executive Council were drawn from the Assembly, which

also elected the Prime Minister; 7 others, mostly officials, were nominated by the Governor. The Governor retained control of defence and foreign policy. Ashiqqa boycotted the elections and they were won by the Umma Party, led by Abdullah Khalil.

1951   (27 October) Egypt unilaterally abrogated the Condomimium Agreement of 1899 and proclaimed Farouk King of the Sudan as well as of Egypt.

Attainment of independence

1952   (July) Free Officers' coup in Egypt made new negotiations possible.

1953   (February) Egypt agreed to accept the possibility of Sudanese independence. New elections should be held and the Sudanese decide within three years whether to join Egypt or become independent.

      (November) Elections won by the National Union Party (Ashiqqa and some other groups), led by Ismail al-Azhari, who became Prime Minister. Umma formed opposition. Al-Azhari modified his pro-Egyptian stance.

1954   (January) Sudan achieved internal self-government.

1955   (December) The Sudanese House of Representatives voted for independence.

1956   (1 January) Sudan became an independent state, a republic, which chose not to join the Commonwealth.

Palestine

1897   First Zionist Congress in Basle put forward the idea of a Jewish 'homeland'. Zionist ideas had developed in response to growing anti-Semitism, particularly the 'pogroms' in Russia.

1904   Chaim Weizmann settled in Manchester and became the leader of an effective lobby group, which was particularly influential during the First World War. The Rothschild family, who as prominent bankers and politicians had the entrée into the highest echelons of British society, also played a part.

1905   The Zionist Congress rejected the idea put forward by the British Colonial Secretary, Joseph Chamberlain, in 1903 that they might find such a homeland in East Africa. They had already begun to organise Jewish settlements in Palestine, still part of the Ottoman empire, despite growing opposition from Palestinian Arabs.

1915   (March) Herbert Samuel, a Zionist sympathiser and a member of Asquith's Cabinet, suggested a British mandate over Palestine, coupled with a Jewish homeland there.

1916–17 The British Palestine Committee, in association with Weizmann, pressed the Jewish case and linked it with the British war effort.

1917   (2 November) Balfour Declaration. The British Foreign Secretary, A.J. Balfour, wrote a letter to Lord (Lionel) Rothschild, subsequently published, saying that Britain favoured the establishment of a national home for the Jewish people in Palestine, providing it did not prejudice the civil and religious rights of non-Jews resident there. The situation was complicated by the fact that the British had also encouraged the Arabs to assert their rights throughout the Ottoman empire, as part of the campaign against Germany's ally, Turkey.

   (9 December) General Allenby, the commander of the British Expeditionary Force, entered Jerusalem. In 1918 the British took Damascus, Beirut and Aleppo.

1918   Weizmann headed a Zionist Commission, which went to Palestine, hoping to put the Balfour Declaration into practice. He was opposed there by Feisal (later King of Iraq), the son and spokesman of Hussein, Sharif of Mecca, the leader of the Arab revolt against the Turks.

1919   Paris Peace Conference. Weizmann acted as spokesman for the Zionist cause and envisaged the arrival of 70–80,000 Jews in Palestine each year. An Arab terrorist group, the Black Hand, was formed to fight Jewish settlement.

British mandate

1920   Britain accepted the League of Nations Mandate for Palestine. Zionists were able to influence the wording, which spoke of 'the historic connection of the Jewish people with Palestine'. Arab riots in Jerusalem.

1921   Amin al-Husseini became Mufti (Muslim religious leader) of Jerusalem and led opposition to Jewish settlement.

1922   (22 July) The League of Nations formally approved the terms of the British Mandate over Palestine. This was a Class A Mandate, that is, it obliged the Mandatory Power to work towards independence but it also specifically obligated the British to facilitate the establishment of a 'Jewish national home'.

Winston Churchill, the Colonial Secretary, although himself a Zionist sympathiser, issued a cautious White Paper, warning that immigration must not be allowed to exceed the economic capacity of the country. Lord Curzon, the Foreign Secretary, had already expressed misgivings, doubting whether the promises to the Zionists were compatible with self-determination in a country with 580,000 Arabs and, at most, 60,000 Jews.

1919–31   Jewish population grew to 175,000, rising from 8 to 17.7 per cent of the population.

1922   Sir Herbert Samuel, himself Jewish, was appointed as the first British Governor. The Arabs refused to cooperate in the establishment of a representative council.

1929   Jewish Agency established to assist Jewish immigration and buy lands for immigrants. It became the official representative body of world Zionism to both the British government and the League of Nations. The Jews also set up Haganah, their own defence force.

(August) Arab and Jewish riots in Jerusalem.

1930   The British sent out a Commission of Enquiry under Sir Walter Shaw. A report by Sir John Hope Simpson led the Colonial Secretary, Lord Passfield (Sidney Webb), to conclude that Palestine could barely support its existing population and to issue a White Paper calling for restrictions on immigration.

1930–31   Weizmann and others organised a very effective campaign in London.

1931   (13 February) The Prime Minister, Ramsay MacDonald, wrote a letter to Weizmann, reaffirming Britain's commitment to continued Jewish immigration. This letter was subsequently published and dubbed the 'Black Letter' by the Arabs.
Izz al-Din al Qassam preached holy war in Palestine.

1933   Hitler came to power in Germany.

1935   (September) Nuremberg Laws deprived German Jews of their civil rights. Jewish migration to Palestine peaked at over 61,000.

1936   Followers of Qassam initiated major Arab rebellion, which continued until 1939.

1936–37   Royal Commission under Lord Peel sent to investigate. Reported (June 1937) in favour of the division of Palestine into an Arab state, a Jewish state and a third part of particular strategic or religious sensitivity to remain under British mandate. The idea of partition was never completely dropped thereafter, but with the approach of the Second World War and the need to conciliate Arab opinion it was held to be impractical.

1937   Irgun Zvai Leumi (National Military Organisation), founded by David Raziel, began to organise a terrorist campaign against the Arabs.

1939   (February) Zionist bombing campaign throughout Palestine in which 38 Arabs died.
(February–March) Round Table Conference in London. Arabs refused to negotiate with Zionists.
(May) British Colonial Secretary, Malcolm MacDonald, issued a White Paper, rejecting the idea of partition and affirming that Britain envisaged an independent Palestine, in which Jews and Arabs would share the government. Targets were set for Jewish immigration: 75,000 would be admitted over the next five years; after that immigration would be subject to Arab consent.

Second World War

The situation was fundamentally changed by Hitler's persecution of the Jews, culminating in the 'Final Solution', in which up to 6 million Jews perished. Zionist lobbying largely switched from London to the United

States. American domestic politics meant that the Jewish vote was crucial to both the Democrat and the Republican Parties. American pressure, when Britain was economically very weak and dependent on American aid after the war, led to the precipitate abandonment of the mandate.

1939   (September) Irgun promised a truce for the duration of the war.

1940   Abraham Stern broke with Irgun and formed Lohame Herut Israel (Fighters for the Freedom of Israel), more generally known as the Stern Gang, which reverted to terrorism, attacking moderate Jews, as well as the British.

1942   Menachem Begin arrived in Palestine from Poland and denounced the British for not doing more to save the Jews of Central Europe. He assumed the leadership of Irgun.

1944   (February) Irgun began to attack police stations, government buildings and immigration offices.

(23 March) Stern Gang killed seven British policemen in Tel Aviv.

(April) Anglo-American discussions. The British told the Americans that they could contain the situation so long as the Americans did not support militant Zionists. The Americans replied that they could exercise little control in an (American) election year.

(27 June) The Republican Party adopted a platform calling for the opening of Palestine to unrestricted immigration for the victims of Nazi persecution, unrestricted Jewish landownership and the establishment of Palestine as a free and democratic commonwealth.

(15 October) President Roosevelt (Democrat) promised that, if re-elected, he would work for 'the establishment of Palestine as a free and democratic Jewish Commonwealth'.

(6 November) Lord Moyne, British Minister Resident in the Middle East, murdered in Cairo by the Stern Gang.

(17 November) Churchill made it plain that his previous sympathy with Zionism had evaporated. Short-lived cooperation during which the Jewish Agency and even Haganah handed over members of Irgun and the Stern Gang to the British authorities.

1945   (May) End of the war in Europe. Full horror of the concentration camps now known.

(July) Labour victory in the British general election. New Foreign Secretary, Ernest Bevin, had been a Zionist sympathiser but now concluded that to back Jewish immigration to Israel would cause unacceptable damage to Britain's relations with the Arab states and might be of no service to Jews, who should be helped to re-establish themselves in Europe, rather than shipped out to fight hostile Palestinians.

(October) Completion of alliance between Haganah, Irgun and even the Stern Gang to launch military campaign to establish a Jewish state in Palestine. Began attacks on bridges, railways and British troops.

(9 November) Bevin announced the appointment of an Anglo-American Commission of Enquiry. The mandate would need to be converted into a United Nations trusteeship agreement and Bevin suggested the Commission should seek a permanent solution of the problem to put before the United Nations.

1946   (25 April) Seven British soldiers killed by the Stern Gang in Tel Aviv.

(30 April) The American President, Harry Truman, accepted Congress recommendation that 100,000 certificates should be issued to allow the immediate entry of Jewish refugees into Palestine.

(1 May) The British Prime Minister, Clement Attlee, told the House of Commons that it would be impossible to absorb so many refugees so quickly.

(22 July) A series of terrorist outrages culminated in the blowing up of the King David Hotel in Jerusalem, in which 91, mainly civilians, died.

(5 August) The Jewish Agency suggested a partition plan.

(4 October) President Truman indicated sympathy with the partition plan.

1946–47   (Winter) Security situation seriously deteriorated. Britain evacuated non-essential personnel. Martial law imposed for a time in Tel Aviv, following the murder of British soldiers.

1947   (February) Britain announced that she was referring the Palestinian question to the United Nations.

(April–May) Britain protested to the United States about the open collection of large sums of money to run illegal immigrant ships to Palestine and arm terrorists.

(May) United Nations Special Committee on Palestine (UNSCOP) set up with broad powers of investigation.

(July) British public opinion particularly horrified by the circumstances of the hanging of two British sergeants and the booby-trapping of their bodies. An illegal immigrant ship, the *Exodus*, was intercepted and the 4,493 refugees aboard sent back to Germany, from where they had come.

(31 August) UNSCOP's majority plan proposed a partition, into an Arab state and a Jewish state, with the city of Jerusalem remaining under international trusteeship. Britain should administer the mandate during the interim period and admit 150,000 refugees.

(26 September) Bevin announced that, if no satisfactory solution could be found, Britain would simply surrender its mandate and withdraw its forces and administration by June 1948 at the latest.

(28 November) David Ben-Gurion arranged a secret purchase of arms, mainly from Eastern bloc countries, although bought with American money.

(29 November) The United Nations General Assembly voted for partition. The Mufti of Jerusalem proclaimed a *jihad*, or holy war, complaining that the Jews constituted less than a third of the population and owned less than 10 per cent of the land but that the United Nations was awarding them 55 per cent of the land. The Zionists on their side were dissatisfied because they were not given Jerusalem.

(December) General fighting broke out between Arabs and Jews.

(4 December) The British Cabinet resolved that British troops would be withdrawn by 15 May 1948.

1948   (March) Communications seriously disrupted throughout Palestine.

(22 March) The British government instructed Chief of Staff to accelerate British withdrawal.

(April–May) Zionists had about 60,000 men under arms in various capacities. Captured Haifa and Jaffa. Many Arabs fled to avoid the fighting, some under truces arranged by the British.

(13 April) Arabs attacked convoy of, mainly Jewish, doctors and nurses on road to Mount Scorpus; 77 were killed.

(15 April) Bevin told the American ambassador, Lewis Douglas, that British public opinion would not tolerate further British

military involvement and suggested that the Americans send troops.

(4 May) Washington suggested cease-fire and extension of the mandate. Bevin refused.

(9 May) Massacre at Deir Yassin: 245 Arab villagers killed by Irgun and Stern Gang, under Haganah command. This was believed to have been done with the approval of Ben-Gurion to encourage Arabs to flee their lands.

(14 May) British troops evacuated Jerusalem. Arabs and Israelis seized parts of the city.

(14 May) Establishment of Jewish state to be called Israel proclaimed by Ben Gurion, with Weizmann as President and Ben Gurion as Prime Minister.

(14 May) United States recognised the state of Israel.

(15 May) Armies of neighbouring Arab states entered Israel and first Arab–Israeli war began.

1949   (24 February) Armistice signed at Rhodes between Israel and Egypt, followed by further agreements with Lebanon, Jordan and Syria. By these agreements, Israel retained nearly 80 per cent of the area covered by the Palestine mandate and 20 per cent more than had been allocated to it by the United Nations partition plan. But Jerusalem remained divided.[12]

Transjordan (Jordan)

Creation

1918   After Turkish surrender, General Allenby allowed Feisal, the son of Hussein, Sherif of Mecca, and commander of the Arab forces, to administer Damascus and Beirut.

1919   Paris Peace Conference. Feisal asked the Great Powers for independence for Arab states in line with the Fourteen Points. The Great Powers determined on the mandate system.

1920   (March) Elected assembly in Damascus proclaimed Feisal King of an independent state of Syria, which included Palestine, Lebanon and what became Transjordan. American Commission of

---

[12] For events after 1949 see R. Ovendale, *Longman Companion to the Middle East since 1914*, 1992.

Enquiry had found strong opposition to the separation of Syria and Palestine.

(April) San Remo Conference allocated mandates for Syria and Lebanon to France, and for Palestine and Mesopotamia (Iraq) to Britain.

1921 British Colonial Secretary, Winston Churchill, created the state of Transjordan in the northern Arabian desert plus the territory east of the River Jordan, with a capital at Amman (then a village), to be ruled over by Abdullah, another son of Hussein.

1922 (September) Britain made it clear that commitments to providing a Jewish homeland would not apply to Transjordan.

(December) Britain recognised the existence of self-government in Transjordan but took close interest in the army, the Arab Legion, founded by Glubb Pasha in 1920, and controlled foreign policy, reinforced by an agreement in 1928.

Independence

1942 Abdullah and Nuri es-Said (of Iraq) developed the idea of 'Greater Syria', a union of Transjordan, Syria and Palestine, which would later include the Lebanon, and be in a close relationship with Iraq and Saudi Arabia.

1944 Transjordan, with British encouragement, joined the Arab League.

1946 (22 March) Britain recognised the independence of Transjordan, now called Jordan, and concluded a formal alliance with new state. Jordanians were invited to London to negotiate about the future of Palestine. Abdullah was prepared to accept the Jewish state within defined limits but wished to control the rest of Palestine. Ernest Bevin was sympathetic to the view.

1948 War with Israel. The attitude of the Arab Legion, as the best Arab army, was regarded as crucial. Jordan occupied East Jerusalem and territory on the West Bank of the Jordan.

1967 New war with Israel. Israel occupied East Jerusalem and Jordanian West Bank.

Iraq (Mesopotamia)

British interest in Mesopotamia, the land of the two rivers, the Tigris and Euphrates, was originally strategic and connected with possible routes to India. In the twentieth century another very important dimension was added, that of oil.

Acquisition

1908   First important oil strike – in Persia.

1918   Mesopotamia came under Anglo-Indian administration.

1919   Britain and France signed an agreement about oil in the former Ottoman empire.

1920   (April) San Remo conference gave Britain the mandate over Mesopotamia.
       (April–July) Feisal had been installed as the ruler of Syria. Following the San Remo Conference, which gave France the mandate over Syria, he was expelled by French troops.
       (June) Rebellion in Iraq, which was put down with difficulty. Britain suggested that Feisal should become King.

1921   (August) Feisal confirmed as King after a referendum.

1925   Constitution agreed in Iraq.

1930   (30 June) Anglo-Iraqi Treaty gave Iraq full independence, although with a promise of consultation on foreign affairs.

1932   (October) Iraq became a member of the League of Nations.

1933   Death of Feisal inaugurated a period of political confusion.

1938   Nuri es-Said, Feisal's former right-hand man (who had negotiated the 1930 treaty) and was pro-British, brought to power by army officers.

1939–45 Iraq broke off relations with Germany on the outbreak of war. Britain's need to keep on good terms with Iraq (and other Arab states) was a factor in restricting Jewish immigration to Palestine.

1945–58   Nuri-es-Said continued pro-British policy: supported Baghdad
Pact and opposed Nasser.

1958   Nuri-es-Said and King (Feisal II) overthrown and murdered in
a coup, which brought the army to power.

Aden

Acquisition

1839   Britain took possession of the port of Aden, near the southern
extremity of the Red Sea, to safeguard India at a time when
French influence was growing in Egypt. It was originally under
the authority of the government of Bombay. Treaties with local
rulers created the Protectorate of Aden in the hinterland.

1869   With the opening of the Suez Canal, Aden became a busy port.

1920s   With the collapse of the Ottoman empire, the ruler of neighbouring Yemen tried to extend his authority. The British used
air power (an early example of such a policy) to stop him.

1937   Transferred to the jurisdiction of the Colonial Office.

Independence

1947   Indian independence.

1951–54   British Petroleum lost privileged position in Iran.

1954   British Petroleum built large new facility in Aden.

1955   Four elected members added to the Legislative Council in the
colony but on an extremely restricted franchise, designed to
exclude all immigrant workers, who made up the majority population in Aden itself.

1956   Britain told representatives of Aden that, although they could
have more internal self-government, the British government
could not 'relax their responsibilities' for the colony, i.e. no
independence.

After the Suez crisis Arab nationalist feeling began to grow. At the same time Aden came to seem of increasing importance to Britain as a military base and staging post for troops.

1959   Britain helped to establish the Federation of Arab Emirates of the South in the Protectoratc. This was attacked from the Yemen.

1962   The Legislative Council in the colony voted to join the Federation, henceforth called the Federation of Southern Arabia. Feudal government in the Yemen was overthrown by revolution backed by Nasser's Egypt. Powerful trade unions in Aden began to cooperate with Yemen. The British Foreign Office (and the United States) favoured an accommodation with the new government in (North) Yemen. But the revolution there was incomplete and Macmillan's Conservative government opted to support the opposition in the Yemen.

1963   Britain offered Aden and the Federation independence under its existing rulers, but this encountered resistance from the National Liberation Front.

1967   Britain ceded power to the National Liberation Front and the country became independent as the People's Democratic Republic of Yemen (sometimes called South Yemen). Did not join the Commonwealth.

1990   (22 May) United with North Yemen to form Yemen Republic.

United Arab Emirates (Trucial States)
These sheikhdoms on the Persian Gulf and the Gulf of Oman were never strictly part of the British empire but they had close treaty relations with Britain, which came to control their foreign policy.

1820   The Sheikhs signed a treaty with Britain guaranteeing permanent peace. This was followed by other agreements, including some for the suppression of the slave trade.

1853   Perpetual Maritime Truce.

1892   Exclusive Agreement. By this the Sheikhs bound themselves and their heirs and successors not to enter into agreements or cede territory to any Power but Britain.

1971   Britain withdrew forces from Persian Gulf and on 2 December Britain's special treaty relations came to an end and a new independent state, the United Arab Emirates, was formed by Abu Dhabi, Ajman, Dubai, Fujirah, Sharjah, Umm al-Qaiwan and Ras al-Khaimah (last joined February 1972). The UAE concluded a treaty of friendship with Britain.

Iran (Persia)

Iran was never formally part of the British empire, but in the twentieth century it was a client state, whose fate was intimately bound up with that of the empire. Britain's first interest in Persia (as it was known until the 1920s) was strategic. Control of the Persian Gulf was of great importance to the security of the Indian empire. But in the twentieth century, oil became the most important factor.

Background

1901   First concession to exploit oil granted to an Englishman, William Knox d'Arcy.

1907   Anglo-Russian Agreement divided Persia into three parts: a Russian sphere of influence in the North, including the capital Teheran; a British sphere in the South, including the Persian Gulf coast; and a neutral sphere between.

   The Shah granted a constitution. First reform movements in Iran paralleled those of Young Turks in Ottoman empire. Britain favoured liberals (who included Mohammed Mossadeq), as against Russians who favoured conservative monarchists.

1908   First important oil strike near Abadan.

1909   Anglo-Persian Oil Company established.

1914   On the outbreak of war the British government bought a controlling interest in the Anglo-Persian Oil Company. British and Russian troops were stationed in the country but Russians withdrew after the 1917 revolution.

1919   (August) A treaty was drawn up by which, in return for a loan, Persia would have accepted British advisers to reorganise the army and the finances. This would have created a quasi-protectorate but was never ratified.

1921   Reza Khan became Prime Minister.

1925   Reza Khan elected Shah in place of last of Qajar Dynasty, Sultan Ahmed Shah. He insisted on use of the name Iran in place of Persia.

1933   Agreement on Anglo-Iranian Oil Company profit-sharing with Iran.

1939   On the outbreak of the Second World War, the Iranian government declared for neutrality but showed sympathy with Germany.

1941   When Germany invaded Russia, both British (Indian) and Russian troops entered Iran. On 16 September the Shah abdicated in favour of his son, Mohammed Reza Shah Pahlavi, regarded by the Allies as weak and malleable.

1945–46   British, and subsequently, Russian troops withdrawn.

Oil crisis

1948   Labour government in Britain, faced with a financial crisis, required all British companies to limit dividend payments. This affected the Anglo-Iranian Oil Company's payments to Iran.

1949   New agreement negotiated but figures revealed that the British government was receiving $79 million, Iran only $37.8 million.

1950   The new Prime Minister, General Razmara, attempted to secure the agreement of the Majlis (Parliament) to the 1949 agreement. This was opposed by Mossadeq, who declared Iran should never have granted such concessions to a foreign company.

1951   (March) Razmara assassinated by a fanatic.
   (29 April) Mossadeq elected Prime Minister.
   (2 May) Iranian oil industry nationalised.
   Britain appealed to the United Nations and to the International Court of Justice against this unilateral abrogation of the 1933 Agreement. Covert operations began to bring down Mossadeq. Oil Company refused to cooperate with Iranian government.
   (July) All exports ceased. Americans attempted to mediate.

(September) Iranians occupied Abadan refinery. British government seriously considered use of military force. Law Officers advised that that would be illegal.

(October) Britain evacuated Abadan.

1952   (22 July) International Court of Justice ruled it had no jurisdiction.

(11 August) Mossadeq given dictatorial powers by Iranian Parliament. Further negotiations with Britain broke down.

(22 October) Iran broke off diplomatic relations with Britain.

(October–December) America now alarmed by Mossadeq's Soviet associations. CIA and MI6 began to plan Mossadeq's overthrow in 1953. The principal agents were Kermit Roosevelt and C.M. Woodhouse.

1953   Mossadeq began to offend Islamic leaders by secular reforms and his position was weakened.

(29 July) American President, Eisenhower, warned Mossadeq that he would get no further American aid unless he settled the nationalisation dispute with Britain.

(August) American-led coup. The Shah agreed to dismiss Mossadeq but fled to Rome. On 19 August Mossadeq was deposed by troops. On 22 August the Shah returned. American, not British, influence was now dominant.

1954   (5 August) New oil deal. Anglo-Iranian (now British Petroleum) owned 40 per cent of new company; American companies, 40 per cent; Royal Dutch Shell, 14 per cent; and French Petroleum Company, 6 per cent.

Cyprus

The island of Cyprus, 40 miles from Turkey and 500 miles from mainland Greece, but predominantly Greek in population, has always been regarded as strategically important in the Eastern Mediterranean, despite its lack of deep water harbours. From the setting up of an independent Greek state in 1830, Greeks wished for *enosis* (union between Cyprus and Greece). (Britain had returned the Ionian Islands, a British Protectorate since 1815, to Greece in the 1860s.)

1878   Britain leased the island from the Sultan of Turkey.

1914   (5 November) After Turkey had declared for the German side in the First World War, Britain annexed Cyprus.

1915   Many British Philhellenes (including Winston Churchill) had sympathised with Greek ambitions and Britain now offered to cede Cyprus to Greece if she would come into the war against Germany. Greece refused.

1925   Cyprus became a Crown Colony. Britain, now a dominant power in the Eastern Mediterranean, was less sympathetic to Greek aspirations than in the past.

1931   Riots. Britain suspended the constitution.

1931–39   Little political activity or agitation.

1943   Cypriot Communist party (AKEL) did well in municipal elections.

1944–45   Civil war in Greece. Communists defeated.

1945   British Labour government promised to call a consultative assembly in Cyprus to discuss constitutional and other reforms but did not offer self-determination. As the Cold War developed, Britain became involved in a difficult balancing act between two allies, Greece and Turkey, both of whom now put forward claims in Cyprus.

1948   Britain put forward new constitutional proposals, which would have ensured a Greek majority in legislature, but these were rejected because they did not offer *enosis*.

1950   Makarios, then Bishop of Kition, organised a plebiscite among the Greek Orthodox, who voted 96 per cent in favour of *enosis*. Later in the year Makarios became Archbishop and formal religious leader of the Greek Cypriots.

1952   Makarios recruited Colonel George Grivas to organise EOKA (National Organisation of Cypriot Fighters) to organise the military wing of the *enosis* movement, possibly without realising his reputation for violence and ruthlessness.

1954   Britain finally withdrew troops from the Suez base and looked to Cyprus as a possible alternative.
          (28 July) Henry Hopkinson, Minister of State at the Colonial Office, incautiously said in the House of Commons that Cyprus could 'never expect to be fully independent'. This caused an

outcry from the Labour opposition and the Greek government took the matter to the United Nations, who however refused to consider it.

1955   (April) Grivas and EOKA launched a brutal terror campaign which lasted four years. Field Marshal Sir John Harding, the Chief of the Imperial General Staff, was appointed Governor to deal with it and a State of Emergency was later declared in November.

1956   (March) Archbishop Makarios exiled to the Seychelles.
    The Suez crisis and its aftermath altered British strategic thinking: Britain was less concerned with keeping conventional forces in Cyprus, and attached more importance to air bases.

1957   (April) Makarios allowed to return to Athens, but not to Cyprus.

1957–58   Violence began between Greek and Turkish Cypriots, each side receiving covert support from the Greek and Turkish governments.

1957   (December) The British Prime Minister, Harold Macmillan, signalled a policy change by appointing Sir Hugh Foot as Governor. Although a career civil servant, then serving in Nigeria, Hugh Foot was the brother of Michael Foot, a leading Labour politician, known to be sympathetic to decolonisation. The Turks were suspicious and began to ask for the partition of the island.

1958   (November–December) Direct talks began between Greece and Turkey, initially between respective Foreign Ministers, Evangelos Averoff and Fatim Zorlu, in New York.

1959   (February) Zurich meeting of Greek and Turkish Prime Ministers, Constantine Karamanlis and Adnam Mendere.
    (19 February) Agreement signed in London between Britain, Greece and Turkey, despite last-minute objections from Makarios. *Enosis* was rejected. Cyprus was to become an independent republic with power-sharing arrangements: a Greek Cypriot President and a Turkish Cypriot Vice-President, and a House of Representatives with 35 Greek and 15 Turkish members. As NATO allies, Britain, Greece and Turkey all retained some rights to a military presence on the island – in Britain's case air bases, which remained under British sovereignty.
    (December) Elections. Makarios became President.

1960   (16 August) Cyprus became an independent republic within the Commonwealth.

Events after independence
Communal troubles between Greeks and Turks continued.

1964   (March) United Nations peace-keeping force sent.

1974   (July) Makarios overthrown by more extreme supporters of *enosis*. Turks invaded and occupied northern third of the island.

1983   Turkish Cypriots announced the setting up of Turkish Republic of Northern Cyprus but this was not internationally recognised.

Oceania

Ellice Islands (Tuvalu)

1892   Became British Protectorate.

1916   Annexed and became British Crown Colony (administered with Gilbert Islands).

1942   Occupied by Japanese.

1963   Advisory Council set up.

1970   Legislative and Executive Councils established.

1974   Ministerial system of government instituted.
        (1 October) Referendum went in favour of separating from the Gilbert Islands.

1978   (1 October) Became independent member of the Commonwealth under name of Tuvalu.

Fiji

1874   Became British colony.

1970   (10 October) Became independent state within the Commonwealth.

1986   Census revealed that native Fijians were a minority because of immigration from the Indian sub-continent: 48.6 per cent Indian; 46.2 per cent Fijian; 5.2 per cent other races.

1987   (14 May) Military coup overthrew government.

       (7 October) Government of Colonel Sitiveni Rabuka declared Fiji a republic and did not seek continued membership of the Commonwealth.

1990   New constitution reserved 37 seats (out of 70) in the House of Representatives for 'indigenous Fijians'.

Gilbert Islands (Kiribati)

1892   Became British Protectorate.

1916   Annexed and became British colony (administered with Ellice Islands).

1942   Occupied by Japanese.

1974   (1 October) Referendum went in favour of separating from the Ellice Islands.

1979   (12 July) Became independent republic within the Commonwealth under the name of Kiribati.

Hong Kong

1842   Island of Hong Kong ceded to Britain by the treaty of Nanking.

1860   Britain also acquired the Kowloon Peninsula.

1898   Britain began a 99-year lease on the 'New Territories', mainland territories vital for, among other things, an adequate water supply.

1942–45   Japanese occupation.

1982   British talks with China on the 1997 expiration of the lease.

1984   (26 September) Agreement on Hong Kong becoming a 'special administrative region' of China on the expiration of the lease.

1997   (1 July) Hong Kong restored to Chinese sovereignty.

Maldives

1887   Protectorate arrangement formalised.

1948   Remained a Protectorate when Ceylon became independent. Britain controlled external relations but undertook not to interfere in internal affairs.

1960   Maldives allowed to conduct certain foreign relations themselves in return for permitting British air base on Gan island.

1965   (26 July) Became fully independent and Britain ceased to be responsible for either defence or foreign policy.

1976   British forces withdrew.

1982   (1 July) Became a 'special' (in effect, associated) member of the Commonwealth.

1985   (20 June) Became full member of the Commonwealth.

Malta

1798   Captured from the French during the Napoleonic Wars.

1814   Confirmed in British possession. Governed as a Crown Colony but Advisory Council included Maltese from an early date.

1921   Bi-cameral Legislature established: Senate, partly nominated, partly elected; Legislative Assembly, wholly elected. System of Dyarchy established. The Governor remained responsible for foreign policy, defence and the language question.

1921–36   Constant political crises.

1936   Constitution revoked.

1939   Reverted to Crown Colony status.

1939–45   Of exceptional strategic importance during the Second World War, blockaded and heavily bombed.

1947   Self-government restored but with defence and some other matters still reserved for the Governor. Single chamber, elected legislature.

1953   Nationalist coalition government asked for Dominion status. Britain was unwilling to agree for strategic reasons and made the unique offer of integration in the United Kingdom with representation in Westminster Parliament. This was not accepted.

1955   Labour administration of Dom Mintoff in Malta.
(December) Round Table Conference. The Labour Party would have accepted representation at Westminster. The National Party wanted independence within the Commonwealth. Britain wished to continue to control foreign policy and defence.

1956   (February) Referendum in Malta showed 76 per cent in favour of integration with Britain. This was accepted in principle by British government but negotiations broke down on details.

1958   (March) Both the governing Labour Party and opposition asked for independence.

1959   Britain resumed direct government.

1960   Maltese constitutional commission.

1962   (March) New constitution restoring internal self-government. Nationalist Party, led by Dr Borg Olivier, successful at the polls.

1963   The Malta Independence Conference in London was inconclusive but Olivier subsequently produced a new constitution, which was approved by a referendum.

1964   (21 September) Became independent within the Commonwealth.

1974   (December) Became a republic.

Mauritius

1810   Taken from France during the Napoleonic Wars. (As the Île de France had attracted French settlers but population later predominantly Indians, who came to work in the sugar plantations.)

1810–1903   Administered with the Seychelles as a single colony.

1886   Some elective element in Council.

1903   Became separate colony.

1947   New constitution established first Legislative Council, elected on a wide franchise. (Became universal suffrage in 1958.)

1957   Ministerial system introduced.

1965   Constitutional conference. Independence promised after new elections if the Legislative Council wished it.

1967   Strong local opposition to independence but the Alliance Independence Party, which favoured it, won the elections.

1968   (12 March) Became an independent state within the Commonwealth.

Nauru

A small Pacific island with a population in 1992 of about 10,000, dependent on single industry, phosphates. A doubtful starter for nation status.

1888   Became German possession.

1920   Mandate shared by Britain, Australia and New Zealand but actually administered by Australia.

1942   Occupied by Japanese.

1947   Became trusteeship territory.

1968   (31 January) Became an independent republic with special (in effect, associate) membership of the Commonwealth.

New Hebrides (Vanuatu)

1906   Anglo-French Condomimium established.

1922   Details of arrangement revised.

1974   Anglo-French agreement on independence.

1975   Elections.

1977   Vanua'aku Party (VP) organised a boycott of the political process because they disliked some constitutional provisions.

1979   Constitutional conference.
         (23 October) Britain and France agreed a new constitution by an exchange of notes.

1980   (May) A Francophone group on the island of Santo tried to break away from the rest of the group.
         (24 July) British and French troops sent.
         (30 July) New Hebrides became independent and a member of the Commonwealth under the name Vanuatu. Politics continued to be turbulent.

Papua New Guinea

1884   British Protectorate established on South Coast of New Guinea. (Germans established to the north.)

1902   Placed under Australian authority.

1920   Australian mandate established.

1942   Japanese occupation.

1949   Became trusteeship territory. Legislative Council established with small elective element.

1963   House of Assembly with elected majority.

1965   House appointed Select Committee on constitutional development.

1971   Committee reported in favour of self-government.

1973   (December) Self-government established.

1975   (16 December) Became an independent state within the Commonwealth.

Seychelles

Consisted of 115 islands with a population in 1992 of 70,763 of very mixed ethnic origin.

1810   Taken by the British during the Napoleonic Wars.

1810–1903   Regarded as a dependency of Mauritius.

1903   Became Crown Colony with a Governor and Legislative and Executive Councils.

1976   (29 June) Became independent with its first constitution.

1977   (June) A coup established single-party government.

1991   Decision taken to hold plebiscite on multi-party system.

1993   New constitution. Commonwealth observers supervised referendum and elections.

Solomon Islands

1893–1900   British Protectorate established.

1942   Japanese occupation.

Post 1945   Masino Ruu movement rejected cooperation with the West and tried to organise own society with promises of earthly paradise.

1952   Partly to combat this a Provincial Council (later Assembly) was organised.

1974   New constitution provided for an elected Legislative Council of 24, which chose the Chief Minister.

1976   Elections.

1977   Constitutional conference drew up a new constitution.

1978   (7 July) Became an independent state within the Commonwealth.

Tonga (Friendly Islands)

1826 onwards   Close missionary ties with Britain.

1900   Became a British Protected State. Retained its own monarchy and control of internal affairs.

1970   (June) Britain ceased to be responsible for external relations. Tonga became a member of the Commonwealth.

Western Samoa

1899   Annexed by Germany.

1919   New Zealand became the Mandatory Power.

1946   Became United Nations trust territory.

1947   Legislative Assembly established.

1959   Cabinet government established.

1960   Constitutional conference.

1961   (May) Plebiscite, held under the auspices of the United Nations, voted overwhelmingly for independence.

1962   (1 January) Became independent.

1970   (August) Became a member of the Commonwealth.

The (British) Commonwealth

Membership as at January 1997
(with date of joining)

Antigua and Barbuda (1981)
Australia (1931)
The Bahamas (1973)
Bangladesh (1972)
Barbados (1966)
Belize (1981)

Botswana (1966)
Brunei (1984)
Cameroons (1995)
Canada (1931)
Cyprus (1961)
Dominica (1978)

The Gambia (1965)
Ghana (1957)
Grenada (1974)
Guyana (1966)
India (1947)
Jamaica (1962)
Kenya (1963)
Kiribati (1979)
Lesotho (1966)
Malawi (1964)
Malaysia (1957)
The Maldives (1982)
Malta (1964)
Mauritius (1968)
Mozambique (1995)
Namibia (1990)
Nauru (1968)
New Zealand (1931)
Nigeria (1960)*
Pakistan (1947)
Papua New Guinea(1975)

St Christopher and Nevis (1983)
St Lucia (1979)
St Vincent and the Grenadines (1979)
Seychelles (1976)
Sierra Leone (1961)
Singapore (1965)
Solomon Islands (1978)
South Africa (1931)
Sri Lanka (1948)
Swaziland (1968)
Tanzania (1961)
Tonga (1970)
Trinidad and Tobago(1962)
Tuvalu (1978)
Uganda (1962)
United Kingdom
Vanuatu (1980)
Western Samoa (1970)
Zambia (1964)
Zimbabwe (1980)

*Membership suspended in 1995.

Countries which have left the Commonwealth
Fiji (1987)
Republic of Ireland (1949)
Pakistan (1972, rejoined 1989)
South Africa (1961, rejoined 1994)

Dependent Territories (of the United Kingdom)
Anguilla
Bermuda
British Antarctic Territory
British Indian Ocean Territory
British Virgin Islands
Cayman Islands
Falkland Islands
Gibraltar
Montserrat
Pitcairn Group
St Helena, with Ascension Island and Tristan da Cunha
South Georgia and South Sandwich Islands
Turks and Caicos Islands

Origins

The Commonwealth grew out of the development of Colonial (later Imperial) Conferences. The first meeting was in 1887, when leading men from the colonies happened to be in London for Queen Victoria's golden jubilee. The 1907 meeting gave a formal shape to the organisation. Meetings were to take place every four years under the chairmanship of the British Prime Minister and discuss 'questions of common interest'. Canada, Australia, New Zealand and South Africa objected to being called 'Colonies' and the communiqué at the end of the meeting spoke of 'His Majesty's Government and his Governments of the self-governing Dominions beyond the Seas'. The term 'Dominion' (first coined to avoid offending American susceptibilities by using the word 'Kingdom' in the 1867 Act establishing Canadian Federation) came to have a quasi-legal meaning of a self-governing state within the British empire. In 1920 the status of Eire (Southern Ireland) was assimilated in all respects to that of Canada.

Between the wars a distinction was drawn between the Commonwealth of the Dominions and the Empire of countries still more or less directly governed from Britain. The classic definition of the Commonwealth at this time was given in the Balfour Report on Inter-Imperial Relations of 1926. They [the Dominions] are

> autonomous Communities within the British Empire, equal in status, in no way subordinate one to another in any aspect of their domestic or external affairs, though united by a common allegiance to the Crown, and freely associated as members of the British Commonwealth of Nations.

Legislative effect was given to this by the Statute of Westminster (1931). At this time the Dominions were all 'white' former colonies of settlement but after the Second World War, as the British colonies and dependencies became independent, they showed a desire (rather to the British surprise) to remain members of the Commonwealth.

A particular difficulty was caused by the wish of some members to become republics. This was held to be technically incompatible with the 1926 wording of 'united by a common allegiance to the Crown' and when Eire became the Republic of Ireland in 1948 it left the Commonwealth. But the 1949 Commonwealth Conference provided a solution by defining the British monarch only as a 'symbol' and the 'Head of the Commonwealth', and India and Pakistan remained members on becoming republics in 1950. In 1961, however, the need for a member becoming a republic to seek confirmation of its membership from the rest of the

Commonwealth proved a convenient device for excluding South Africa, whose *apartheid* policies were unacceptable to the rest.

At the time of writing in 1997, of the 53 member states, 32 are republics, 16 accept Queen Elizabeth II as their monarch and 5 have national monarchies. In the 16 which still retain Elizabeth II as their Queen, she is represented by a Governor-General, now chosen on the advice of the government of that country. One relic of the fact that the British empire was once a single state in international law is the convention that members of the Commonwealth maintain High Commissioners, not Ambassadors, in each other's countries.

The Commonwealth originally consisted entirely of states which had been part of the British empire and so regarded themselves as having a common heritage, but in 1995 Mozambique, a former Portuguese colony, was admitted to membership because of its close ties with neighbouring Commonwealth countries.

It was assumed that the Commonwealth would fade away as the first generation of colonial nationalists, who often had personal links, left the stage. It was confidently assumed that the 1966 Commonwealth Conference would be the last – despite the fact that the Commonwealth Secretariat, funded by all members, had been established in 1965. But the Commonwealth proved unexpectedly tough. The adjective 'British' was dropped. Heads of Government meet every two years to discuss matters of common interest, finance ministers annually. Besides intergovernmental links, 300 non-governmental organisations cooperate in a wide variety of fields, including sport.

In 1993 criteria for membership were defined in human rights terms, following the Harare Declaration of 1991 on democracy, rule of law, human rights and social justice. The Commonwealth was important in its condemnation of the Unilateral Declaration of Independence in Rhodesia and *apartheid* in South Africa. In 1995 it suspended the membership of Nigeria for human rights violations.

3   The French Empire

The French were more inclined than the British to fight to retain their empire and the effect of its loss on the politics of metropolitan France was proportionately greater. The difference had its origins in their different philosophies of empire. The British empire had always inclined towards devolution and London was reluctant to interfere in local affairs. The French ideal was *assimilation*. The principles of the Revolution of 1789 were held to be of universal application. Eventually, the inhabitants of their colonies would become educated French men and women, enjoying all the rights of French citizenship and electing Deputies to sit in the National Assembly in Paris. In a burst of enthusiasm during the Second Republic in 1848, full citizenship was offered to the inhabitants of the colonies, Senegal (the original colony only), Guadeloupe, Martinique and Réunion (sometimes later referred to as the 'old colonies'). Representatives of these colonies did sit in the Chamber of Deputies of the Third Republic but these tended to be expatriate Frenchmen. The first black African to sit there was Blaise Diagne, who was elected to represent Senegal in 1914.

With the rapid expansion of the empire in the late nineteenth century, it was realised that full assimilation would never be attained, partly because of the diversity of the colonial cultures, some of which were strongly resistant to the imposition of French ideas, partly because of the sheer numbers. The idea of *association* was substituted. By the time of the Second World War it was accepted that assimilation would apply only to an elite, the *evolués*, in each colony. The French did create an educated class, some of whom, for example Leopold Senghor, made their names as intellectuals before they turned to politics. They were employed as civil servants in the colonies, as well as sometimes sitting in the Chamber of Deputies and being employed in official positions in France. There was no exact parallel in British practice and France's former colonies did start with an important cadre of men with governmental experience. But between the wars, and for a time after the war, colonial politicians tended to associate with the political parties of metropolitan France and to link parties in the colonies closely with them, for example the early association of the *Rassemblement Démocratique Africain* (RDA) in West Africa with the French Communist Party.

Despite the French concern for system and order and a reluctance to tolerate the untidiness which characterised the British empire, the French empire in 1945 was very diverse, ranging from Algeria, which had been incorporated into metropolitan France as a Department, through conventional colonies in black Africa, to a virtual puppet regime in Indo-China and the 'Protected States' of Tunis and Morocco.

The French Union, 1946

The whole French political system had to be reorganised after the Second World War and a new constitution (the Fourth Republic) was adopted in 1946. The empire too was reorganised. During the war the Free French had proposed reforms in a bid for the support of the colonies against the Vichy regime. They also hoped to impress the Americans. The most important discussions were those at the Brazzaville Conference (30 January–8 February 1944). Although General de Gaulle was present, this was a meeting of officials, not representatives of the colonies, and it only had power to make recommendations. It advocated further integration of the colonies with France, promised representation for the colonies in the Constituent Assembly at the end of the war, hinted at a possible federal solution and suggested greater involvement for both 'natives' and resident Europeans in the decision-making process in each colony.

First Constituent Assembly (elected October 1945)
The Socialists and Communists had a majority in the First Constituent Assembly. Some 63 out of its 522 members came from overseas but the use of a two-roll electoral system in the colonies meant that 25 of the 63 were Frenchmen. The overseas representatives belonged to the French political parties and, with the exception of the Madagascans, did not generally raise nationalist issues. But some important legislation was passed:

11 April 1946   Houphouët-Boigny Act abolished forced labour in the colonies.

30 April 1946   FIDES (Fonds d'investissement pour le développement économique et social) – comparable to the British Colonial Development and Welfare Act of 1945 – provided for investment for colonial development.

7 May 1946   Lamine Gueye Act declared all inhabitants of the colonies to be citizens of the Republic, thus doing away with the distinction between 'citizens' and 'subjects'.

The First Constituent Assembly had also arrived at a number of definitions, which were carried forward into the second assembly, but the constitution they proposed was rejected by a referendum on 15 May 1946 and a new assembly was summoned.

Second Constituent Assembly (elected June 1946)

Although the Second Constituent Assembly was more conservative than the first, colonial representatives played a bigger part. Black politicians had had a chance to meet one another and the Madagascan nationalists were now joined by thirteen Algerian nationalists. The most important colonial politicians who sat in one or both assemblies were Félix Houphouët-Boigny (Ivory Coast), Léopold Sedar Senghor (Senegal), Sourou M. Apithy (Dahomey-Togoland), Gabriel d'Arboussier (Gabon-Congo), Aimé Césaire (Martinique), Joseph Raseta (Madagascar), Joseph Ravoahangy (Madagascar) and Ferhat Abbas (Algeria). The constitution drawn up by this assembly was confirmed by a referendum on 13 October 1946.

The Republic, including the 'overseas territories', was declared to be one and indivisible, but (Article 41) conceded 'France forms with the overseas territories on the one hand, and with the associated states on the other, a union freely entered into' and 'the Republic recognises the existence of territorial units which govern themselves freely in accordance with the laws of the French nation'.

The constitution of the 'French Union' formed Chapter 8 of the constitution of the Fourth French Republic. The Union had four component parts: (1) metropolitan France, which included Algeria and the 'old colonies', which had been declared to be Departments of France on 12 March 1946, (2) the overseas territories (*territoires d'outre-mer*), such as West and Equatorial Africa, (3) the 'associated territories', that is, the trust territories, Togoland and the Cameroons, which were assimilated for practical purposes to the overseas territories, and (4) the associated states (formerly Protected States), Indo-China, Tunis and Morocco.

The overseas and associated territories would have some kind of elected assembly in each territory, although the franchise was often narrow and weighted against the *indigènes* (natives) and would also elect representatives (by direct election) to the National Assembly in Paris and (by indirect elections) to the Council of the Republic, which scrutinised but could not ultimately reject legislation from the National Assembly.

The *Loi Cadre* (June 1956)

In January 1956 the Socialist, Guy Mollet, became Prime Minister. He appointed Gaston Deferre as Minister for Overseas Territories, and the West African Félix Houphouët-Boigny as Minister of State. Indo-China had been lost and the war in Algeria was going badly. The Union was no longer viable in its original form and his government passed the *loi cadre* (sometimes called the 'skeleton law'), which opened the way for change. This marked the final end of the ideal of *assimilation*. Each overseas territory was now able to embark on the course to independence as a separate nation. Despite right-wing opposition in the National Assembly, it passed by 477 votes to 99.

In 1957 the *loi cadre* was put into operation in West and Equatorial Africa, and elsewhere. The territorial assemblies were now elected by single-roll procedure (universal suffrage) and had extended powers, in particular they could appoint councils to assist the governors; in effect members of the councils were ministers, elected by the assemblies. West and Equatorial Africa no longer had central councils in Dakar and Brazzaville and this was opposed by some African politicians.

The French Community

In May 1958 the Fourth French Republic collapsed, brought down by events in Algeria, and General de Gaulle returned to power. He set out to formulate a new structure for the empire at the same time as the new constitution of the Fifth Republic was drawn up. This time colonial politicians were consulted and Félix Houphouët-Boigny played a leading role. Overseas representatives would cease to sit in the National Assembly in Paris, although overseas territories would vote in Presidential elections. The French Community, as it would now be called, would have its own Executive Council, chaired by the French President, consisting of the heads of government of each member state and the responsible French ministers. It would also have a Senate, representing the parliaments of its members with membership in proportion to population, which would debate matters of common interest before they went to individual legislatures. Each territorial member would have the right to change its status at the request of its legislature confirmed by a referendum. This proposal was submitted to a referendum in the colonies on 28 September 1958, the same day that France voted on the new constitution. It received overwhelming endorsement everywhere, except in Guinea, where Sekou Touré's opposition secured a decisive rejection. France then withdrew all economic and other aid from Guinea, which turned to the Eastern bloc for assistance.

The French Community did not last long. Most former colonies wished to become completely independent, although keeping some economic and other links with France. In May 1960 Mali (a federation of Senegal and the French Sudan) was given independence within the Community. In August 1960 the remaining states of French West Africa, the Ivory Coast, Niger, Dahomey and Upper Volta, asked for independence outside the Community, although as a preliminary to negotiating a new relationship with France. France agreed, wishing to avoid the complete break which had occurred with Guinea. The former colonies marked their independence by becoming members in their own right of the United Nations, but close economic and other ties with France did remain.

Africa

i. The Maghreb (Morocco, Tunisia and Algeria)

Morocco
A Protected State, which came under the jurisdiction of the Foreign, not the Colonial, Office.

1912   (30 March) Treaty giving France a Protectorate over Morocco. The Sultan remained in office but France was represented by a Resident-General, who controlled foreign policy and exercised supervision over internal affairs.

1924–25   Abd-el-Krim (Rif) rising. The Protectorate was virtually replaced by direct rule.

1930s   Beginnings of diverse nationalist movements. Moroccan graduates of French universities formed 'Young Moroccans', founded two newspapers, *Le Maghreb* and *L'Action du peuple*, and campaigned both in Paris and Morocco for more freedom and modernisation. They recognised the Sultan as a possible leader and (May 1934) hailed him as 'Malik' (Chief).

1934   Principal nationalist leaders formed the Comité d'Action Marocaine and (1936) drew up reform plan.

1943   (January) Sultan Mohammed ben Yusuf met President Roosevelt at the time of the Casablanca Conference. Hopes of American support rose.

1944   (January) Various nationalist movements united to form Istiqlal (Independence Party).

(11 January) Istiqlal issued a manifesto, asking for independence, constitutional monarchy and membership of the United Nations. Leaders of Istiqlal were imprisoned by the French.

1946   Disappointed to remain a Protectorate.

(March) A brief attempt, with Erik Labonne as Resident-General, to implement liberal reforms met with distrust from Istiqlal and hostility from French settlers.

1947   (May) General Juin, now Resident-General, instructed to follow authoritarian policy. Sultan sided with nationalists and pan-Arabists.

1950   (October) Sultan asked for revision of Protectorate treaty.

1951   (26 January) Sultan given ultimatum: he must either disavow Istiqlal or abdicate. Sultan yielded.

1952   (7 December) Nationalists had gained support of trade unions. Strike in protest against assassination of Tunisian leader, Ferhat Hached, crushed with serious loss of life, especially in Casablanca. United Nations put Morocco on its agenda.

1953   French played Sultan off against Berber leader, Thami al-Glaoui, pacha of Marrakesh. Sultan forced into exile (20 August 1953) and replaced by compliant Mulay Arafa. Moroccan nationalists created National Liberation Army and prepared for armed struggle. French government divided. E. Faure wished to negotiate.

1955   (August) Conference at Aix-les-Bains between French ministers and Moroccan leaders.

(September) A. Pinay travelled to see Mohammed ben Yusuf in exile in Madagascar. Agreed to settlement by which Morocco would be 'free and sovereign' but would accept 'links of interdependence with France'. Arafa abdicated. Moroccan 'national army' began rebellion.

(5 November) Declaration of La Celle-St Cloud, signed by Pinay and Sultan. Agreed Sultan would form a government and start negotiations for settlement on basis of independence but with 'links of interdependence'. Sultan returned to Rabat.

1956   (February) In negotiations involving French President, R. Coty, Sultan made it a condition that independence must have precedence.

(20 March) Joint Declaration acknowledged full and immediate independence of Morocco and abrogated Protectorate treaty of 1912.

(28 May) Agreements signed defining interdependence simply as cooperation in certain fields and reaffirming Morocco's complete independence even in foreign policy.

Tunisia
A Protected State, under the jurisdiction of the Foreign, not Colonial, Office.

1881   (May) Treaty of Bardo (Kasser-Said). Tunisia became a French Protectorate, although governed more like a colony. The Bey (Tunisian ruler) remained in office but was 'advised' by French Resident-General.

1906   'Young Tunisians' formed, inspired by 'Young Turks' and had links with pan-Islamic and pan-Arab groups.

Pre-1914   Substantial French settlement, especially in better agricultural areas.

1912   Disturbances.

1919   Destour (Constitution) party formed. Sought a modern constitutional state, with the franchise confined to Tunisians, who would be admitted to all administrative offices, and the buying out of French settler property.

1927   Henri Bourguiba returned from France.

1932   Bourguiba launched new journal *L'Action Tunisienne*, which advocated economic reform and promised no religious discrimination.

1934   Bourguiba formed Neo-Destours party, inspired by the French Revolutionary tradition, and asked for universal suffrage and independence by stages. French Governor, Peyrouton, muzzled press and sent leaders to detention camps.

1936–38   Popular Front governments in France were more sympathetic to Tunisian demands, but after the fall of Blum in June 1937 relations worsened again.

1938   (April) Demonstrations led to new repression.

1940   Defeat of France. Germans played off nationalists against the French and allowed Bourguiba, in detention in France, to return to Tunisia.

1943   (May) Bourguiba declared for France, saying 'I am convinced that the French nation, once freed from the Nazi yoke, will not forget her true friends, those who stood by her in her hour of trial. What matters most now is to win the war.'[1] The French, influenced by settler opinion, did not respond. They deported the Bey and would have arrested Bourguiba but for American protection.

1945–47   In post-war settlements, Tunisia remained a Protected State. Some concessions were made. The Bey, Lamine, was allowed to return and Tunisians were promised equality of numbers with the French in government ministries and in the Grand Council, which supervised the Budget. Despairing of further concessions, Bourguiba organised resistance from Cairo and made common cause with Ferhat Abbas in Algeria. In Tunisia, the Moderates joined with the Neo-Destour to form the Tunisian Front, which gained the support of the trade unions and professional groups.

1950   (April) The Bey prepared the way for Bourguiba to negotiate with President Auriol in Paris. Settlers, organised in the Rassemblement Français de Tunisie, opposed concessions but French socialists were more sympathetic.

(June) Robert Schuman, French Foreign Minister, promised immediate political reforms, which would lead ultimately to independence. Settlers gained the support of the French army and right-wing parties. The alarmed French government suspended negotiations.

(25 November) Enfidaville riots.

1951   (7 February) Administrative reforms, which promised the end of direct rule but stopped short of giving internal autonomy.

---

[1] Quoted in Henri Grimal *Decolonization*, trans. S. de Vos, 1978, p. 117.

The French floated the idea of 'co-sovereignty', but this was unacceptable to Tunisians. Terrorist attacks from both the Tunisian and the French settler side.

(December) French re-affirmed permanent nature of links between France and Tunisia.

1952   United Nations Assembly urged setting up of 'free institutions' in both Tunisia and Morocco.

1954   (21 July) Cease-fire signed in Indo-China.

(31 July) P. Mendès-France, French Prime Minister, went to Carthage and promised virtual autonomy for Tunis.

1955   (3 June) Agreement signed, by which Tunis secured internal autonomy, although defence and foreign policy were still ultimately controlled by France. Arabic became the official language but with safeguards for French.

1956   (February) Morocco became independent. Neo-Destour demanded the same for Tunisia.

(20 March) Protocol signed, which granted Tunisia independence within a freely accepted framework of interdependence.

1956–58   Further conventions clarified this to confirm full Tunisian independence.

Algeria

This was exceptionally difficult to decolonise because it had been incorporated into metropolitan France. Under the Third Republic it came under the Ministry of the Interior, not the Foreign or Colonial Offices.

1830   Charles X occupied the coastal region to eliminate the threat from pirates and score a foreign policy success.

1830–48   The Orleanist Monarchy found it politically impossible to withdraw and went on to conquer the whole country, particularly during the campaigns of Marshal Bugeaud in the 1840s. He encountered strenuous resistance from Abd-el-Kadar. Some limited French settlement followed the conquest.

1871   Following the French defeat in the Franco-Prussian War, there were serious risings in Algiers and Constantine. Despite further risings in 1876, 1879 and 1881–84, the Third Republic encouraged large-scale settlement.

1887 Naturalisation Act. This extended French citizenship to the considerable number of non-French Europeans resident in Algeria. A settler class was thus supcrimposcd on the existing mixed population of Berbers and Arabs, who were bound together only by a common religion, Islam.

1895 Senatus consultus. This allowed non-Europeans to escape *indigénat* (native) status by applying for French citizenship. Although this conferred French civil rights and made an individual subject to French, not Islamic law, it was not attractive to Algerians, who saw it as abjuring their religion.

1900–14 Opposition groups began to form but were divided between those who felt primarily Muslim and those, such as Les Jeunes Algériens, who had taken advantage of French education and looked for secular reforms.

1919 Act which extended the provisions of the Senatus consultus and allowed some Muslims to sit on government bodies in Algeria.

1920s Writings of Ferhat Abbas, who maintained that it was possible to be both French and a Muslim. But others such as the Muslihim, who published *al-Muntaqid* (the *Critic*), rejected the idea of assimilation, arguing that Algeria had its own language, history and religion and they must revitalise Islam.

1922 Ali Abd-el-Kader started a movement for Algerian independence among Algerians in Paris, the Étoile Nord-Africaine, initially a Friendly Society among working-class Arabs.

1927 Messali Haj became leader of the Étoile Nord-Africaine and gave it a strongly nationalistic character.

1931 Ben Badis founded Ulama at a Muslim Conference in Jerusalem, clearly anti-western in tone, and declaring 'Islam is our religion, Algeria our country, Arabic our language'.

1936 Following the Popular Front victory in France, a conference met in Algiers, bringing together Ulama, representatives of Les

Jeunes Algériens and the Algerian Communist Party (which had been independent of the French Communist Party since 1935), which drew up a charter of political demands.

1937 Blum–Violette proposals. These would have allowed 20–30,000 Algerians to acquire the franchise, without giving up their personal status. This was dropped because of settler opposition.

Messali Haj, who had dissociated himself from the 1936 Charter, founded a new party, the Parti Populaire Algérien (PPA, Algerian People's Party), calling for independence in collaboration with France. This was particularly influential in urban areas in Algeria.

1943 Ferhat Abbas drew up the Algerian Manifesto, in an attempt to unite the disparate movements, calling for an autonomous and democratic Algeria in a federal relationship with France.

1945 (May) Serious riots in Sétif. Although these were as much economic as political in origin, they were severely repressed.

1946 Ferhat Abbas founded L'Union Démocratique du Manifeste Algérien (UDMA, the Democratic Union for the Algerian Manifesto). He played an important role in the second French Constituent Assembly but no final decision was taken on the status of Algeria.

1947 (20 September) Algerian Statute. This defined Algeria as 'a group of provinces' with its own identity. It maintained the distinction between French nationals with full rights of citizenship and others who had not renounced their 'personal Muslim status' and would continue to be governed by their own laws. Many laws passed by the French National Assembly were automatically applicable to Algeria but Algeria now also had its own Algerian Assembly of 120 members: 60 were elected by those on the first roll (i.e. French citizens) and 60 by those on the second roll of those who had retained their personal Muslim status.

1947–54 Ferhat Abbas's UDMA and Messali's party, now the Mouvement pour le Triomphe des Libertés Démocratiques (MTLD, Movement for the Triumph of Democratic Liberties), contested elections, but settler influence, exercised through the French authorities, ensured that the elections were rigged.

1954   (1 November) The Algerian insurrection began. Masterminded by the Revolutionary Committee for Unity and Action (CRUA, *Comité Révolutionnaire d'Unité et d'Action*), largely operating from Cairo, it brought the different groups together in the FLN (*Front de Libération Nationale*, Front for National Liberation). Various French targets were attacked in Algeria. Moderates, like Ferhat Abbas, reluctantly gave the movement their blessing and were counted among the 'historic chiefs'.

1954–61   Algerian War of Independence. This was fought with increasing savagery on both sides.

1956   (August) Armée de Libération Nationale formed. This eventually engaged the greater part of the French army (over 400,000 men).

(February) The government of Guy Mollet, while declaring Algeria indissolubly linked with France, offered fresh negotiations on its status, subject to a cease-fire. The FLN was not interested in a cease-fire. Neither was the French army until it had secured victory. But the most effective opposition came from the *colons* or *pied noires* (settlers, numbering about one million), who adopted the slogan *Algérie Française* (Algeria is French). Mollet was compelled to dismiss his comparatively liberal Governor-General, Georges Catroux, and replace him with a hard-line conservative, Robert Lacoste.

(March) Special Powers Act increased repression and military effort in Algeria.

1957   Lacoste brought para-units, led by General Jacques Massu, into Algiers, where they had some military success, although the French Left protested against the brutality of their methods.

1958   (February) French air force bombed a Tunisian village suspected of harbouring FLN guerrillas. This action was condemned in the United Nations.

(13 May) Settlers began a general strike in Algiers in protest at what they saw as the weakness of their government in heeding international criticism. They had the sympathy of the army.

(June) President Coty, fearing civil war, called on General de Gaulle to form a government.

(3 October) De Gaulle launched his Constantine plan for the economic development of Algeria (but also removed army officers of doubtful loyalty).

1959   (September) De Gaulle proposed three options: (1) Algeria should secede from the French Union, but without the Sahara (where oil was now known to be an important resource), (2) assimilate with France, or (3) become autonomous but with France still controlling foreign and economic policy.

1960   (January) The settlers rose in Algiers but this time the army did not support them. De Gaulle held secret talks with the FLN, at the same time backing a military campaign against them to lessen their bargaining power.

1961   (January) De Gaulle secured the right in a French referendum to impose his own solution on the Algerian problem.

(April) Failed army revolt in Algiers followed by the formation of the OAS (*Organisation Armée Secrète*, Secret Army Organisation), composed of army and settler extremists, which carried out acts of terrorism. Attempted assassination of de Gaulle.

(May) The French government began discussions at Evian with representatives of what now called itself the Algerian Provisional Government (GPRA), operating from Tunis.

1962   (18 March) Agreement reached at Evian. The French had hoped to keep some control of the Saharan gas and oil fields and to protect the rights of the settlers. They had to settle for guaranteed rights to lease some Saharan developments and the settlers were compelled, in effect, to choose between French and Algerian nationality. Most settlers returned to France.

(8 April) A referendum in France approved the settlement overwhelmingly. In Algeria the approval rate was almost 100 per cent.

(3 July) Algeria became independent.

ii. French Equatorial Africa

In 1945 this consisted of Chad, Gabon, Middle Congo and Ubanghi-Shari (in the post-colonial period, Chad, Gabon, the Congo Republic and the Central African Republic respectively). The French had established a station on the Gabon River in 1839 and a further settlement there (Libreville) to provide a home for freed slaves in 1849. Most of the territory had been acquired during the Scramble for Africa period. It was very important during the Second World War in declaring against Vichy France and providing a base for the Allies, but in both political and economic development it lagged far behind French West Africa.

Acquisition

1849   Libreville established, the nucleus of Gabon and later its capital.

1879–82   Explorations of Savorgnan de Brazza, who established Brazza-ville and concluded treaties (popularly known as Makoko treaties) with chiefs.

1882   (November) France ratified 'Makoko' treaties.

1885   France ceded some territory, including Kinshasa, to the Congo Free State.

1885–91   Following the Berlin West Africa Conference of 1884–85, France claimed Gabon and Middle Congo and began to extend control into Ubanghi-Shari and Chad.

1913   Chad region finally conquered.

1919   Regained some corridors of land, ceded to Germany in 1911.

Early developments

1910   French Equatorial Africa established as an administrative unit, comprising Gabon, Middle Congo and Ubanghi-Shari. Each territory had a Governor, with a Governor-General in Brazzaville.

1920   Chad added to French Equatorial Africa.

Inter-war period   Equatorial Africa remained poor and with little political activity.

Second World War

1940   (26 August) The Governor of Chad, Felix S. Eboué, himself a Negro of West Indian origin, rejected Vichy and declared for de Gaulle and the Free French. Other territories of French Equatorial Africa followed.

1940   (November) Brazzaville became the capital of the Free French in Africa and Eboué was appointed Governor-General. French

Equatorial Africa became an important base for Allied operations in Africa.

1941–42   Eboué issued circulars with proposals for the future development of French Africa. He favoured more decentralisation and the incorporation of traditional institutions into the administration, and played a part in the summoning of the Brazzaville Conference.

1944   (January–February) Brazzaville Conference of all the Governors of French African territories. De Gaulle attended. Discussed plans for future development. Generally looking towards a closer integration in the French system, with more representation for colonial views, rather than to decolonisation as it was later understood.

Developments after the Second World War

1945   Elections for Constituent Assembly in Paris. Little political organisation among Africans, who failed to take advantage of the opportunity. All their representatives were Europeans, except Jean-Felix Tchicaya from Middle Congo.

1946   Reorganisation of the French empire abolished the distinction between citizen and subject. The constituent parts of French Equatorial Africa became Overseas Territories. Each territory had a Governor, answerable to a High Commissioner in Brazzaville. Chiefs were appointed by the administration. Each territory had an elected assembly – albeit elected on a still narrow franchise. These assemblies had control of the budget and elected the members of the Grand Council of French Equatorial Africa, which met in Brazzaville. French Equatorial Africa had 5 deputies in the National Assembly in Paris (directly elected), 8 representatives in the Council of the Republic (indirectly elected) and 7 councillors in the Assembly of the French Union (indirectly elected).

Post 1946   Political parties began to appear, but the conservatism of the area was demonstrated by the fact that the most successful was the Rassemblement du Peuple Français (RPF), de Gaulle's own party, which was heavily backed by the administration. Other metropolitan parties, mainly the communists and socialists, tried to establish themselves but achieved little. The Rassemblement Démocratique Africain (RDA), already strong in West Africa, had more success. Affiliated parties, the Parti Progressiste Tchadien (PPT), the Parti Progressiste Congolais, and the Union Oubanguienne, were established in Chad, Middle Congo and Ubanghi-Shari respectively. Gabon developed its own parties, the Union Démocratique et Sociale Gabonaise of Jean Aubame and the Bloc Démocratique Gabonaise of Leon M'ba.

1951   Franchise widened.

1956   *Loi cadre* extended franchise and powers of territorial assemblies.

1957   New elections. Divergence of interests was now becoming apparent between the four territories. Gabon, the most prosperous, resented subsidising the rest.

1958   (September) De Gaulle's referendum on the establishment of the French Community. All four territories voted by massive majorities in favour of the Community but they were divided in that attitude to the continuation of any federation between them. Henceforth their histories divide, although in January 1959 they negotiated a tariff, trade and transport union.

Gabon

The two leading politicians were Jean Aubame, who had links with Leopold Senghor and the Indépendants d'Outre Mer (IOM) in Senegal, and Leon M'ba, whose links were with Houphouët-Boigny and the RDA. But both wished to keep strong ties with France while rejecting any strong federation in Central Africa.

1960   (August) Became independent with M'ba as President.

Ubanghi-Shari

Immediately after 1946, Antoine Darlan, a man of mixed race and himself a communist, began the protest movement, but after 1952 Barthélemy Boganda, the leader of the Mouvement pour l'Évolution Sociale de l'Afrique Noire (MESAN), was the dominant figure. He favoured not only a continuation of a federation of the old French Equatorial Africa but a wider grouping including the (Belgian) Congo and Angola. Even before he was killed in an air crash in 1959, it seemed unlikely that he would fulfil even part of this ambition.

1958   (December) Ubanghi-Shari became a member state of the French Community under the name of the Central African Republic. Boganda became President.

1959   David Dacko succeeded him as President.

1960   (August) Central African Republic became independent.

Chad

Chad was the most populous territory in French Equatorial Africa and had the complication of a serious religious division between the Muslim North and the mainly Christian South. The most important political leaders of the post-war era were Gabriel Lisette, associated with Houphouët-Boigny, and Ahmed Koulamallah, whose support came from the Muslim North. Lisette became Prime Minister after the 1957 elections. He at first had some sympathy for Boganda's federal ideas but swung against them. Koulamallah wanted the maximum autonomy.

1958   Chad became a republic and a member of the French Community.

1959   Although the PPT won a majority in elections, there were disturbances and dangerous signs of disunity.

1960   Formation of new Muslim party, Parti National Africain (PNA).
         (August) Chad became independent. François Tombalbaye, now the leader of the PPT, became President.

1961   Tombalbaye secured merger with PNA.

Middle Congo

Divisions here tended to follow tribal groupings. The most important politicians to emerge were Jacques Opangault, who led the Mouvement Socialiste Africain (MSA), which was connected with the Section Française de l'Internationale Ouvrière (SISO); Jean Felix Tchicaya, who led the PPC; and, after 1956, Abbé Fulbert Youlou, who drew his followers from the Balili, a section of the Bakongo, and formed the Union Démocratique de la Défense des Intérêts Africains (UDDIA).

1957   Elections resulted in a dead heat between the MSA and the UDDIA, who formed a coalition.

1958   Middle Congo became autonomous within the French Community.

1957–59   Struggles, and even serious violence, between the parties.

1959   Youlou managed to crush his opponents and secure a large majority in elections. He secured a new constitution and combined the offices of President and Prime Minister.

1960   Youlou tried to revive the ideas of Boganda and restore a federation of the old Equatorial Africa and perhaps reunite the Bakongo tribe, which had been split between the Middle Congo, the Belgian Congo and Angola, to form a much larger unit. He could not persuade the other leaders of the former Equatorial Africa and he had little chance of wresting the leadership of the Bakongo in the former Belgian Congo from Kasavubu.

(August) The Middle Congo became independent as the Republic of the Congo.

iii. French West Africa

French West Africa covered one-sixth of the whole of Africa and, together with French Equatorial Africa, gave France control of a vast territory, stretching from the Mediterranean to the Congo. In 1925 its constituent parts were Senegal, French Guinea, Ivory Coast, Dahomey, Upper Volta, Niger territory, French Sudan and Mauritania, plus parts of Togoland, which was a mandated territory and administered separately. After decolonisation it dissolved again into separate countries. It was both richer and far more politically advanced than French Equatorial Africa.

Acquisition

1645   Factory established at the mouth of the Senegal River (St Louis).

1848   During Second French Republic, citizenship conferred on inhabitants of 'ancient communities' of St Louis, Gorée, Dakar and Rufisque.

1854–65   Commandant Louis Faidherbe subdued the hinterland of Senegal and conceived idea of linking Senegal with the Upper Niger.

Most of French West Africa was acquired during the Scramble for Africa:

1876–98   Penetration of Upper Niger. Timbuktu reached in 1893.

1887–89   Conquest of Ivory Coast, despite strenuous resistance by Samory (comparable to that of Abd-el-Kader in Algeria).

1889–94   Conquest of Dahomey.

1890 and 1898   Agreements with Britain to demarcate boundaries.

Early developments

1895   French West Africa constituted. High Commissioner in Dakar and Governors in each of the then 8 territories.

1899   Dahomey included in French West Africa.

1904   Reorganised into a more coherent federation with Governor-General in Dakar.

1910 and 1916   Revolts in Upper Volta led to it being separated from the Ivory Coast. (Reunited with Ivory Coast in 1933 but separated again in 1947.)

1914   Blaise Diagne of Senegal was the first full-blooded African to represent a colony in the Chamber of Deputies in Paris.

1914–18   First World War. West African soldiers served with French forces.

Inter-war period   There was little overt political organisation in French West Africa, although a Socialist Party, affiliated to the French Socialist Party, the Section Française de l'Internationale Ouvrière (SFIO), was formed in Senegal. More important was the steady advance of education, which created the *evolué* class, teachers and civil servants, conversant with western ideas of liberty and self-determination.

1940   Fall of France during the Second World War. Unlike Equatorial Africa, West Africa, did not immediately declare for General de Gaulle. The Governor-General, Pierre François Bisson, initially supported Vichy and repelled a British attack on Dakar.

1942   (November) Bisson and West Africa generally transferred their loyalties to the Free French.

Developments after the Second World War

1946   Constituent Assembly. A number of West Africans, notably Leopold Senghor, Félix Houphouët-Boigny and Lamine Gueye, played a very important role.

Abolition of the distinction between citizen and subject. New constitution in the colonies. Each of the territories making up West Africa was to have an elected assembly, which would vote on the budget. These territorial assemblies also elected representatives for the grand council in Dakar. West Africa sent 20 directly elected deputies to the National Assembly in Paris; 20 indirectly elected representatives to the Council of the Republic and 26 indirectly elected representatives to the Council of the French Union. Africans gained experience of sitting in the Chamber of Deputies and were, not infrequently, employed in official positions in Paris. Senghor, for example, was Secretary of State in the Prime Minister's Office in Faure's administration and Houphouët-Boigny held various ministerial appointments in 1956–58.

(October) Bamako Conference. Called mainly by West African leaders, who had signed a manifesto calling for a common front in the struggle for democracy in Africa. Attended by several hundred delegates from French Africa. This led in turn to the setting up of the Rassemblement Démocratique Africain (RDA). This came to centre on the Ivory Coast, with Houphouët-Boigny as its leader, but affiliated parties were set up in most of the states of West and Equatorial Africa, e.g. Parti Démocratique de Guinée, Union Soudanaise, Parti Progressiste Tchadien, Parti Progressiste Congolais and Union Oubanguienne. It attracted the support of most, although not all, the early nationalist leaders (Leopold Sengor, for example, was not a member). It looked for advance within the French Union and the abolition of distinctions between white and black 'Frenchmen', i.e. assimilation. It had close associations with the French Communist Party, and when the Communist Party left the French government in 1947, its policy became somewhat contradictory.

1948   Senghor founded the Indépendants d'Outre Mer (IOM) in Senegal.

1949–50   Disturbances on the Ivory Coast.

1950   Houphouët-Boigny broke with Communists in the RDA and sought closer cooperation with the French government.

1951   Qualifications for the franchise were lowered and the electorate considerably increased. Senghor defeated Lamine Gueye in Senegal.

1953   IOM held conference in Upper Volta at which it put forward plans for French West Africa to be replaced by two federations, although still within the French Union.

1954–55   Economic problems led to widespread strikes.

1955   Partly under pressure from the United Nations Trusteeship Committee, France gave Togoland internal self-government. This influenced the thinking of the other territories.

Guy Mollet formed socialist government in Paris, and included Houphouët-Boigny in his Cabinet.

1956   (June) *Loi cadre* passed, which in effect abandoned the idea of assimilation and accepted that each territory would become a separate nation. Territorial assemblies were to be elected by universal suffrage. This represented the policy of Houphouët-Boigny but not of Senghor, who saw it as attempt to divide and rule.

1957   *Loi cadre* put into operation.

(September) RDA met at Bamako. Conflict between Houphouët-Boigny and Leon M'ba, who favoured separate states, and Sekou Touré and Modibo Keita, who preferred to keep federal structure.

1958   Formation of Parti de Regroupement Africain (PRA), which was led by Sengor, included most parties not committed to RDA and stood for continuation of the West African federation.

(May) Fourth Republic collapsed and de Gaulle returned to power.

(June–September) De Gaulle appointed Houphouët-Boigny one of his Ministers of State. Influenced proposals for French Community. The African territories would no longer send deputies to the National Assembly, although they would vote in the

Presidential elections. The Community would have its own Executive Council, chaired by the President, consisting of the heads of government of each member state and the responsible French ministers. It would also have a Senate, representing the parliaments of its members in proportion to population, which would debate common issues before they went to the individual legislatures. Each territorial member would have the right to change its status at the request of its legislature confirmed by a referendum.

(July) RDA and PRA held joint discussions and issued a manifesto, strongly influenced by Houphouët-Boigny, calling for a federal republic of autonomous states. (PRA held subsequent conference at Cotonou to strengthen federal proposals.)

(September) Constitution of the Community confirmed by referenda in every West African state except Guinea, where Sekou Touré, the leader since 1954, had opposed it. France immediately cut off all aid to Guinea.

(December) Senghor called new conference in Bamako to try to resurrect federation idea. Delegates of Senegal, Soudan, Upper Volta and Dahomey attended but Upper Volta and Dahomey were persuaded by the French to withdraw.

1959   (April) Federation of Mali created by Senegal and Soudan, with Senghor as President and Keita as Prime Minister.

1960   (June) Mali was recognised as independent, although remaining a member of the French Community.

(August) Federation collapsed, although Soudan retained name of Mali. Houphouët-Boigny tried to create loose federation of Ivory Coast, Upper Volta, Niger and Dahomey. Idea collapsed and with it much of the substance of the French Community, which was also under presure from Togoland and the Cameroons. All the remaining states of the former French West Africa became independent and members of the United Nations.

The French administered the mandated territories of Cameroon and Togo separately from French West Africa.

Cameroon

1919   German colony of Kamerun divided between Britain and France, the majority going to France.

1922   League of Nations' mandate formally constituted.

1946   Became United Nations' Trusteeship territory.

1955   New constitution widened franchise.

1960   Became independent as the Federal Republic of Cameroon (later United Republic of Cameroon).

1961   After plebiscite the Southern part of the British mandated territory of the Cameroons joined the Republic of Cameroon.

Togo

1922   The eastern part of the German colony of Togo became a French mandate.

1946   Became a United Nations' Trusteeship Territory.

1956   Became an autonomous republic within the French Union.

1960   Became independent as the Republic of Togo.

iv. Madagascar

Acquisition

France had had trading interests in Madagascar since the seventeenth century. England and France had contended for influence there in the nineteeth century but England would probably have been content to come to an accommodation with the Hova dynasty, which was emerging as the unifying force on the island.

1885   France established a virtual Protectorate by gaining control of Malagasy foreign relations.

1894   French military expedition.

1896   (August) Madagascar became a French colony.

Early developments

Although Madagascar had a very mixed population, derived from Arab countries and various parts of Asia, Melanesia, Indonesia, Malaya and India, as well as Africa, it had attained a degree of unity under the Hova kings, which was reinforced by early French administration. Consultative assemblies, although with little real power, were established from an early date. Malagasy troops served in the First World War in France and Syria. Education was comparatively good. By 1940, 8,000 of Madagascar's 4,000,000 population had gained French citizenship by meeting the necessary criteria. It was from this class that the first nationalists arose.

1916   Joseph Ravoahangy was exiled for seven years to the Comoro Islands for campaigning for home rule.

1920s   Ralaimongo, a teacher who had served in the First World War, started a journal, *L'Opinion*, asking for true assimilation. He was banished to a remote area in 1929.

1936   Appearance of Popular Front government in France again encouraged nationalists to look for progress through assimilation but this ran counter to a, possibly stronger, tendency of returning to their own traditions.

1940   During the Second World War the French administration declared for Vichy.

1942   Occupied by British forces (to prevent Japanese occupation).
(November) French National Committee (Free French) appointed a High Commissioner and took over administration.

Developments after the Second World War

1946   Political parties were formed, the Malagasy Democratic Party, which was favoured by the administrators, and the more radical and popular Mouvement Démocratique de la Révolution Malgache (MDRM, Democratic Movement for Malagasy Revival/ Revolution). Two leaders of the MDRM, Joseph Raseta and Joseph Ravoahangy, were members of the French Constituent Assembly, where they played an important role.

1947   Serious rebellion centred on the east coast, which was severely repressed by the French. An estimated 20,000 people were killed. The country was economically devastated. The MDRM was banned and several of its leaders, including Ravoahangy and Raseta, sentenced to death, although all were eventually reprieved and were released at various dates after 1954.

1956   *Loi cadre* established a federal form of government for the island with provincial assemblies and a central council. Gave Malagasy nationalism a chance to re-establish itself.

(December) Philibert Tsiranana, already a deputy in the French National Assembly and associated with Guy Mollet's Socialist Party, formed the Parti Social Démocrate (PSD, Social Democratic Party) in Madagascar.

1958   Tsiranana secured a vote in favour of the French Community in the referendum, despite a strong call for complete independence from some younger politicians, especially those who looked back to the traditions of the Hova monarchy.

1959   Tsiranana became President.

1960   (26 June) Madagascar became independent as the Malagasy Republic, although remaining within the French Community.

Asia

Indo-China

The French had established missionary and trading connections with Indo-China in the eighteenth century but only in the latter half of the nineteenth century did they conquer it. The Japanese occupied Indo-China during the Second World War and after the war the general assumption, particularly in the United States, was that the French would concede independence to Indo-China, much as the British were conceding it to India. In fact the French tried to re-establish their control until they were militarily defeated in 1954.

Indo-China, more than any other colonial area, became a pawn in the Cold War between the United States and the Soviet Union and, more particularly, China, after China became communist in 1949. American feelings shifted from sympathy with the Vietnamese to support for the French and eventually to direct intervention, until they too were militarily defeated in 1975.

Acquisition

1787   First treaty between France and the Emperor of Vietnam (which had gained independence from China in the fifteenth century).

1852   French Emperor, Napoleon III, began a series of expeditions to protect French missionaries in Vietnam.

1861   French captured Saigon.

1862   Vietnamese Emperor, Tu Duc, signed treaty granting French concessions.

1863   French extended influence to Cambodia.

1873   French extended influence to Tonkin.

1883   French established a Protectorate over Annam and Tonkin.

1887   French created Indochinese Union of Cochinchina, Annam, Tonkin and Cambodia.

Political developments

1930   Ho Chi Minh and others established Indochinese Communist Party in Hong Kong.

1932   Bao Dai came to power as Emperor but under French tutelage.

1936   Popular Front government in France attempted reforms.

Developments during and after the Second World War

1941   Ho Chi Minh founded Vietminh to work for Vietnamese independence.
    (September) Japanese occupied Indo-China but allowed French (Vichy) colonial administration to continue to operate.

1944   Vo Nguyen Giap formed Vietminh army.

1945   (9 March) Japanese took over administration throughout Indo-China.
    (11 March) Bao Dai proclaimed Vietnam independent of the French empire.
    (July) Potsdam Conference. Allied leaders assigned British to disarm Japanese in South Vietnam and Chinese Nationalists to do the same in North Vietnam (north of 16th parallel).
    (18 August) Japanese transferred power to Vietminh.
    (23 August) Bao Dai abdicated.
    (29 August) Ho Chi Minh proclaimed provisional government in Hanoi.

(2 September) Ho Chi Minh proclaimed independence of Vietnam.

(13 September) British forces landed in Saigon and returned authority to the French.

1945–46   Famine in North Vietnam.

1946   Chinese withdrew from North Vietnam. Replaced by the French.

(March) France recognised Vietnam as a 'free state' within the French Union and promised a referendum to determine whether Tonkin, Annam and Cochinchina should be reunited.

(May–September) Ho Chi Minh negotiated in Fontainebleau. Only a limited agreement reached.

(23 November) French warships bombarded Haiphong.

(December) Vietminh forces withdrew from Hanoi after attacking French garrison. Ho Chi Minh created a rural base. War with the French began.

1947   United States formulated the doctrine of 'containment' of communism world-wide, which took shape in the Truman Doctrine.

(December) Bao Dai (in exile in Hong Kong) reached preliminary agreement with Émile Ballaert, French High Commissioner, for limited Vietnamese independence.

1949   (8 March) Elysée Agreement. Bao Dai and French President, Vincent Auriol, agreed Vietnam should be an 'Associated State' in the French Union; France to retain control of finances, as well as foreign policy and defence.

(April) Bao Dai returned to Vietnam.

(1 October) Communists completed conquest of China. Mao-Tse-Tung proclaimed the establishment of the People's Republic of China.

1950   (14 January) Ho Chi Minh declared Democratic Republic of Vietnam was the only legal government. Recognised by the Soviet Union and China.

(7 February) United States and Britain recognised Bao Dai's government. Chinese began to supply arms to Vietminh.

(26 June) Korean War began.

(26 July) President Truman signed legislation granting $15 million in military aid to French for war in Indo-China.

(6 December) General Jean de Lattre de Tassigny became military commander. Blunted General Giap's offensive in Red River Valley.

1952   (11 January) Death of Lattre de Tassigny of cancer in Paris.

1953   (27 July) Armistice in Korea.

(October) France granted Laos full independence as a member of the French Union.

(9 November) Prince Norodim Sihanouk took command of the Cambodian army and declared Cambodia independent of France.

(November) French forces re-occupied Dien Bien Phu.

(December) Vietminh forces pushed into Laos.

1954   (January) At meeting in Berlin, the United States, Britain, France and the Soviet Union agreed to hold a conference in Geneva on Korea and Indo-China.

(13 March) Battle of Dien Bien Phu began.

(7 May) French defeated at Dien Bien Phu.

(April–July) Geneva Conference.

(8 May) Discussions on Indo-China began with Britain and the Soviet Union acting as co-chairmen.

(16 June) Bao Dai selected Ngo Dinh Diem as Prime Minister. Diem, a Roman Catholic in a Buddhist country, had a very narrow power base.

(17 June) Pierre Mendès-France became the Prime Minister of France and pledged to bring about a cease-fire in Indo-China within a month.

(July) Agreement reached in Geneva for cessation of hostilities in Vietnam, Cambodia and Laos. Provided for a provisional demarcation on the 17th parallel, pending national elections to be held within two years. The United States expressed reservations and Bao Dai denounced the settlement.

(9 October) French forces left Hanoi.

1955   French and Vietnamese allies withdrew to the South. The United States gave financial aid to the Diem governmment. Pro-French refugees fled from the North to the South. Vietminh regrouped in the North.

(July) Diem (with United States' approval) rejected Geneva agreement and refused to participate in elections.

(July) Ho Chi Minh in Moscow accepted Soviet aid.

(23 October) Diem defeated Bao Dai in (heavily rigged) referendum to become Head of State.

(26 October) Diem proclaimed Republic of Vietnam with himself as President.

1956   Diem clamped down on Vietminh sympathisers in the South. In the North sweeping land reforms were carried out and landlords put on trial.

1957   (October) Communist insurgency began in earnest in the South.

1958   (July) Phoui Sananike adopted anti-communist stance in Laos with American support.

1959   Communists infiltrated the South via the Ho Chi Minh trail. In August Diem clamped down still further on dissent.

1960   Conflict spread to Laos.

(December) Hanoi leaders formed National Liberation Front (Vietcong) to operate in South.

1961   (May) Geneva Conference on Laos.

1962   Number of American military 'advisers' in South Vietnam increased significantly.

(23 July) Geneva Accord on neutrality of Laos signed.

1963   North Vietnam adopted China, rather than Russia, as its ally. Internal struggles in South Vietnam led to the overthrow and subsequent assassination of Ngo Dinh Diem, and his influential brother, Ngo Dinh Nhu, by the military.

1964   (2 August) North Vietnamese patrol boats attacked American destroyer, *Maddox*, in Gulf of Tonkin.

1965   Americans bombed North Vietnam.

1965–75   Vietnam War.

1975   (30 April) Communist forces captured Saigon (and renamed it Ho Chi Minh City). American forces left.

The Middle East

Syria

Syria, which included what became the Lebanon and Palestine, was a province of the Ottoman empire. It was at the forefront of growing Arab national consciousness in the nineteenth century.

The French Mandate

1914   Outbreak of First World War. On 14 November Turkey entered the war on the side of Germany. Germany and Western allies manoeuvred for the support of the Arabs within the Ottoman empire. The French had already been seeking a privileged position in Syria.

1915   (15 July) Hussein, Sherif of Mecca, offered assistance to Britain in return for recognition of the independence of Arab states within a defined area.

(24 October) British High Commissioner in Egypt, Sir Henry McMahon, sent a cautious reply, knowing French sensitivities, specifically reserving position in certain areas, including western Syria.

(21 December) French willing to consider possibility of Arab confederation but wanted British and French commercial spheres recognised.

1916   (26 April) Agreement (later rendered of no effect by the Russian Revolution) between Russia, France and Britain on the partition of Asiatic Turkey after the war. In an 'independent' Arab confederation, Britain was to have a sphere of influence in Mesopotamia and the ports of Haifa and Acre in Syria; France, the western part of Syria, Cilicia and Southern Kurdistan; and Russia, Armenia, part of Kurdistan and northern Anatolia.

(9 May) Sykes–Picot Agreement between British and French officials, later formally accepted by their governments, which divided the region into areas of economic primacy. France was to have Mosul, Homs, Hama, Aleppo and Damascus within her sphere.

(June) Hussein raised Arab revolt.

1917   (November) Bolshevik government in Russia published details of Sykes–Picot Agreement. Arab opinion alarmed.

1918   (8 January) The twelfth of President Woodrow Wilson's Fourteen Points spoke specifically of opportunities for 'autonomous development' for non-Turkish parts of Ottoman empire.

(30 October) Turkey capitulated. Allies already in control of Damascus and Aleppo.

(November) French took over administration of Syria and what became the Lebanon, removing the Arab leader, Feisal, whom General Allenby had placed in control of cities.

1919   Paris Peace Conference. Feisal asked for independence for all the Arab countries. American mission found that Syrians were hostile to the idea of a French mandate.

1920   (March) Elected assembly in Damascus proclaimed Feisal King of the independent state of Syria, including Palestine, Lebanon and what became Transjordan.

(April) San Remo Conference gave France a mandate over Syria and Lebanon.

(14 July) Feisal compelled to accept French ultimatum.

(25 July) French troops seized Damascus.

1925   Syrians particularly resented French action in setting up an enlarged Lebanon. Rebellion broke out in July, followed by demands for independence for a re-united Syria and the withdrawal of foreign troops. French bombarded Damascus in October (and again in May 1926).

1930   (22 May) New constitution in Syria but with France retaining control of defence and foreign policy. Constitution in suspension, 1932–37.

1936   (9 September) Franco-Syrian treaty. Mandate to end in three years but Lebanon to remain separate.

1939   Outbreak of Second World War.

Developments during the Second World War and the end of the mandate

1940   Mandated territories technically non-belligerent but, with the fall of France, the Vichy government ordered the High Commission in Beirut to cooperate with the Axis Powers. German aircraft used Syrian airfields.

1941   (8 June) British and Free French, under General de Gaulle, attacked and occupied Syria and Lebanon.

(16 September) Free French reluctantly approved the proclamation of Syria as an independent nation.

1942   Nuri es-Said of Iraq and Abdullah of Transjordan proposed the idea of 'Greater Syria'.

1943   (22 December) France transferred all powers under the mandate to the Syrian government.

1945   (26 February) Syria joined United Nations.

Lebanon

The Ottoman empire had regarded the Lebanon as part of the vilayet (province) of Syria. Its distinctive character arose from the existence of a Maronite Christian community, in communion with Rome, around Mount Lebanon, of whom France constituted itself the guardian. The Maronites had particularly strained relations with the Druze community, a heretical Islamic sect.

Background

1860   Massacre of Maronites by Druzes. French sent an expedition, which led to an international agreement setting up an autonomous region of Mount Lebanon, still within the Ottoman empire, but to be governed by a Christian governor and a Maronite-dominated council.

1913   The French attempted to build on their influence in the Lebanon to secure a strong economic position throughout Syria. This was resented in Syria.

The First World War and the establishment of a mandate

Discussions during the war left Lebanon within the French sphere of influence.

1918   French made clear that they had prior claims and compelled Feisal to lower his flag in Beirut.

1919   Feisal's requests for Arab independence rejected by Paris Peace Conference.

1920   (April) San Remo Conference. France given mandate over Lebanon.

1925   Druze resentment at the enlargement of Lebanon and what they saw as the French favouring the Maronites led to a rebellion, in the course of which the French bombarded Damascus.

1926   French imposed a constitution on the Lebanon, based on the religious communities.

The Second World War and independence

1940   After the fall of France, the Vichy government ordered the High Commission in Beirut to collaborate with the Axis Powers.

1941   (June–July) British and Free French forces under General de Gaulle entered and occupied Lebanon.
            (26 November) Lebanese government proclaimed Lebanon to be an independent sovereign state.

1943   The major religious communities agreed on a National pact. On the basis of the census of 1932, there should be a Maronite Christian President; a Sunni Muslim Prime Minister; and a Shiite Muslim Speaker of the Legislative Assembly. Seats in the assembly and the Cabinet were also determined on a religious basis, which guaranteed the Maronites a small majority.
            (November) The Lebanese government passed legislation removing from the constitution all clauses inconsistent with Lebanese independence. The French Delegate-General suspended the constitution and arrested the President. Britain and the United States supported the Lebanese and the French were compelled to back down.
            (22 December) France transferred all mandate powers to the Lebanese government.

1946   (March) All British and French forces evacuated.[2]

---

[2] For later history see R. Ovendale, *Longman Companion to the Middle East since 1914*, 1992.

4 The Dutch Empire

The Dutch empire was an old one, dating from the seventeenth century, but the Dutch had been selective in their acquisitions and, conspicuously, had not joined in the Scramble for Africa in the nineteenth century. By the time of the Second World War their empire consisted of the Dutch East Indies, the Dutch West Indies and Surinam. Their system of government had approximated more to British ideas of Indirect Rule than to French ideas of assimilation, but the empire had played an important role in the Dutch economy. After the Second World War the Dutch intended that their empire should continue and were even prepared to fight for it, although, when their initial plans broke down, they looked for a solution which had an obvious model in the British Commonwealth.

Asia

Dutch East Indies

1908   First nationalist movements.

1927   Ahmed Sukarno founded National Indonesian Party (PNI).

1928   Sukarno brought about a federation of diverse nationalist groups in the Union of Indonesian Political Associations (Permufakatan Perhimpunam Politiek Kebangsaan Indonesia, PPPKI), of which he became President.

1932   Sukarno published *Towards Independence for Indonesia.*

1942–45   Japanese occupation. Japanese encouraged Indonesian nationalism in opposition to Europeans. Sukarno cooperated for a time but (like Aung San in Burma) dissociated himself as the Japanese position weakened. The Allies encouraged guerrilla movements against Japanese (which would later be turned against the Dutch).

183

1945   (17 August) Sukarno proclaimed Indonesian Republic in Batavia (Jakarta). The Republic claimed to govern the whole of the Dutch East Indies but only set up government in Java and Sumatra.

(29 September) British troops arrived. Used Japanese troops to establish order. Indonesians had some success in resisting Japanese.

(October) Dutch troops arrived. Took possession of Borneo, the Moluccas, Celebes and some other areas without difficulty, but guerrilla war on Bali and Celebes cost many casualties.

1945–46   Fighting between rival Indonesian groups, as well as with Dutch.

1946   (July) Dutch Governor-General, Hubertus van Mook, convened a conference at Malino of representatives of islands not in sympathy with the Republicans in Jakarta, which led to the setting up of the State of Eastern Indonesia (including islands such as Bali, Ambon, Celebes and Banka) under Sukawati, who wished to cooperate with the Dutch.

(November) British troop withdrawal completed. International pressure on Dutch to find settlement. Sukarno and other senior leaders were prepared to negotiate.

(15 November) Preliminary Linggadjati (Cheribon) Agreement (signed 25 March 1947). The Dutch recognised the jurisdiction of the Indonesian Republic over Java, Madura and Sumatra and both sides agreed to work for a wider Indonesian federation. Indonesia and the Netherlands would form a union under the Dutch Crown. Van Mook conducted negotiations but public opinion in the Netherlands was turning against it and the agreement broke down.

1947   (21 July) The Dutch attacked in Java.

(30 July) India and Australia brought the matter before the United Nations Security Council and a cease-fire was agreed. But the Dutch were able to consolidate their position in the part of Indonesia still under their control.

(October) A 'good offices committee', proposed by the United States and consisting of one Belgian, one American and one Australian, arrived in Indonesia.

1948   (17 January) Agreement reached on board USS *Renville* that the Dutch would not cross the cease-fire line of August 1947 but

Sukarno's republic would continue on reduced territory with Jakarta as its capital. Plebiscites would eventually be held to allow territories to decide whether they wished to join the republic or the Malino group.

(Summer) General election in the Netherlands resulted in victory for right-wing parties determined to re-establish position in Indonesia. Constitutional arrangements put in train for federal solution, which would leave control of foreign policy and defence in The Hague.

(September) Sukarno and other Republican leaders suppressed Communists. Sympathies of American President, Harry Truman, began to shift towards the Indonesians.

(19 December) In an attempt to regain the initiative, the Dutch (who had replaced van Mook with the hard-liner, Louis van Beel) launched surprise attack on Jakarta and seized Sukarno and other leaders. The United Nations Security Council called for an immediate cessation of fighting and the release of the Indonesian leaders. The United States stopped Marshal Plan payments to the Netherlands. The Dutch withdrew to the Renville lines.

1949   (January) Good Offices Committee was changed to United Nations Commission for Indonesia (UNCI) with extended powers.

(August) Round Table Conference in The Hague. The Netherlands agreed 'the unconditional and complete transfer of sovereignty of the entire territory of the former Dutch East Indies (except Western New Guinea) to the Republic of the United States of Indonesia by 30 December 1949 at the latest'. A Dutch-Indonesian Union was to be created with the Queen as its Head but cooperation was to be based on equality, with both partners having equal rights in foreign affairs and defence, as well as in financial and other matters. The Dutch parliament ratified the agreement, despite strenuous right-wing opposition.

(27 December) Transfer of sovereignty took place. A few days earlier Sukarno had been elected President of the United States of Indonesia.

1950   (17 August) The federal structure agreed in 1949 was dissolved in favour of a unitary state.

1956   (13 February) Sukarno denounced Union between the Netherlands and Indonesia, after he had failed to secure the accession of Dutch New Guinea.

1962   (15 August) Treaty signed for transfer of Dutch New Guinea.

1963   Western (Dutch) New Guinea (Irian) joined the Republic but at the same time strong separatist movements developed in Sumatra and Celebes.

1960s   Struggles between Indonesia and Malaysia over disputed territories.

1968   General Suharto became President.

1969   Referendum in Irian Jaya (formerly Dutch New Guinea). Result rejected by Papua Independent Organisation (OPM) which began guerrilla warfare.

1975   Indonesia seized East Timor.

The Caribbean

Netherlands Antilles

Curaçao, Bonaire, St Maartens, St Eustatius and Saba remain Dutch dependencies although they have a 22-member Federal Parliament and have been largely self-governing since the 1954 Realm Statute. Aruba, formerly part of the Netherlands Antilles, became a separate territory, although still within the Kingdom of the Netherlands, on 1 June 1986.

Dutch Guiana (Surinam)

Dutch Guiana was acquired by the Dutch from the British in 1667 in exchange for the New Netherlands (later New York) in North America. On 25 November 1975 it became independent under the name of Surinam.

5 The Portuguese Empire

This was the first of the European maritime empires, dating from the late fifteenth century. It was also the last to be dissolved, although Portugal had lost her most important overseas possession, Brazil, in 1822. Her empire had become moribund in the nineteenth century but she revived her claims, notably to Angola and Mozambique, in the Scramble period at the end of the century. The government of the empire was centred on Lisbon and tended to be authoritarian. This was intensified during the Salazar period from 1932 to 1968.

Portugal had remained neutral during the Second World War and had no plans to decolonise at the end of the war. On the contrary, Salazar wished to integrate the colonies much more closely with Portugal. Portugal fought fiercely to retain her empire with profound results for domestic politics.

Africa

Although it was true that the Portuguese were less resistant to the idea of marrying non-Europeans than the northern Europeans were and the existence of communities of mixed race in the colonies was an additional complication, the numbers involved were actually small: about 70,000 in Angola and 30,000 in Mozambique (with populations of 4 million and 5 million respectively). Legislation under Salazar in the 1930s had divided the inhabitants of the colonies into two distinct categories: the *indigenas* (natives) and the *civilisados/cidadoes* (civilised people/citizens). The latter included all Europeans, Goans, peoples of mixed race and the African *assimilados*. An African had to meet tough conditions of education and status to become an *assimilado*. In 1950 there were about 30,000 in Angola and about 4,000 in Mozambique.

After the Second World War, Portugal pursued a deliberate policy of encouraging emigration to the colonies. Partly to facilitate this, in June 1951, the colonies were redefined as 'Overseas Provinces'. By 1970 there were 250,000 to 300,000 recent settlers in Angola and about 130,000 in Mozambique. Most of these settlers constituted a 'poor white' class and greatly increased the tension with the black population.

In 1961–62 the Salazar government initiated some tentative reforms, the most important of which was the abolition of forced labour. The 1950s saw the foundation of political movements or parties in various parts of Portuguese Africa but all needed a base in exile and this resulted in considerable interaction with other countries.

Angola

1956   Movimento Popular de Libertação Angola (MPLA, Popular Movement for the Liberation of Angola) founded in Luanda, mainly by *assimilados* and men of mixed race. Communist-orientated.

1959   Holden Roberto re-formed Union of Peoples of North Angola, set up in Leopoldville in Congo in 1958 as a politico-cultural organisation among the Bakongo people, as the União das Poulacoes de Angola (UPA), a more clearly political organisation which demanded the liberation of the whole of Angola.

1960   Roberto attended the All-African People's Conference in Tunis.

1961   (4 February) MPLA implicated in attack on prison of São Paulo in Luanda. Began series of disturbances, including sporadic attacks on white settlers.
(15 March) UPA launched mass rebellion in northern Angola. Portuguese made military response. Acts of terrorism committed by both sides. The UPA were pushed back to mountainous zone in interior.

1960s   State of virtual civil war continued. MPLA leaders went into exile in Algeria and Guinea, where they received aid. Containment of both MPLA and UPA damaged the Portuguese economy and compelled constant recall of men to the colours to the point where Portugal itself was destabilised.

1968   Salazar finally compelled to relinguish power by failing health. Regime survived until the 1974 revolution.

1974   (25 April) Revolution in Portugal.

1975   (15 January) Main liberation movements, MPLA, Frente Nacionalde Libertação de Angola (FNLA) and Uniho Nacional Par a

Independencia Total de Angola (UNITA) signed agreement with Portugal. FNLA and UNITA, unlike MPLA, were anti-Marxist. (11 November) Angola became independent.

1975–89 Civil war continued between Angolan factions. Aid from Soviet Union and Cuba helped MPLA to defeat most of its rivals and, in 1976, Angola became a one-party state. But South African forces crossed into Angola to support UNITA. Clashed with Cuban troops. Conflict intensified in 1981. (South African support for UNITA was designed to counter Angolan support for guerrillas in Namibia.)

1989 (April) Cease-fire arranged which led to withdrawal of both South African and Cuban forces.

1993 Civil war resumed between MPLA and UNITA.

1994 (November) Civil war ended by United Nations mediation by Lusaka Protocal, but by that time UNITA was virtually defeated.

Mozambique

1962 Frente de Libertação de Mocambique (FRELIMO) founded in Dar-es-Salaam in Tanganyika.

1964 (September) FRELIMO launched first attacks in Mozambique and gained control of large parts of country despite Portugal maintaining large concentration of troops there.

1974 (25 April) Revolution in Portugal. New government opened negotiations with FRELIMO.

(3 September) White settlers in Lourenço Marques started insurrection.

(7 September) Cease-fire with FRELIMO, followed by agreement of independence date.

1975 (25 June) Mozambique became independent. Became one-party state.

1976–92 Civil war. FRELIMO opposed by MNRM, which at first had backing from Rhodesia and South Africa, which wished to counter Mozambique's support for Mugabe's military wing of ZANU.

1992   (October) Peace accord signed.

1994   Elections.

1995   (January) Last United Nations troops withdrawn.
            (13 November) Became a member of the Commonwealth.

Portuguese Guinea (Guinea-Bissau)

1956   Partido Africano da Independeñcia da Guiné a Cabo Verde
            (PAIGC) founded. Amilcar Cabral, who had worked as a civil
            servant in Angola in 1955, became the Secretary-General. The
            movement was inspired from Senegal.

1959   (August) PAIGC called a dockers' strike which was severely
            repressed by police. Cabral fled to Conakry in (French) Guinea,
            where Sekou Touré aided him.

1963   Campaign of armed resistance began.

1973   (24 September) PAIGC unilaterally claimed independence.

1974   (10 September) Portugal recognised independence of Guinea.

1975   Cape Verde Islands became independent as a separate entity
            from Guinea-Bissau.

São Tomé e Principe

1522   Became colony.

1951   Became Overseas Province of Portugal.

1975   (12 July) Became independent state.

Asia

Goa

1510   Albuquerque took Goa from the Sultan of Bijapur.

1961   (December) India occupied Goa and subsequently declared it
            to be Indian territory.

Macao

1557 Macao became Portuguese colony.

1887 (December) China recognised Portuguese sovereignty over Macao.

1951 Portugal declared Macao an 'Overseas Province'.

1974 Portugal changed Macao's status to that of 'territory under Portuguese administration'.

1986 (June) Sino-Portuguese negotiations on transfer of administration.

1987 (13 April) Agreement signed by which Macao would be transferred to China on 20 December 1999.

East Timor

1859 Treaty dividing the Island of Timor, which had been in dispute between the Portuguese and the Dutch since the seventeenth century. Portuguese retained the eastern part.

1974 (April) Revolution in Portugal.

1975 (June) Portuguese promised independence and immediate elections.

 (August) Fighting broke out between communist FRETILIN and more moderate UDT, which wished to continue links with Portugal. Refugees fled into Indonesian West Timor.

 (December) Indonesia sent troops into East Timor and took control.

1976 (17 July) Indonesia declared East Timor to be integrated into Indonesia.

1976–97 FRETILIN continued guerrilla warfare with a high casualty rate: an estimated 200,000 dead. Indonesia settled 150,000 Muslims in East Timor to counter the predominantly Christian population. Indonesian control not recognised by the United Nations, which still regards Portugal as the sovereign power.

6 The Spanish Empire

Spain had had one of the first European empires, and at its zenith it had been highly organised, but its most important parts, in South and Central America, had become independent in the early nineteenth century. Some of the remainder, Cuba and the Philippines, had been lost to the United States in 1898 during the Spanish-American war. (Cuba finally became independent of the United States in 1909, the Philippines in 1946.) By the Second World War, Spain had only a few remnants of empire in Africa. It regarded the Canary Islands, although they were off the African coast, as part of metropolitan Spain.

Spain had remained neutral during the Second World War and the authoritarian government of General Franco had no plans for decolonisation at the end of the war. At the same time Spain had no intention of wasting her substance, as Portugal had done, on a last-ditch defence of her empire. The picture was rather one of gradual disengagement.

Morocco

1956–58 French Morocco became independent (March 1956). Spain withdrew from her protectorates in the north (1956) and the south (1958) which joined independent Morocco. She retained Ceuta and Mellila and the enclave of Ifni.

1957 (23 November) Moroccan irregulars attacked Ifni but were repulsed.

1969 (January) Ifni transferred to Morocco. (Ceuta and Mellila remain part of metropolitan Spain.)

Equatorial Guinea

1959 Constituted as two provinces of metropolitan Spain.

1963 Became autonomous.

1968   (December) Rio Muni, Fernando Po and a few small islands were granted independence and joined together to form Equatorial Guinea.

Spanish Sahara (Western Sahara, Rio de Oro)

Spain was more reluctant to relinquish this because of the discovery, in 1972, of rich phosphate deposits. There was the added complication that the territory was claimed by Morocco and Mauritania and, more dubiously, by Algeria.

1973   Polisario movement Frente Popular para la Liberacion de Saguia y Rio de Oro, which demanded complete independence for the Western Sahara, formed with Algerian support.

1975   (November) King Hassan of Morocco demonstrated claim by sending 350,000 unarmed Moroccans into the territory.

(14 November) Madrid Agreement by which Spain would withdraw and the administration be divided between Morocco and Mauritania.

1976   (26 February) Madrid Agreement became operative but Polisario proclaimed independent Saharan Arab Democratic Republic. Serious fighting followed. France assisted Mauritania and the Organisation of African Unity tried, unsuccessfully, to mediate.

1979   (5 August) Mauritania came to terms with the Polisario and renounced its share. Morocco refused to recognise Polisario claims and fighting continued.

1984   Morocco built a defensive wall to protect the north of the territory.

1988   Morocco and Polisario accepted United Nations compromise and agreed to a referendum. Although a cease-fire came into effect in September 1991, the referendum has not yet taken place.

7   The Belgian Empire

This consisted of one colony (the Belgian Congo) and one mandated territory (Ruanda-Urundi). The colony had been acquired by the King, Leopold II, in the 1880s as a kind of personal fief, but had passed under the regular jurisdiction of the Belgian Parliament in 1908, following the international scandal of the cruel exploitation of the Congolese in the production of raw rubber. Ruanda-Urundi had been part of German East Africa.

In 1945 the Belgians had no plans for decolonisation and the lack of opportunities for education beyond the simplest primary and vocational level meant that the Congolese were late in developing their own nationalism, compared with many other European colonies. The hasty decolonisation, with virtually no preparation, in 1960 resulted in violence and anarchy, unparalleled elsewhere in Africa. The situation was made worse by the artificial nature of the boundaries, drawn up during the Scramble period in the late nineteenth century.

Congo

1954   Liberal-socialist government elected in Belgium. Made first cautious moves towards political reform in the Congo.

1955   Joseph Kasavubu organised Alliance des Bakongo (ABAKO), previously a cultural organisation among the large Bakongo tribe, into a political party.

1957   ABOKO won the first municipal elections held in the Congo.

1958   Patrice Lumumba and others founded Mouvement National Congolais (MNC, Congolese National Movement).
Liberal-socialist coalition fell. Political impetus for change slackened. An economic crisis developed in the Congo, triggered by a fall in the world price of copper, the Congo's principal export.
Lumumba attended All-African Conference in Accra in Ghana.

1959   (January) Lumumba returned to the Congo and announced that the objective was immediate independence.

(4–6 January) Serious riots in Leopoldville, the Congolese capital, partly political, partly economic in origin. Severely repressed by Belgian authorities.

(13 January) King Baudouin promised in radio broadcast that the Congo would be given its independence, although no time scale was indicated.

Various political parties formed in the Congo but all tended to have a tribal or regional base. Among them were the Confédération des Associations tribales du Katanga (CONAKAT), led by Moise Tshombe, and the Parti National du Progrès (PNP), led by Godefroid Munongo.

1960   (January–February) Conference in Brussels worked out a plan for Congolese independence. The Congolese were divided between those who wanted a federal and those who wanted a more centralised system.

(19 May) *Loi Fondamentale* (Fundamental Law) set up a federal state of six provinces with some rights of autonomy but with ultimate power vested in the central government. At the centre power was divided between the President and the Prime Minister.

(May) Pre-independence elections. Because of the splintered nature of the parties, the results were not decisive. The 137 seats of the House of Representatives were divided: Lumumba's (centralist) wing of the MNC and allies, 41; PNP and allies, 15; Parti Solidaire Africain (PSA), 13; ABAKO, 12; CONAKAT, 8; Federalist wing of MNC, 8; the rest were divided between a number of smaller parties.

(30 June) Power transferred to Democratic Republic of the Congo. Kasavubu became President; Lumumba became Prime Minister.

(4–9 July) Disturbances in various areas. Belgians, who still commanded the Force Publique (Congolese army), intervened. The Congolese army mutinied. Period of anarchy and atrocities.

(11 July) Moise Tshombe announced secession of Katanga from Congo. Belgian paratroopers intervened. Lumumba asked for a United Nations force.

1960–63 Civil war in Congo. United Nations force sent. Secretary-General of United Nations, Dag Hammarskjold, who had largely masterminded the operation, was killed in plane crash flying to meet Tshombe in Northern Rhodesia (September 1961).

1960   (September) General Joseph Mobutu ousted Lumumba and, temporarily, Kasavubu from their offices.

1961   (January–February) Lumumba killed in mysterious circumstances.

1963   Katanga secession ended.

1963–65   Tshombe gained control of whole country.

1965   (November) Mobutu led army coup which overthrew Tshome and himself took control.

1971   Name changed to Zaire.

1997   Mobutu overthrown by Laurent Kabila. Restored name: Democratic Republic of the Congo.

Ruanda-Urundi (Rwanda and Burundi)

1920   Part of former German East Africa, mandated to Belgium.

1946   Became trusteeship territory.

1959   Hutu majority population rose against ruling Tutsis. Massacres followed and many Tutsis fled to Uganda.

1962   (1 July) Belgian trusteeship ended after United Nations intervention. Ruanda-Urundi became two separate independent states – Rwanda (capital Kigali) and Burundi (capital Usumbura).

8 The Italian Empire

This was of very recent creation, having been all acquired after the unification of Italy in 1871. During the Scramble for Africa period in the late nineteenth century, Italy had gained Eritrea and Italian Somaliland but had failed to secure Abyssinia (Ethiopia). The Italian defeat at the battle of Adowa in 1896 was one of the few defeats suffered by a European Power at African hands at this time and left a permanent sense of humiliation in Italy. There had been Italian investment in, and even emigration to, North Africa in the nineteenth century, but France secured control, except in Libya, which the Italians acquired from the Ottoman empire in 1912. Italy also failed to secure what she regarded as her fair share of mandated territories after the First World War.

In 1935–36 she conquered Abyssinia, despite widespread international condemnation and the ineffective application of League of Nations sanctions. Italy was defeated in the Second World War and her colonial empire was not restored to her at the end.

Abyssinia (Ethiopia)

1941   British forces drove out the Italians. Country restored to its ruler (expelled in 1936), the Emperor Haile Selassi. Ethiopia became a member of the United Nations, as she had been a member of the League of Nations.

Eritrea

1941   Liberated by British forces.

1941–52   Remained under British protection and administration.

1952   United with Ethiopia.

Italian Somaliland

1941   Liberated by British forces.

1941–50   Remained under British control.

1950   Placed under Italian administration by the United Nations.

1960   (July) United with British Somaliland to form Somali Democratic Republic.

Libya

1912   Italy acquired Libya from Ottoman empire.

1941–43   Battlefield between Axis and Allied Powers.

1945   United Nations gave it trusteeship status and entrusted the administration to Britain and France.

1951   (24 December) Became independent with monarchical form of government, under King Idris.

SECTION FOUR

Biographies

(In this Section, the biographies of western politicians generally only include information relevant to their role in the decolonisation process.)

Abbas, Ferhat (1899–1985) Algerian politician. Born at Taher, the son of a civil servant. Educated at the lycée of Constantine and the University of Algiers, where he took a degree in pharmacy. President of the Algerian Muslim Student Union. In 1931 published his first book, *Le Jeune Algérien.* Became a pharmacist in Sétif in 1933. At this time he wanted political progress but believed it to be possible to be both an Algerian Muslim and French. He joined the French army during the Second World War and was dismayed by France's defeat. In November 1942 he met President Roosevelt's special envoy, R. Murphy, and believed the principles of the Atlantic Charter should be applied to Algeria. In 1943 he published 'Manifesto of the Algerian people', which called for an autonomous Algerian state within the French Union. The organisation he founded to work for reform, Les amis du manifeste et de la liberté (The friends of the manifesto and of liberty), was composed of moderate Muslim leaders but it was dissolved after riots in Sétif in May 1945 and Abbas interned. In 1946 he founded a party, l'Union Démocratique du Manifeste Algérien (UDMA, the Democratic Union for the Algerian Manifesto) and the same year played an important part in the second French Constituent Assembly. Like other moderates he at first opposed the rebellion of November 1954 but gave his public blessing to the aims of the FLN (National Liberation Front) after April 1956, when a peaceful solution came to seem impossible because of the opposition of the French settlers. He was Prime Minister of the provisional government in Tunis, 1958–61, and after Algerian independence he became President of the National Assembly, 1962–63, but resigned because of differences with Ben Bella. Ben Bella exiled him to a distant part of the country and in 1965 the Boumédienne regime placed him under house arrest. He was only completely rehabilitated in 1984. Always distrusted as too pro-French by more radical politicians, his main service to his country was to make Algerian nationalism respectable in the eyes of the world by his moderation and international diplomacy, especially in the period 1958–61.

Abd-el-Kedir (1807–83) Algerian resistance fighter. Led the opposition to the French occupation from 1832 and was the principal adversary of Marshal Bugeaud. Surrendered in 1847 and imprisoned in France until 1852, when he went into exile in Damascus. Refused offer from Emperor Napoleon III in 1865 to become Viceroy of Algeria.

Abdullah (1882–1951) King of Jordan. Born in Mecca, a son of Hussein ibn Ali. Educated in Constantinople. In 1908 represented Hejaz Province of western Arabia in Ottoman parliament. Became active in movement for Arab independence before 1914. Took part in Arab revolt of 1916. Helped British forces drive Turks out of Syria. In 1920 the Arab National Congress, meeting in Damascus, elected Abdullah King of Iraq but he was driven out by the French. Abdullah accepted the British offer of the emirate of the newly created state of Transjordan. Transjordan became independent in 1946 and in 1949 Abdullah became King of the Hashemite Kingdom of Jordan. Participated in first Arab-Israeli war, 1948–49, and Abdullah's Arab Legion held central Palestine for the Arabs, but its annexation as part of Jordan in 1950 aroused the hostility of Palestinians. Abdullah was assassinated by a Palestinian in Jerusalem on 20 July 1951.

Adams, Sir Grantley Herbert (1898–1971) Prime Minister of the Federation of the West Indies. Born in Barbados. Educated at Harrison College and Oxford University. Called to the Bar, 1923. Practised law in the West Indies and his politics became more radical in the face of the poverty caused by the Depression. In 1934 he was elected a member of the House of Assembly. After the 1937 riots he went to London to press for a royal commission, as a result of which the Moyne Commission was appointed in 1939. While in London he came to know Stafford Cripps and Arthur Creech-Jones. In 1938 he founded the Barbados Progress League, from which both the Barbados Workers' Union and the Barbados Labour Party (which he led) emerged. He was appointed to the Executive Council in 1942 and, when the Barbados Labour Party won a majority in 1946, became Leader of the House of Assembly. He was a member of the British delegation at the first meeting of the United Nations. Became Prime Minister of Barbados in 1954. He believed in a federal solution to the problems of the West Indies and attended the conferences at Montego Bay in 1947 and in London in 1953 and 1956. He became the first (and only) Prime Minister of the Federation in 1958. When the Federation collapsed in 1962 he returned to Barbadan politics but was in opposition when independence came in 1966. He retired from politics because of ill-health in 1970.

Adoum, Tchere (b. 1925) Chad politician. Joined the French army and fought with Free French during Second World War. Awarded the Légion d'Honneur and Croix de Guerre. In December 1958 he became Minister of Social Affairs and Labour, and in 1964 he became President of the National Assembly.

Aggrey, James Emman Kwegyir (1875–1927) African missionary and teacher. Born at Anamaba on the Gold Coast. Educated at a Methodist missionary school and at Livingstone College, North Carolina, where he graduated in 1902. Returned to Africa after further work in America. Joined staff of Achimota College, one of the few institutions in Africa at this time above the secondary level. Became the first African Vice-Principal. Exercised an important influence on the first generation of West African nationalist leaders, especially in inspiring them to go to the United States for their education. Strongly advocated the need for cooperation between whites and blacks and coined the famous metaphor of the need for both the black and white keys of the piano.

Ahidjo, Ahmadou (1924–89) Cameroun politician. A Fulani, he was born at Garoua, Northern Cameroun. Was elected to the first Assembly of the French trust territory of Eastern Cameroun in 1947. Secretary of Assembly of French Union, 1954. In 1957 he was elected President of the Cameroun Assembly and became Deputy Prime Minister of the first pre-independence government. In February 1958 became Prime Minister. In January 1960 signed independence agreement with France for Eastern Cameroun. Became President of the Republic of Cameroun in May 1960. Responsible for union with British-administered territory of Western Cameroun in 1961, forming Federal Republic of Cameroun. Re-elected President in 1965. Resigned in 1982 and spent last years in exile.

Ahomadegbe, Justin (b. 1917) Dahomey politician. Born in Abomey. Studied medicine and dentistry. Founded Dahomey Democratic Union, 1956. In 1959 became President of Dahomey National Assembly. Imprisoned for alleged subversion 1961–62. Took office in Soglo government 1963. Prime Minister 1964–65 and, briefly, President. Forced out of office in November 1965.

Akintola, Chief Samuel L. (1911–66) Nigerian politician. He taught at the Baptist Academy in Lagos, 1930–42, but then resigned in sympathy with three colleagues who were dismissed for trade union activities. He worked for a short time as a clerk with the Nigerian railways but then turned to journalism. Edited an important newspaper, the *Daily Service*, until 1946. Went to London on a British Council scholarship, studied law and was called to the Bar in 1949. He returned to Nigeria in 1950 and in 1951 joined Awolowo's Action Group, later becoming Deputy Leader. He was a member of the Federal House from 1952 and led the Opposition there, 1954–57. Succeeded Awolowo as premier of the Western Region in 1959, when Awolowo transferred his interests to the Federal House. In 1962 he quarrelled seriously with Awolowo and founded a new party, the United People's Party. In the 1964 Western Region elections Akintola's party, now the Nigerian National Democratic Party, retained power, with the help of the Northern People's Congress. He was among those assassinated in the massacre of Nigeria's leading politicians in January 1966.

Alexander, Albert Victor, Earl Alexander of Hillsborough (1885–1965) British Labour politician. First Lord of the Admiralty in Churchill's wartime coalition government. In June 1946 travelled to Bordeaux to try to secure French promise that their fleet would not fall into German hands. When that appeal failed he authorised the use of force against the French ships at Oran in Algeria in July. Went with Sir Stafford Cripps and Lord Pethick-Lawrence on 'Cabinet Mission' to India in 1946.

Allenby, Edmund Henry Hynman, Field Marshal, 1st Viscount Allenby of Megiddo (1861–1936) British soldier. Fought in Boer War, 1899–1902, and in France, 1914–17, but best known for his success against the Turks in 1917–18. In the course of the campaign his troops captured both Jerusalem and Damascus. Famously preferred to enter Jerusalem on 11 December 1917 on foot 'as a pilgrim', instead of on horse-back as a conqueror. High Commissioner for Egypt, 1919–25. Released Saad Zaghlul from gaol and oversaw the end of the British Protectorate.

Ambedkar, Dr Bhimrae Ramji (1891–1956) Indian political leader. Born at Mhow in Madya Pradesh of the Mahars caste, an 'Untouchable'. Educated at Columbia University and received his Ph.D. in 1926. Throughout his life he campaigned for justice for the Untouchables. In 1924 he organised the Depressed Classes Institute of Bombay and subsequently became a member of the Bombay Legislative Council. He attended the Round Table Conferences in London in 1930–32 and clashed with Mahatma Gandhi, who believed that the Untouchables were adequately represented by the Indian National Congress, whereas Ambedkar believed that they must have the facilities to campaign for themselves. He continued to organise the Untouchables after the Government of India Act of 1935 and became the Legal member of the Viceroy's Executive Council in 1942. In this capacity he had influence on the drafting of the Indian constitution. Just before his death in December 1956, he converted to Buddhism and a large number of Mahars followed his example.

Amin, Col. Idi Dada Oumee (b. 1925) Ugandan soldier and politician. Came from West Nile district of northern Uganda. Joined army as a private in the 4th Battalion of King's African Rifles in 1943. Served in Burma during Second World War and in Kenya during Mau Mau emergency. Commissioned in July 1961. Became Deputy Commander of Ugandan army after a mutiny in 1964. Played leading role in 1966 crisis, which forced the resignation of the Kabaka, Sir Edward Mutesa, and the adoption of a new constitution. As army commander he overthrew the government of Milton Obote in January 1971. He ruled as a dictator, 1971–79, presiding over a particularly brutal and bloodthirsty regime. Among his victims was Archbishop Luwum. In 1971 he expelled the large and prosperous Asian community from Uganda. He was overthrown by military intervention from neighbouring Tanzania in 1979 and went into exile.

Andriamanjato, Richard (b. 1930) Malagasy politician. Studied at the universities of Montpellier and Strasbourg and was president of the Association of Malagasy students when in France, 1956–57. Mayor of Tananarive, 1959. From 1959 also leader of Congress for Independence Party (AKFM), a left-wing nationalist party, which opposed the ruling Social Democratic Party.

Apithy, Sourou-Migan (1913–89) Dahomey politician. Born in Porto Novo. Studied in Paris and became an accountant. In 1946–58 represented Dahomey in the French National Assembly. Elected to Dahomey Constituent Assembly in 1958. Minister in President Hubert Maga's first two governments. After Maga's overthrow he was elected (January 1964) President and Prime Minister. Deposed by Assembly in November 1965.

Appiah, Joseph Emmanuel (1918–90) Ghanaian lawyer and politician. Went to London to study law in 1943. President of West African Students' Union. Close friend of Kwame Nkrumah. In 1953 married Peggy Cripps, the daughter of Sir Stafford Cripps. Returned to Gold Coast in 1954 but broke with Nkrumah and joined National Liberation Movement in Ashanti. In 1957 joined Busia's United Party. Was imprisoned by Nkrumah, 1961–62. After coup against Nkrumah in 1966, joined new government.

d'Arboussier, Gabriel (1908–76) Nationalist leader in French West Africa. Born in French Soudan, the son of Henri d'Arboussier, a distinguished administrator. Educated in France as a lawyer, then at the École Normale de la France d'Outre-Mer, the training ground for senior colonial civil servants. Joined the colonial administration in French West Africa. Represented French Equatorial Africa in the Constituent Assembly in 1945. Became involved in nationalist politics and participated in the Bamako Conference of 1946, which led to the formation of the RDA. In 1949 became the general secretary of the RDA and the editor of its journal, *Réveil*. Elected to the French National Assembly in 1947 and the representative of the Ivory Coast on the Grand Council of the French Union, he began a campaign against the colonial authorities in the Ivory Coast in 1950. When Houphouët-Boigny decided to cooperate with the French and the RDA split, d'Arboussier was first dismissed as general secretary and then (1952) expelled. In 1957 he was elected to represent Niger in the Grand Council of French West Africa. After the break-up of the Mali Federation in 1960, he made his career in Senegal, becoming Minister of Justice, then Ambassador to France (1963) and to West Germany, Austria and Switzerland (1968–72).

Arden-Clarke, Sir Charles N. (1898–1962) British colonial governor. Born in India, the son of a missionary. Served in the First World War. Joined the Colonial Service in 1920 (inspired by the example of Lord Lugard). Served in Nigeria, 1920–36, and Bechuanaland, 1936–42. Resident Commissioner, Basutoland, 1942–46. Governor of Sarawak, 1946–49. Governor of the Gold Coast, 1949–57, where he was instructed to channel, rather than check, the nationalist spirit and achieved a good working relationship with Kwame Nkrumah. Although asked to stay on, he retired almost immediately after independence. He subsequently (1958) chaired the United Nations 'good offices' committee on Namibia. In 1960 he sat on the Monckton Commission on Central Africa and in 1961 acted as constitutional adviser on Swaziland independence.

Aridy, Célestin (b. 1919) Malagasy politician. A teacher by profession. Closely associated with Philibert Tsiranana in setting up the Social Democratic Party in 1956.

Attlee, Clement (1883–1967) British politician. He was educated at Haileybury, by this time a public (independent) school but originally a college for training men for service in India. Went to the University of Oxford and subsequently became a lawyer. Shocked by the conditions he had seen in the East End of London, he became a member of the Labour Party and its leader in 1935. He held various Cabinet offices in Winston Churchill's wartime coalition government, including that of Deputy Prime Minister, 1943–45. After Labour's landslide victory in the 1945 general election, he was Prime Minister, 1945–51. He had sat on the Simon Commission, 1927–29, and by 1945 was committed to Indian independence, which he personally piloted through in 1947. It was followed by the related transfer of power in Burma and Ceylon.

Aubame, Jean-Hilaire (b. 1912) Gabon politician. Worked as a minor civil servant. More radical and socialist in his proposed solutions than his main rival Leon M'ba, he founded his Gabonese Democratic and Social Union (UDSG) in opposition to M'ba's Gabon Democratic Bloc after the Second World War. The UDSG had links with Leopold Senghor's African Regroupment Party (PRA). He sat in the National Assembly in Paris as the Gabon representative, 1946–59. M'ba and Aubame cooperated in the 1958 referendum, which led to the substitution of the French Community for the French Union and the eventual independence of Gabon. The two leaders were in coalition after the 1961 elections but Aubame was gradually side-lined by M'ba. In 1964 there was an attempted coup in Aubame's name. When it failed, Aubame was tried and sentenced to imprisonment.

Aung San (1915–47) Burmese nationalist. Aung San was committed to the cause of Burmese independence from an early age. He was sent to one of the high schools set up by Burmese nationalists and then to the University of Rangoon, where he was President of the Students' Union and a founder of the All-Burmese Students' Union. He was expelled for publishing a critical article in his journal, *Oway*. Although it had not been on a nationalist topic, it led to a general students' strike in 1936, which was important in shaping the nationalist movement. He was on the editorial staff of *New Burma* and, with U Nu, founded the anti-colonial Red Dragon Book Club. In 1938 he became the general secretary of Thakin (Our Own Masters' Party) and helped to found the All-Burma Peasants' League. With Ba Maw, he established the Freedom Bloc to present a united front to the British. In 1940 he went underground and visited Japan. In 1941 he returned to Japan with companions, the 'Thirty Comrades', planning to lead a Burmese army from Thailand in 1942. After the Japanese occupation of Burma he became, in 1943, Minister of War in Ba Maw's government. Aung San, however, was intent on playing both sides off against each other and in August 1944 he was the driving force in establishing what eventually became the Anti-Fascist People's Freedom League (AFPFL), which was to govern Burma after independence. In March 1945 he led what was now called the Patriot Burmese Force into rebellion against the Japanese. In 1945 he became president of AFPFL. When British rule was restored the Governor, Sir Reginald Dorman-Smith, deeply distrusted Aung San, but his successor, Sir Hubert Rance, reached an accommodation with him. In January 1947 Aung San led a delegation to meet the British Prime Minister, Clement Attlee, in London and on his return negotiated the Panglong Agreement, which provided for various frontier peoples to join the Union of Burma. On

19 July 1947 (six months before independence) Aung San and other leaders were assassinated by order of a rival, U Saw.

Auriol, Vincent (1884–1966) French President. Lawyer. An admirer of Jean Jaurès, he joined the Socialist Party and was a member of the 1936 Popular Front government. He opposed Pétain in 1940, escaped to London and joined General de Gaulle. Sat in Consultative Assembly in Algiers, 1943, 1944. President of both Constituent Assemblies, which drew up 1946 constitution. President of France, 1947–54. Instrumental in bringing ministries of both Faure and Pinay to power at a time of great instability. Played a part in bringing back General de Gaulle in 1958.

Awolowo, Chief Obafemi (1909–87) Nigerian politician. A Yoruba and the son of a farmer from western Nigeria. He received his early education in Protestant schools and trained as a teacher in Wesley College in Ibadan. After working for a time as a clerk, he became a trader and journalist. In the late 1930s he organised the Nigerian Produce Traders' Association and became secretary of the Nigerian Motor Transport Union. In 1943 he was the co-founder of the Trade Union Congress of Nigeria. He edited the *Nigerian Worker.* In 1940 he had also become the secretary of the Ibadan branch of the Nigerian Youth Movement. He thus played a key role in the two organisations – the trade unions and the youth movements – which spear-headed the African drive for independence. He was in London 1944–47, studying law. In 1947 he published an important book, *Path to Nigerian Freedom.* On his return to Nigeria he combined legal practice with political activities and played a key role in forming the Action Group (a predominantly Yoruba organisation) which won the Western Region elections in 1951. He was Leader of Government Business in the Western Region, 1951–54, and then became the first premier of the Western Region. He resigned the premiership in 1959 to contest the Federal elections, subsequently becoming Leader of the Opposition in the Federal House of Assembly. He led his party's delegation to the constitutional conferences in London in 1953 and in Lagos in 1954 and 1958, which prepared the way for independence in 1960. In 1962 he was arrested and imprisoned after a split in the Action Group, in which Awolowo's opponents were backed by the Northern politicians. He was released in 1966 after further political turmoil in Nigeria. He supported the Federal Government during the Biafran civil war and ran unsuccessfully for President against Shehu Shagari in 1979 and 1983. Prolific writer.

Azikiwe, Nmandi (1904–96) Nicknamed 'Zik' and generally regarded as the father of Nigerian independence. Born at Zunguru, Northern Nigeria, where his father, an Ibo from the Eastern Region, was working as a clerk. He was educated at the Hope Waddell Institute, Calabar, and the Methodist Boys High School, Lagos. Worked in the Treasury Department in Lagos, 1921–25, when he stowed away on a ship bound for the United States. Studied at Storer College, West Virginia, and at Howard and Lincoln Universities, did post-graduate work at the University of Pennsylvania and lectured at Lincoln University, before returning to West Africa in 1934. He founded the *African Morning Post*, published in the Gold Coast. After successfully fighting a charge of sedition, he returned to Nigeria in 1937. He set up other newspapers, including the *West African Pilot*, which he edited. In 1942 he founded a political party, the National Council of Nigeria and the Cameroons. In 1944 it merged with the Nigerian National Democratic Party, led by Herbert Macaulay, but retained the acronym NCNC. It aimed to be an all-Nigeria party, transcending tribal divisions. In pursuit of this policy, in the 1951 elections under the Macpherson constitution, Azikiwe stood in Lagos in the Western Region. He was elected but his party failed to carry the day. In the 1954 elections he stood in the Eastern (Ibo) Region, subsequently becoming the Prime Minister of the Eastern Region. When Nigeria became independent in 1960, he became Governor-General, and when it became a republic in 1963 he was the first President. He was in London when he was deposed by the violent coup of 1966. His sympathies were with his fellow Ibos of Biafra during the Nigerian civil war. He ran unsuccessfully for the Presidency in 1979.

Ba, (Mamour) Ousmane (b. 1919) Mali politician. Studied medicine in Dakar. Leading member of African Democratic Rally (RDA), founded in Bamako, the capital of Mali, in 1947. Was Minister of Civil Service in Government Council in Upper Volta, 1957–58, after which he returned to Mali and held various ministerial posts, becoming Minister for Foreign Affairs in 1964.

Bakary, Djibo (b. 1922) Niger politician. Trained as a teacher. Became founder secretary-general of Niger section of African Democratic Rally (RDA), the Niger Progress Party. He was active in the Niger section of the CGT (the French Communist trade union.) When the African Democratic Rally broke with the CGT in 1950, Bakary broke with RDA and set up the Niger Democratic Union. He opposed the proposal for association with France in General de Gaulle's 1958 referendum and lost influence. The Niger Democratic Union was renamed Sawaba (Freedom) Party but the party was dissolved by the Niger government and Bakary went into exile in October 1959.

Balewa, Sir Abubakar Tafawa (1912–66) Nigerian politician. He was Ahmadu Bello, the Sardauna of Sokoto's, lieutenant in the Northern People's Congress (NPC), the main political party in Northern Nigeria. When, in the 1954 elections, the Sardauna preferred to stand in the Northern Region, Balewa, who had previously been little known outside his own region, became an important figure as the leader of the NPC in the federal capital, Lagos. He formed an administration in 1957, to which he tried to give a genuinely federal character. After the 1959 elections he led a coalition of the NPC and Azikiwe's NCNC. He was assassinated in the coup of January 1966.

Balfour, Arthur James, 1st Earl of Balfour (1848–1930) British politician. The nephew of the 3rd Marquess of Salisbury, the British Prime Minister. Became Conservative MP, 1874. Succeeded his uncle as Prime Minister, 1902. During First World War, Foreign Secretary in Lloyd George's wartime coalition. In 1917 issued what became known as the Balfour Declaration, promising the Jews a homeland in Palestine. Responsible for the Balfour Report, accepted by the 1926 Imperial Conference, defining equality of status for the Dominions in the British Commonwealth.

Banda, Dr Hastings Kamuzu (1906–97) Malawi (Nyasaland) politician. Member of Chewa tribe. Received first education at Livingstonia mission of Church of Scotland. Walked to South Africa in search of education at age of 13. Worked as a clerk on Rand Goldfields. Inspired by lecture by Dr J.E. Aggrey to go to the United States. Studied at Indiana University and University of Chicago. Qualified in medicine at Meharay Medical Centre, Nashville, Tennessee, in 1937. Studied medicine further in Universities of Glasgow and Edinburgh and became an elder of the Church of Scotland. Practised medicine in Liverpool, North Shields and London. While still in Britain formed ties with Kwame Nkrumah and Jomo Kenyatta, and founded Nyasaland African Congress in 1950. Opposed Central African Federation. Moved to Gold Coast and practised medicine in Kumasi. Returned to Nyasaland in 1958 and became president-general of Nyasaland African Congress. The Congress was banned in March 1959 and Banda arrested following allegations of a plot to murder Europeans, which were subsequently discredited. He was released from prison in April 1960 and was a principal architect of the 1960 consitution which gave the Africans a majority on the Nyasaland Legislative Council. Banda's party, now the Malawi Congress Party, gained the majority in the 1961 elections. He became the first Prime Minister of an independent Malawi in 1964 and the President when Malawi became a republic in 1966. He subsequently maintained a virtual one-party state, becoming President for life in 1971. He lost power in 1993.

Bao-Dai, Emperor (1913–97) The last emperor of Vietnam. He succeeded his father in 1925 at the age of twelve but did not ascend the throne until 1932. He cooperated with the Japanese during the Second World War but abdicated in 1945 to join the Vietminh. Quickly went into exile but was brought back by the French to rule as Head of State, 1949–55. He was then ousted by Ngo Dinh Diem. Went into exile in France.

Baring, (Charles) Evelyn, 1st Baron Howick of Glendale, (1903–73) British colonial governor. The third son of Evelyn Baring, Lord Cromer, one of the most famous of British 'pro-consuls' and virtual governor of Egypt, 1883–1907. Inspired by father's example to seek similar career. Educated at Winchester and Oxford. Entered Indian civil service, 1926. Indian career terminated in 1932 by amoebic dysentery. Worked in banking and business until Second World War. Became Governor of Southern Rhodesia, 1942. In 1944 became High Commissioner to South Africa, which involved being both, in effect, Ambassador to the Union of South Africa and governor of the three protectorates, Bechuanaland, Swaziland and Basutoland. Governor of Kenya, 1952–59. During this time he had to deal with the Mau Mau emergency. He took advantage of the emergency legislation to put through some far-reaching reforms. He had considerable sympathy with the African desire for economic change and neither in Rhodesia nor in Kenya did he support the white settlers in the way they had hoped. From 1960 to 1963 he was Chairman of the Colonial Development Corporation.

Begin, Menachem (1919–92) Prime Minister of Israel, 1977–82. Born in Poland. Inspired by Zionism and helped to organise illegal emigration. Reached Israel himself in 1942. In 1943–48 led the Irgun, the terrorist organisation responsible for the blowing up of the King David Hotel and other atrocities. In 1948 founded right-wing Herut Party. Led Likud bloc, 1977–82. Advocated further expansion of Israel and clashed with Ben Gurion but later negotiated the Camp David accords and a peace treaty with Egypt in 1978.

Bello, Ahmadu (1909–66), Sardauna of Sokoto, Nigerian political leader. He founded the Northern People's Party, which because of the large population of Northern Nigeria, compared with the South, was in a position to dominate Nigerian politics at the time of independence. Bello preferred to operate from his home base, Northern Nigeria, and his lieutenant, Abubakar Tafawa Balewa, led the party in the Federal capital, Lagos. Bello was assassinated, with members of his family, in the January 1966 coup.

Ben Barka, el-Mehdi (1920–65) Moroccan politician. Born in Rabat and active in opposing the French even when at school. A member of the Comité d'Action Marocaine and (1944) Istiqlal Party. Imprisoned for being a signatory of the Manifesto demanding the end of the Protectorate. When the Sultan was exiled, Ben Barka was sent to southern Morocco. President of independent Moroccan Consultative Assembly, 1956. Left Istiqlal and founded rival party in 1959. Fled to Paris in 1961 and was an important figure in the Afro-Asian Solidarity Conference in Conakry in 1961. Kidnapped and murdered in Paris in October 1965.

Ben Bella, Mohammed Ahmed (b. 1916–98) Algerian soldier and politician. Served in the French army, 1937–40, and fought with the Allies, 1943–45. On returning to Algeria he joined the Movement for the Triumph of Democratic Liberation in 1946. He joined the SO (Special Organisation) which was preparing for an armed struggle with France and became its chief in Oran province in 1947 and in the whole country in 1948. He was jailed in 1950 for involvement in an armed robbery in the post office at Oran but escaped in March 1952 and joined other exiles in Cairo. In March 1954 he promised support for the armed insurrection that broke out on 1 November and was accounted one of the nine 'historical chiefs' of the Front de la Libération Nationale (FLN). He travelled widely in the cause, but in October 1956 an aircraft taking him from Rabat to Tunis was forced down over Algiers and he was again arrested. He spent the years 1956–62 in prison in France, thus avoiding the internecine quarrels of the other leaders. He was freed under the Evian Agreement in 1962. With the help of Boumédienne he became President of Algeria in 1963. But he was ousted by the army in 1965 and remained under house arrest until 1979.

Ben Gurion, David (1886–1973) First Prime Minister of Israel. Born in Russian Poland. Became an ardent Zionist and went to Israel in 1906. When Turkey entered the First World War on the German side, he went to the United States. Enlisted and fought with the British army in Palestine in 1918. Helped to found Mapai (Socialist Party) in 1930. Became Chairman of Zionist Executive and Jewish Agency in 1935. Organised Haganah (Jewish Defence Force). By 1942 he wanted a separate Jewish state and theoretically accepted United Nations' partition plans. On 14 May 1948 he proclaimed the independent state of Israel in Tel Aviv. Prime Minister, 1948–53 and 1955–63. Colluded with the British and French in the Suez crisis of 1956. Retired from office in 1963.

Benn, (William) Wedgwood, Viscount Stansgate (1877–1960) British politician. Educated at Lycée Condorcet in Paris and University College,

London. Shocked by conditions in London's East End. Became Liberal MP, 1906. Joined Labour Party in 1927 and resigned seat. Elected at by-election, 1928. Secretary of State for India in Labour government, 1929–31. Authorised the Viceroy, Lord Irwin, to declare that Dominion status was the legitimate goal of Indian aspirations. Refused to join National (coalition) government in 1931.

Bevin, Ernest (1881–1951) British Labour leader and politician. Only had elementary education. Led the Dockers' Union, 1910–21. General secretary of the Transport and General Workers' Union, 1921–40. Entered Parliament, 1940. Minister of Labour and National Service, 1940–45. Foreign Secretary, 1945–51. Had to deal with the Palestine problem. Despite his left-wing background, he took a firm line against the Soviet Union in the Cold War.

Biko, Steve Bantu (1946–77) Founder of South African 'Black Consciousness' movement. The son of a clerk, he was expelled from school in 1963 for political activities but subsequently entered the University of Natal Medical School. He joined the multiracial National Union of South African Students but felt it was dominated by the whites. In 1968 he co-founded the all-black South African Students' Organisation. Its aim was 'Black Consciousness' to make blacks proud of their race and heritage. He felt it necessary to concentrate on the conversion of the young and helped to found the South African Students' movement for high school pupils and became honorary president of the Black People's Convention, an umbrella organisation for young professionals. He was subjected to a 'banning' order in February 1973 which severely curtailed his activities. He was arrested several times during 1975–77. His death in police custody in September 1977 caused an international outcry.

Blyden, Edward Wilmot (1832–1912) Writer and philosopher. Born at St Thomas in the Virgin Islands, probably of Ibo descent. His parents were both free and literate. Brought up a Presbyterian and later ordained, he went to the United States in 1850 to study theology but was turned down because of his race. In 1851 he went to Liberia, becoming in 1858 Principal of the Alexander High School in Monrovia and, 1862–71, Professor of Classics at the new Liberia College (of which he was subsequently President). He also held government posts. From 1871 until his death he lived sometimes in Liberia, sometimes in Sierra Leone and sometimes in Lagos. He stood, unsuccessfully, for the Presidency of Liberia in 1885. He acted as Liberian Ambassador to both Britain and France and was in 1896–97 government agent for native affairs in Lagos.

But his most lasting influence was as a writer, instilling pride into the black races and arguing that the negro was different from the white man but in no way inferior. He wished to build bridges between Christianity and Islam and hoped that a West African state, perhaps centred on Liberia, would arise to become a focus of Pan-Africanism. He edited the *Sierra Leone News* and the Freetown *West African Reporter* and wrote for the *Lagos Weekly Record*, but he also wrote many books and pamphlets. His most important book was *Christianity, Islam and the Negro Race* (1887).

Boganda, Barthélemy (1910–59) Politician of French Equatorial Africa. Born in Ubangi-Shari. His mother was murdered by guards in charge of rubber gathering and he was brought up by Catholic missionaries. Ordained as a priest in 1938. His early political involvement was encouraged by the Church. In November 1946 he was the first African elected to represent Ubangi-Shari in the French National Assembly. A member of the MRP (Mouvement Républicain Populaire) he made a powerful speech to the Assembly on 4 August 1947. In 1949, with others, he founded MESAN (Mouvement d'Évolution Sociale de l'Afrique Noire, Movement for the Social Evolution of Black Africa). MESAN became more militant in the face of continued coercive practices to develop cotton growing. Briefly imprisoned in 1951 but returned with big majority to National Assembly. In 1952 MESAN won control of the Ubangi-Shari Territorial Assembly. After the passage of the *loi cadre* in 1956, Boganda, now President of the Grand Council of French Equatorial Africa, wished to keep a federal structure in being and keep strong economic links with France. In August 1958 he put MESAN under the umbrella of Senghor's PRA. But in the referendum of September 1958, Congo, Gabon and Chad all voted for individual membership of the French Community. On 1 December 1958 he had to proclaim a Central African Republic which consisted only of Ubangi-Shari. During the ensuing election campaign he died in an air crash on 29 March 1959.

Bokassa, Jean-Bedel (1921–96) Politician of Central African Republic. Son of a village chief but orphaned as a child, he was educated at mission schools. Joined the French army in 1939 and fought with the Free French. He also served in the French campaign in Indo-China. In 1960 President Dacko asked him to set up the Central African army and in 1964 he became Central African Chief of Staff. In 1966 he organised a coup d'état and became President of the Central African Republic. Overthrown in 1979 and took refuge in France. Sent back to Central African Republic in 1986 to face charges of murder, cannibalism and embezzlement. Sentenced to life imprisonment but released 1993.

Boumédienne, Houari, pseudonym of Mohammed Ben Brahim Bou Kharouba (1927–78) Algerian soldier and politician. Son of a peasant family. Educated at Muslim schools and the al-Azhar University in Cairo. He joined the armed Algerian resistance to France in 1954. By 1958 he was coordinating military operations. In September 1962, in the first Ben Bella government, he became Minister of National Defence. He overthrew Ben Bella in a coup in June 1965 and set about the economic development of Algeria. Although strongly anti-imperialist, he kept Algeria non-aligned during the Cold War.

Bourguiba, Habib (b. 1903) Tunisian politician. Went to Paris to study law in 1924 and subsequently practised as a lawyer in Tunisia. He joined the moderate Destour party, which was working for constitutional reform, and founded a newspaper, *Tunisian Action.* In 1934 he founded the more radical Neo-Destour party. He was exiled to the south of the country but in 1936 he was freed by the new Popular Front government in Paris and took part in talks. Always an anti-communist, he detached the Tunisian workers from the CGT and founded an autonomous Tunisian labour union, the UGTT. He was arrested in April 1938 and imprisoned in France until March 1943, when he was freed by the Germans who tried, unsuccessfully, to recruit him to the Axis cause. When he returned to Tunisia in April 1943 he persuaded the Neo-Destours to support the Allies. He was disappointed by the French attitude after the war but tried to negotiate with them, while also seeking American and Arab support. In 1950 he appealed directly to the United Nations and prepared for military action. He was imprisoned from January 1952 to July 1954. When, in 1955, the French Prime Minister, Pierre Mendès-France, offered Tunisia internal autonomy, Bourguiba persuaded his fellow nationalists to accept. He took advantage of France's offer of independence to Morocco in 1956 to win the same concession for Tunisia. In April 1956 he became President of the Constituent Assembly. In 1959 he was elected President of Tunisia under the new constitution. Although a Muslim, he believed in a secular state. He remained strongly anti-communist and pursued a pro-western policy, even when relations with France were severely strained by the war in Algeria. He stood down in 1969 because of ill-health but continued to exercise considerable influence.

Brook, Norman C., Baron Normanbrook (1902–67) British civil servant. Held key offices during the decolonisation era as Cabinet Secretary, 1947–62, combined after 1956 with being Joint Permanent Secretary to the Treasury and Head of the Home Civil Service. Responsible for crucial cabinet committee system.

Burke, Edmund (1729–97) British politician and writer. His views influenced British colonial thinking. He believed that society was an organic growth and could not be 'made over' according to theories and philosophical blueprints. In his pursuit of the East India Company at the time of Warren Hasting's impeachment, he developed ideas of universal natural laws and the concept of 'trusteeship' as the only justification for rule over other peoples.

Burns, Sir Alan Cuthbert Maxwell (1887–1977) British colonial governor. Born in St Kitts. Educated in England but returned to work (like his father) in the civil service in the West Indies. Supervisor of customs in Nigeria, 1912. Served in First World War and acted as private secretary to Lord Lugard. Colonial Secretary of the Bahamas, 1924–29. Governor of British Honduras, 1934. Governor of the Gold Coast, 1941. In 1942 he persuaded the Colonial Office to allow him to admit Africans to his Executive Council and to appoint Africans as District Commissioners. Was closely associated with the 1946 constitution which, although it was quickly overtaken by events, was regarded as very advanced at the time. British representative on the Trusteeship Committee of the United Nations, 1947–56. He published a number of books including a *History of Nigeria* (1929) and a *History of the British West Indies* (1954).

Busia, Dr Kofi A. (1913–78) Ghanaian politician. A member of the royal house of Wenchi in north-west Ashanti. An academic, until he entered politics, believing that the well-educated must play their part. He taught at Achimota College before taking up a scholarship at the University of Oxford. He subsequently became a lecturer in African studies at the new University College of the Gold Coast. When the United Gold Coast Convention, the original nationalist party, was split by Nkrumah's formation of the Convention People's Party in 1952, Busia became the leader of what remained of the UGCC, under the name Ghana Congress Party. In 1957, when various opposition parties merged to form the United Party, he became its leader. In 1959 he went into exile. He returned in 1966 after Nkrumah had been toppled by a coup d'état and became an adviser to the ruling National Liberation Council. He became Prime Minister in 1969, when there was an attempt to return the country to civilian government, but was overthrown by the military in January 1972 and went into exile again.

Bustamente, Sir (William) Alexander (1884–1977). First Prime Minister of Jamaica. Born William Alexander Clark in Jamaica, the son of an Irish father and a Jamaican mother. He had a colourful early career, working in Cuba and Panama and going to New York under the name of Alejandro Bustamenti, a Spanish gentleman. He reputedly made a fortune on the New York Stock Exchange and returned to Jamaica in 1934 to open a money-lending office in Kingston. In 1937 he became treasurer of the Jamaica Workmen's and Tradesmen's Union and in 1939 registered the Bustamente Industrial Trade Union (BITA), of which he was life president. Suspected of subversion during the Second World War, he was interned 1940–42. During this time Norman Manley looked after BITA but, on his release, Bustamente broke with Manley and founded the Jamaica Labour Party (JLP). The JLP won the 1944 and subsequent elections and in 1953 Bustamente became Chief Minister but was defeated in 1955. Bustamente had never been a strong supporter of the West Indian Federation. He was president of the West Indies Democratic Labour Party, 1958–60, but resigned to campaign for Jamaica's withdrawal from the Federation. He succeeded in obtaining the 1961 referendum which led to Jamaica withdrawing. The JLP won the 1962 elections and Bustamente became Jamaica's first Prime Minister. He retired in 1967. A Roman Catholic, he was never a Marxist and was economically and socially a conservative, although concerned for the welfare of the poor.

Butler, Richard Austen (Rab), Baron Butler of Saffron Walden (1902–82) British conservative politician. Born in India, the son of high-ranking member of the Indian Civil Service. Educated at Marlborough and Cambridge. Entered Parliament, 1929. In 1931 became private secretary and later (1932–37) parliamentary under-secretary to Sir Samuel Hoare, Secretary of State for India. Impressed by Gandhi at the second meeting of the Round Table Conference. Defended the India Bill (Government of India Act 1935) against the attacks of Winston Churchill and others. Chancellor of the Exchequer, 1951–55. His belief in consensus politics gave rise to the word 'Butskillism' to describe policies common to Butler and Hugh Gaitskill, the Labour leader. Although applied mainly to domestic politics, this would also describe the attitude to decolonisation. Uneasy about Suez intervention of 1956 but failed to oppose it effectively. Lost premiership to Harold Macmillan when Anthony Eden resigned in January 1957. In March 1962 took charge of new Central African Department and brought about dissolution of Central African Federation in 1963. Later left politics for academic life.

Cabral, Amilcar (1926–73) Nationalist leader in Portuguese Africa. Born in Portuguese Guinea. Educated at University of Lisbon and qualified as an agricultural engineer. Worked for two years for the colonial administration in Guinea, then transferred to Angola because of his political views. Helped to found (1956) MPLA (Popular Movement for the Liberation of Angola) and PAIGC (African Independence Party of Guinea and Cape Verde). In 1959, after the violent repression of a dock strike in Bissau, prepared for armed action. Armed uprising began in January 1963. Cabral organised the government in those regions which PAIGC had cleared of the Portuguese. Assassinated in Conakry, 20 January 1973.

Chamberlain, Joseph (1836–1914) British Colonial Secretary (1895–1903). Believed in modernising and developing the empire. Left a legacy in the 1900 Colonial Stock Act, which although it only facilitated borrowing by colonial governments and did not allocate money to them, set the course which eventually led to the Colonial Development and Welfare Acts.

Chipembere, Henry (1930–75) Malawi (Nyasaland) politician. Educated at Blantyre and Goromonzi Secondary Schools and Fort Hare University College. He was elected a member of the Legislative Assembly in 1955 but opposed the Central African Federation and became secretary-general of the Malawi Congress Party. He was arrested in March 1959 for supposed complicity in the 'Massacre Plot' (to murder Europeans). He was not finally released from prison until 1963. The Prime Minister, Dr Banda, made him first Minister of Local Government and then Minister of Education. In 1964 Banda and Chipembere quarrelled because Chipembere favoured accepting a loan from communist China and subsequently accused Banda of being dictatorial. Chipembere was dismissed with other cabinet ministers and briefly led an armed stuggle against Banda. He then fled into exile.

Churchill, Winston Leonard Spencer (1874–1965) British politician and world statesman. Soldier and writer. Grandson of 7th Duke of Marlborough. Son of Lord Randolph Churchill and his American wife, Jennie Jerome. Educated at Harrow and Sandhurst. Covered, as a journalist, rebellion in Cuba in 1895. Commissioned in army in 1895 and served in India. Seconded to 21st Lancers and fought with Kitchener in Sudan in 1896, including battle of Omdurman. Published *The Story of the Malaband Field Force* (1896) and *The River War* (1899). Resigned from army to enter politics, 1899. In October 1899 went to South Africa as a journalist to cover Boer War. Captured by Boers but escaped. In 1900 entered Parliament as Unionist (i.e. Conservative). Changed to Liberal Party, 1904. Parliamentary Under-Secretary for the Colonies, 1905–8. Wished to modernise and develop the empire. President of Board of Trade, 1908; Home Secretary, 1910; First Lord of the Admiralty, 1911. In 1915, resigned to fight with army in France. Minister of Munitions in Lloyd

George's coalition government, 1917. Colonial Secretary, 1920–22. Created Middle Eastern Department. Chancellor of the Exchequer, 1924–29. In the 1930s emerged as strong opponent of proposed reforms in India. With Lord Salisbury he played important role in delaying reforming Act until 1935. Disagreements about India may have done as much to alienate him from his party as his better-known opposition to the appeasement policy in Europe. In May 1940 became Prime Minister of wartime coalition. Close working relationship with President Roosevelt. Attended all important Allied summit conferences for Britain. Lost 1945 general election, despite tremendous personal prestige as wartime leader. Divisions over India had continued in coalition cabinet and Churchill strongly opposed Attlee's plans for India in 1947. Returned to office as Prime Minister in 1951 but his health was failing and he resigned in 1955.

Cohen, Andrew Benjamin (1909–68) British colonial administrator. Educated at Malvern College and Cambridge. Entered civil service, 1932. Transferred to Colonial Office, 1933. A man of considerable independence, who quickly developed sympathy for the African point of view. Served in Malta, 1940–43. Returned to the Colonial Office to help plan for post-war Africa. In 1947 became Assistant Under-Secretary in charge of the Africa Division. Had a clear vision that the colonies must become self-governing nations 'within the next generation'. Found a sympathetic chief in Arthur Creech-Jones but many administrators did not agree with him. In West Africa he felt that the pace was forced by the Gold Coast and he was not happy at the result. Advocated Central African Federation. Governor of Uganda, 1952–57, and responsible for deporting the Kabaka, Mutesa II in 1953. After 1957 considered entering politics as an MP and in 1959 published a book, *British Policy in Changing Africa*. In 1957–60 served on Trusteeship Council of the United Nations. In 1961 returned to Whitehall to set up Department of Technical Cooperation, which in 1964 became the Ministry of Overseas Development, with Cohen as Permanent Secretary.

Coty, René (1882–1962) French President. Lawyer. A conservative who entered national politics in 1923. Took no part in politics during the Second World War but was elected to the Constituent Assembly in 1945. Had held ministerial office but was an unexpected choice for President in December 1953. Fourth Republic descended into chaos. When in May 1958 revolution broke out in Algeria, Coty, fearing a military coup, turned to General de Gaulle and in January 1959 retired from the Presidency to make way for him.

Coulibaly, (Daniel) Ouezzin (1909–58) Upper Volta politician and founder of first trade union in French-speaking West Africa. Educated at William Ponty School in Dakar, became a teacher and in 1937, with Mamadou Konato of the French Soudan, formed a teachers' union. A chance meeting with Houphouët-Boigny helped his election to the French Constituent Assembly in 1945 and he was elected to the National Assembly in 1946. He became political secretary of the RDA after its foundation in October 1946 and was associated with the PDCI (Parti Démocratique de la Côte d'Ivoire). In 1947 Upper Volta was separated administratively from the Ivory Coast. In September 1950 the RDA disaffiliated from the French Communist Party and in 1951 Coulibaly lost his seat in the National Assembly. Following the *loi cadre* of 1956, Coulibaly became, in March 1957, the Head of Upper Volta's first African government. He died just before the 1958 referendum on the French Community.

Creech-Jones, Arthur (1891–1964) British Labour politician. Always interested in colonial issues. In 1926 advised Clements Kadalie, General Secretary of the South African Industrial and Commercial Workers' Union, on trade union organisation. In 1929 published *Trade Unionism To-day*, which became a handbook in the colonies. In 1935, as an MP, became a member of the Labour Party's advisory committee on imperial questions and its chairman in 1943. In 1937 he also became a member of the Trade Union Congress's colonial affairs committee. By this time he was an acknowledged expert in framing the party's colonial policy. In August 1945 he became Under-Secretary at the Colonial Office and, 1946–50, Colonial Secretary. He founded the Colonial Development Corporation; represented Britain at the United Nations on the debates on the surrender of the mandate over Palestine; piloted through the independence of Ceylon; attended the Montego Bay Conference on West Indian Federation; and attended the first African Conference at Lancaster House in 1948.

Cripps, Sir (Richard) Stafford, (1889–1952) Lawyer and British politician. Educated at Winchester and Oxford. Called to the Bar in 1913. Became a Labour MP in 1931. He was an intellectual Marxist and always on the left wing of the party. During a world tour in 1939–40, he visited India for the first time. In 1940 Churchill appointed him British Ambassador to Russia. On his return Churchill made him a member of the War Cabinet and sent him on his famous mission to India, where he was authorised to offer the Indians a constituent assembly and self-determination (subject to some safeguards for minorities) at the end of the war. In the end he could not convince Gandhi and the Congress Party but the 'Cripps proposals' remained on the table until the end of the war. He was the most dynamic member of the 'Cabinet Mission' to India, led by Lord Pethick-Lawrence, in 1946, which came near to success.

Curzon, George Nathaniel (1859–1925) Viceroy of India. Educated at Eton and Oxford. Travelled extensively in Asia in 1887–94. Under-Secretary at the India Office, 1891–92. Viceroy of India, 1898–1905. His critics called him 'the last of the Mughal Emperors'. Curzon wished to do his best for India and many of his reforms were good, including setting up the Agricultural and Archaeological Departments, but he was fatally authoritarian in his approach. He particularly offended Indian opinion by his Universities Act of 1904 and the partition of Bengal. Part of the Indian National Congress, led by Tilak, was driven to extreme measures to oppose the partition and it did much to radicalise Indian opinion. Curzon resigned in 1905, not because he had offended the Indians but because he had quarrelled with his powerful Commander-in-Chief, Lord Kitchener. He subsequently served in Lloyd George's War Cabinet and was British Foreign Secretary, 1919–24.

Dacko, David (b. 1930) First President of Central African Republic. A teacher by profession. In 1957 became a member of the Territorial Assembly of Ubangi-Shari. When his uncle, Barthélemy Boganda, was killed in April 1959, the Assembly named Dacko as Head of Government. Despite splits in the governing MESAN party, Dacko was re-elected President in 1964. But in January 1966 he was overthrown by a military coup, which led to Bokassa becoming President.

Danquah, Joseph B. (1895–1965) Ghanaian (Gold Coast) politician. The son of a prominent family, in 1915 he became secretary to his elder brother, the paramount chief. He studied in London, 1921–27, where he wrote a doctoral thesis on 'The Moral End as Moral Excellence' and also qualified as a lawyer. He published several books, including *Gold Coast: Akan Laws and Customs* (1928) and *The Akan Doctrine of God* (1944). In 1947 he formed the United Gold Coast Convention to work for constitutional advance but, after 1949, was side-lined by the much more radical Kwame Nkrumah. As Nkrumah became more dictatorial after independence, Danquah was imprisoned in 1961–62 and again in 1964. He died in prison in 1965. It was Danquah who proposed the name Ghana to reconnect the newly independent state with its history.

de Gaulle, General Charles (1890–1970) French soldier and statesman. Rallied the 'Free French' after the fall of France in 1940. In 1943 became Head of Committee of National Liberation, which he claimed to be the French government in exile. Attempted, often successfully, to persuade French colonies to declare for the Free French, rather than Vichy, government. Took part in the unsuccessful attempt to reclaim Dakar in 1940. Attended Brazzaville Conference (1944). Became Head of French provisional government in 1945 but resigned in 1946. Retired to his country home at Colombey-les-deux-Eglises to await recall to power. It came as a result of the Algerian crisis in 1958. President Coty invited him to form a temporary government. The Fourth Republic came to an end and de Gaulle won an overwhelming victory in the referendum to ratify a new constitution. He was elected first President of the new Fifth Republic in 1959. He won another resounding victory in most of the colonies in another referendum in 1958 to transform the French Union into the French Community, which would give the French colonies independence, while maintaining economic and other ties with France. He then addressed the most difficult problem of all, Algeria. The Evian settlement was reached with the Algerian nationalists in 1961–62 and ratified by referenda in France and Algeria. Algeria became independent in July 1963. He survived the near-revolution in France in May 1968 but resigned the following year. The Gaulist party remained, however, one of the strongest forces in French politics.

Delamere, 3rd Baron (Hugh Cholmondeley) (1870–1931) Pioneer settler in Kenya. He first visited the area as a big game hunter in 1897 and returned as a settler and farmer in 1903. Soon established himself as the settlers' leader, becoming president of the Farmers' and Planters' Association in 1903 (Colonists' Association, 1904). He was nominated to the first Legislative Council in 1907 and elected for the Rift Valley in 1920. He led the deputation to the Colonial Office in 1923 to argue against proposals for allowing unrestricted Indian immigration and the extension of the franchise to Indians on a common roll with Europeans. He hoped to see an East African dominion, incorporating Tanganyika and Northern Rhodesia, as well as Kenya, and led another deputation to the Colonial Office in 1930 to advocate this.

Desai, Morarji (1896–1995) Indian politician. Born in Gujerat, the son of a teacher. In 1918 he joined the Bombay civil service but in 1930 resigned to join Gandhi's civil disobedience movement. Several times imprisoned, but in 1937 held ministerial office in Bombay. In post-independence India, in the 1960s, he opposed Indira Gandhi and himself became Prime Minister, 1977–79.

d'Estaing, Valéry Giscard (b. 1926) French President. Member of National Assembly 1956–74 and leader of Independent Republicans. Held various ministerial offices. Elected President of France in 1974 but defeated by François Mitterand in 1981. Relations with the ex-colonies played an important role in his Presidency and he was partly brought down by allegations that he had accepted extravagant gifts from J-B Bokassa, the President of the Central African Republic.

Devlin, Patrick Arthur (Mr Justice, later Lord Devlin) (1905–1992) British lawyer, well-known for trenchant views. Called to the Bar, 1929. Became a judge, 1948. Lord Justice of Appeal, 1960. Headed a number of enquiries including the Nyasaland Inquiry Commission of 1959.

Devonshire, 9th Duke of (Victor Christian William Cavendish) (1868– 1938) British politician. Sat in the Commons, 1891–1908, until he succeeded to the title. Governor-General of Canada, 1916. Colonial Secretary, 1922–24. The period was notable for the British Empire Exhibition at Wembley in 1924, which was a public relations triumph, but more important was the issue of the White Paper, which bore his name, confirming that Kenya was primarily an African country.

Diagne, Blaise (1872–1934) Senegalese politician. Born on the island of Gorée, of a well-to-do African family, who had French citizenship by reason of the 1848 grant. In 1914 he was the first African elected to the National Assembly in Paris, defeating six European candidates. Re-elected 1920 and 1924. In 1916 he secured the passage of the Act which reaffirmed the right of some Africans to French citizenship. In 1917 he was put in charge of recruitment in French West Africa and raised 180,000 men for France. In 1919 he was President of the Pan-African Congress, which met in Paris, working with Dubois and Garvey. In 1931–32 he was Under-Secretary of State for the Colonies. Although he maintained the rights of Africans, he was very throughly assimilated and clearly belonged to an elite. In his later years he was not much in sympathy with men of the new generation, such as Leopold Senghor.

Diallo, El-Hadj Saifoulaye (1916–81) Guinean politician. Descended from a Foulah chieftain family, he became a clerk in the French colonial administration. In 1956 he represented Guinea in the French National Assembly. On the left wing of the RDA, he played an important part in persuading Guinea to vote to stay out of the French Community in the 1958 referendum.

Diori, Hamani (1916–89) Niger politician. Taught after training at William Ponty Teachers' Training College in Dakar. In 1938 invited to go to Paris to teach African languages to French civil servants at the French Institute of Overseas Studies. In 1946 joined Félix Houphouët-Boigny of the Ivory Coast, Ouezzin Coulibaly of Upper Volta and others to form the Rassemblement Démocratique Africain (African Democratic Rally) to fight for independence throughout French West Africa. At the same time he founded, with Boubou Hama, the Parti Progressiste Nigérien (Niger Progress Party), the Niger section of the RDA. He was elected deputy for the Niger in the French National Assemby in November 1946 but lost the seat in the 1951 elections, regaining it in 1956. In 1958 he became Deputy Speaker. He strongly supported a 'Yes' vote in the referendum of September 1958 to support General de Gaulle's plan to replace the French Union with the French Community, with the former colonies still associated with France. He became Chairman of the Government Council of Niger in December 1958, and subsequently Prime Minister and then President of the new Republic of Niger in November 1960. He was overthrown by an army coup in 1974.

Dubois, William Edward Burghardt (1868–1963) Black American academic and Pan-Africanist. Born in Massachusetts, he was educated at Fisk University in Nashville, Tennessee, Harvard, and the University of Berlin. He was awarded his doctorate by Harvard in 1895 and his thesis, *The Suppression of the African Slave Trade to the United States of America, 1638–1870*, which made his name, was published as the first volume in the Harvard Historical Series. He subsequently taught at Wilberforce University, Ohio, the University of Pennsylvania and Atlanta University. He was determined to instil pride in the black race and, in 1905, founded the Niagara Movement, a protest group of black academics and professionals. In 1909 he was one of the founders of the National Association for the Advancement of Coloured People (NAACP) and was, 1910–34, its director of publicity and research. He then resigned because of policy disagreements but returned as director of research, 1944–48, and was very active in lobbying the United Nations. In 1900 he attended the first Pan-African Conference in London and himself organised those of 1919, 1921, 1923 and 1927. That of 1919, in which he cooperated with Blaise Diagne, was particularly important, meeting in Paris at the time of the Peace Conference and trying to influence the fate of the European colonies in Africa. Dubois hoped that the Conferences would bring together men from the British and French colonies but they continued to be mainly Anglophone and the early ones tended to be dominated by the Americans. He chaired the very important 5th/6th Conference in Manchester in 1945 (the discrepancy in numbering arises from doubts as to whether to count the 1900 conference in the sequence), although the initiative had now passed to younger men like Nkrumah and Kenyatta. Du Bois was a socialist, influenced by Marxist thinking. He wrote prolifically, mainly on black America.

Dulles, John Foster (1888–1959) American Secretary of State (1953–59). In January 1954 laid down doctrine of 'massive retaliation', that is the United States would meet any communist aggression 'vigorously at places and means of our own choosing'. This suggested the posibility of nuclear retaliation in local crises. Strongly opposed any recognition of Communist China. Disliked Nasser's nationalisation of the Suez Canal in 1956 but vigorously opposed Anglo-French resort to direct action.

Duncan-Sandys, Duncan E. (1908–87) British politician. Educated at Eton and Oxford. In Diplomatic Service, 1930–35. Entered Parliament as a Conservative in 1935 and married a daughter of Winston Churchill, to whom he was at first politically close. Lost his parliamentary seat in 1945, but returned in 1950 and held ministerial office under both Churchill and Eden. In 1960 became Secretary of State for Commonwealth Relations and, in 1962, Colonial Secretary. Negotiated independence for Cyprus, Malaysia, Nigeria and Uganda. Dismissed by Prime Minister, Edward Heath, for domestic reasons in 1962 and went to Lords 1974.

Eboué, Felix (1884–1944) Governor of Chad at the time of the defeat of France in 1940. A Negro, born in Cayenne, French Guiana (Guyane), and a French citizen from birth. Educated at the Lycée Montaigne in Bordeaux. Having opted for the civil service as a career, he graduated from the Colonial School in Paris in 1908 and accepted a posting to the French Congo. He served in Ubanghi-Shari, 1909–21 and 1923–31. Helped by the patronage of Blaise Diagne, he was named Secretary-General of Martinique in 1932, but after Diagne's death he was transferred in 1934 to Soudan. The Popular Front government in 1936 sent him back to the Caribbean as Governor of Guadeloupe. He was recalled in 1938 after the fall of the Popular Front government. The following year he was sent as Lieutenant-Governor to Chad. In August 1940 he declared for de Gaulle. De Gaulle appointed him Governor-General of French Equatorial Africa, which became an important base for the Free French. He died on a visit to Cairo in 1944.

Eden, Sir Anthony, 1st Earl of Avon (1897–1977) British politician. Sat in the House of Commons as a Conservative, 1925–57. He was Foreign Secretary, 1935–38, when he resigned and won great respect for his opposition to the policy of 'appeasement' of the dictators, Hitler and Mussolini. He again became Foreign Secretary in Winston Churchill's wartime coalition, 1940–45. He was again Foreign Secretary in 1951–55, when he succeeded Churchill as Prime Minister. Eden's own health began to fail and, partly misled by his belief that President Nasser of Egypt represented the same kind of threat to world peace as Hitler and Mussolini had done, he led Britain into the disastrous Suez intervention of 1956, which did much to reveal Britain's decline to the world and helped to hasten the decolonisation process. He was succeeded by Harold Macmillan.

Eisenhower, Dwight David (1890–1969) American soldier and President. Commander of the Allied Forces in North Africa, 1942–44. Supreme Commander of Allied Forces in Western Europe, 1944–45. Chief of Staff of the United States Army, 1945–48. Supreme Commander of NATO forces in Europe, 1950–52. President of the United States, 1953–61.

Ekra, Mathieu (b. 1917) Ivory Coast civil servant and politician. He was trained as an administrator and held various posts concerned with railway and transport in French West Africa. In 1946, when employed in the road transport administration in Guinea, he set up a branch of the Rassemblement Démocratique Africain (RDA, African Democratic Rally). In 1948 he joined the managing committee of the Ivory Coast Democratic Party. He gained a reputation as a militant and was placed in preventive detention by the French for three years, 1949–52. He became a member of the Ivory Coast Assembly in 1959 and after independence he became Minister for Public Affairs and Information in 1961.

Elliott, Sir Charles Norton Edgecumbe (1862–1931) British diplomat. Educated at Cheltenham and Oxford. A formidable linguist. He entered the diplomatic service in 1887. In 1901–4 he was Consul-General at Zanzibar and High Commissioner for the East African Protectorate, where he supported the idea of European settlement and, in 1905, published *The East Africa Protectorate.*

Enahoro, Chief Anthony (b. 1923) Born at Uromi in mid-western Nigeria, he was the descendant of a line of chiefs who had resisted the British. His father, Chief Okotako Enahoro, was a customary court judge, who wanted his son to study law but instead he went to work on the chain of newspapers owned by Nnamdi Azikiwe. In 1944 he became the editor of the *Southern Nigeria Defender.* He edited the *Daily Comet,* 1945–47, and was jailed for sedition. He then became assistant editor of the *West African Pilot* and editor of the *Nigerian Star.* In 1951 he convened a meeting of leaders in the Benin and Warri Provinces to form the Mid-Western Action Group, which merged with Awololwo's Action Group. Between 1951 and 1954 he was a member of both the Western House of Assembly and the Federal House of Representatives. In 1953 he moved in the latter the 'independence motion' asking that 'this House accepts as a primary political objective the attainment of self-government for Nigeria in 1956'. In 1954 he retired from the Federal House to become Minister of Home Affairs in the Western Region government. He attended the All-African Peoples' Conference in Accra in 1958 and Tunis in 1960. In 1959 he returned to the Federal Parliament, in which the Action Group formed the opposition, as the shadow Minister for Foreign Affairs. He was arrested in 1962 and charged with treasonable felony. In September he fled to England. The British courts agreed to extradite him under old legislation which assumed that the law was basically the same throughout the British empire, although the case became a *cause célèbre*, which almost brought down the British government. Although defended by eminent lawyers, he was sentenced to fifteen years' imprisonment. After political changes in Nigeria, he was pardoned in August 1966 and played some further part in Nigerian politics.

Endeley, Dr Emmanuel (b. 1916) Cameroun politician. Born in the British-administered trust territory of Cameroun. Qualified as a doctor in 1942. Became a trade union leader in 1947 when he was asked to organise the workers of the Cameroons Development Corporation. In 1951 he was elected to the Nigerian Eastern Region Assembly. He hoped to keep Southern (British) Cameroun as a separate region of Nigeria and became its first Prime Minister in 1958, but he lost the 1959 election and in 1961 the people of Southern Cameroun voted overwhelmingly to join the Cameroun Republic.

Farouk, King (1920–65) King of Egypt, 1936–52. Made some genuine attempts at economic reform early in his reign but gained an increasing reputation as a playboy. He was compelled to appoint increasingly anti-British governments, 1944–52, but was blamed for Egypt's humiliating military failure against the new state of Israel in 1948 and was eventually forced into exile in 1952.

Feisal I (ibn Hussein) (1885–1933) Third son of Hussein, Sherif of Mecca. Educated in Constantinople. Attracted by the idea of Arab independence and became leader of the Arab revolt against Turkish authority in 1918. Entered Damascus as commander of the Arab army in October 1918 and assumed control of Syria. Represented Arabs at the Paris Peace Conference in 1919. Arab National Congress meeting in Damascus in March 1920 proclaimed him King of Syria but he was driven out by the

French. Winston Churchill proposed that he became King of Iraq (Mesopotamia), and this was confirmed by plebiscite. Responsible for Iraqi
constitution of 1925 and 1930 treaty with Britain by which Iraq became
virtually independent.

Feisal II (ibn Ghazi) (1935–58) Became King of Iraq at the age of three on
his father's death. Educated at Harrow. When he assumed power in 1953
he pursued a pro-British and anti-Nasser line. Assassinated 14 July 1958.

Gaitskill, Hugh Todd Naylor (1906–63) British politician. Leader of the
Labour Party, 1955–63. Powerful opponent of the Suez intervention in
1956.

Gandhi, Mohandas Karamchand (Mahatma – 'Great Soul') (1869–1948)
Indian politician and world figure. Born in Porbandar, a Princely State
in North West India, a member of the Vaisya, or merchant, caste. His
family had traditionally supplied high officials to the rulers of Porbandar.
His father (who died when he was thirteen) was chief minister to
Porbandar and then to Rajkot. His mother was a deeply religious woman,
influenced by the Jains. Gandhi probably took some of his ideas of non-
violence from the Jain tradition of *ahimsa*, avoiding injury to any living
being. He went to England to study law in 1888 and was called to the Bar
in 1891. He returned briefly to India but, finding little chance of employment, he went to South Africa in 1893. He remained there until 1914,
working to end the discrimination against Indian immigrants. He began
to develop the ideas and political techniques which he later perfected
in India. Like many Indians who had received a western education, he
still felt loyalty to the British empire and, finding himself in London at
the beginning of the First World War, he raised an ambulance corps
from Indian students, as he had done during the Boer War. He finally
returned to India in 1915. The Rowlatt Acts of 1919 antagonised him
and he organised a *hartal*, or general strike, against them. During the
1920s and 1930s he organised many campaigns to influence British policy.
It has been said, with truth, that he combined the westernised tactics of
Gokhale with the appeal to tradition of Tilak. But he was never an ordinary politician. His extraordinary influence, not only in India, but throughout the world, depended on the originality of his thinking, which was
as much religious as political. He believed that means shaped ends. He
developed the idea of *satyagraha* ('truth force') which he insisted was
much more than the passive resistance it appeared to be to the world.
His advocacy of *khadi* was not the mere boycotting of western goods but
a return to a simpler economy in which all Indians had a place. His use
of fasting, even, if necessary, to death, which looked like blackmail to

many westerners, had its origins in Hindu tradition. He was not afraid to depart from Hindu traditions when necessary, as in his attitude to the Untouchables, whom he renamed the 'Harijans', children of God. He was revered as a saint by the people, who could recognise in him the traditional Indian holy man and, for the first time, the Indian National Congress changed from being an elite organisation to a mass movement. He could not always control the movements he started. Violence sometimes resulted and Gandhi himself was imprisoned in 1922. But he knew it was essential to convince the British. He found it possible to cooperate with Lord Halifax, when he was Viceroy, and attended the second Round Table meeting in London in 1931. His position became more intransigent during the Second World War and, with other Congress leaders, he was imprisoned after the 'Quit India' resolution in 1942. He was released on health grounds in May 1944. He did his utmost to prevent the partition of India, even suggesting at one point that the Muslim leader, M.A. Jinnah, should become Prime Minister of all India. He was appalled by the violence of the last days of the Raj, going to Bengal to try to calm the rioting after 'Direct Action' Day and fasting to try to end the violence after independence. He was shot by a Hindu fanatic on his way to pray on 30 January 1948.

Garvey, Marcus Mosiah (1887–1940) West Indian writer and early exponent of 'Black Power'. Born in Jamaica, he became a printer and founded the first Jamaican trade union, the Printers' Union. Between 1910 and 1914 he visited central America and England. In England he met African nationalists. On his return to Jamaica in 1914 he founded the Universal Negro Improvement Association (UNIA). In 1916 he went to New York and branches of UNIA sprang up not only in New York but all over the American continent and the Caribbean. At its peak in the 1920s UNIA had 8 million members. It published its own journals, *Negro World* and later *Black Man. Negro World* circulated in Africa even though it was discouraged by the colonial authorities. Garvey, like Blyden, preached pride in the Negro race but he was much more militant in his views, believing the Negro must struggle to be free. At one time he hoped to induce black Americans to return to Africa, primarily to Liberia. He also taught that blacks must become economically self-sufficient. In 1925 he became involved in a shipping venture which failed and he was gaoled for fraud. He subsequently went to England where he died in 1940. He was an important influence on Kwame Nkrumah.

Giap, Vo Nguyen (b. 1912) Vietnamese general. Born into a peasant family, he profited from the education system the French had installed in Indo-China, studying at the Lycée Albert Sarraut and Hanoi University. Although studying law, he was fascinated by military history, particularly the campaigns of Napoleon. He was also already in contact with Vietnamese nationalists. He was first arrested at the age of fourteen. He was permanently embittered by the death of his wife and child in a French gaol in 1941 and the execution of his sister the same year. Ho Chi Minh entrusted him with the formation of the Vietminh organisation. Giap proved to be a brilliant organiser, and later a brilliant general, who was entirely ruthless in his pursuit of Vietnamese independence. He was largely responsible for the French defeat at Dien Bien Phu in 1954 and was the most effective general against the Americans in the Vietnam War, which led to their final evacuation in 1975.

Glubb, Sir John Bagot (Glubb Pasha) (1897–1986) British soldier and Arabist. Educated at the Royal Military Academy, Woolwich. Served in France throughout the First World War. Posted to Mesopotamia (Iraq) in 1920. In 1926 transferred from the army to the British administration in Iraq. Persuaded Bedouin to join armed police and suppress border raiding. In 1930 transferred to Transjordan, where he formed the Desert Patrol, which had similar success. In 1939 came to command Arab Legion. Led them into Syria and Iraq in 1941. In 1948 led Arab Legion to occupy West Bank of the Jordan in accordance with United Nations' partition plans but found he had to fight for it. Lost much of his influence when King Abdullah was assassinated in July 1951. Dismissed by King Hussein on 1 March 1956. Author of a number of books, including *War in the Desert* (1960), recounting his service in Iraq.

Gokhale, Gopal Krishna (1866–1915) Born in Bombay into the Brahmin caste. Educated at Elphinstone College in Bombay, his first career was as a teacher, as a professor at Fergusson College in Poona. But he deserted teaching for politics. Sometimes compared to the British politician, William Gladstone, he was deeply influenced by western liberalism; a moderate, he wished for a steady evolution to self-government. In 1882 he became secretary of the Sarvajanik Sabha and, in 1895, secretary of the Indian National Congress. From 1898 to 1906 he was a member of the Poona municipality and in 1899 was elected to the Bombay Legislative Council. In 1902 he was elected to the Viceroy's Legislative Council and in 1905 became President of the Indian National Congress. The same year he founded the Servants of India Society, members of which took vows of poverty and undertook service to the poorest, including the Untouchables. During these years he visited England and influenced John Morley, the veteran radical who, as Secretary of State for India, introduced the 1909 reforms. In 1912 he visited South Africa and met Gandhi. He died prematurely in 1915.

Gordon-Walker, Patrick (1907–80) British politician. The son of a Scotsman who, as a member of the Indian civil service, was a judge in the Supreme Court of Lahore. Spent his early years in the Punjab. Educated at Wellington College and Oxford. He shared his father's Fabian views. He spent some time in Germany in the 1930s and emerged with a hatred of both Nazism and communism. Worked for the BBC during the war. Entered Parliament as Labour MP for Smethwick at a by-election in 1945. In 1947 became Under-Secretary at the Commonwealth Relations Office. Visited India and played important part in negotiations which allowed India a place in the Commonwealth, after it became a republic. In 1950 became Secretary of State for Commonwealth Relations. Came to be identified with the controversial setting up of the Central African Federation and the equally controversial decision not to recognise Sir Seretse Khama's position in Bechuanaland. When out of office after 1951, travelled widely in the Commonwealth. Was expected to return to high office but lost the Smethwick seat in 1964 because of his opposition to the Conservative Act, limiting Commonwealth immigration. Went to the Lords in 1974.

Gowon, General Yakubu (b. 1934) Soldier and politician. Born in Northern Nigeria, the son of a Christian pastor. After leaving school he joined the Nigerian army in 1954 and trained partly on the Gold Coast and partly in England at Sandhurst and other places. He returned to Nigeria in 1957 and served with the United Nations peace-keeping force in the Congo. In 1963 he was appointed Adjutant-General of the Nigerian army. Following the military coup of January 1966 he was appointed Chief of Staff. In August 1966 he became Head of the Federal Military government and Supreme Commander of the Armed Forces. After the massacre of the Ibos in the Northern Region, he proclaimed (28 May 1967) a state of emergency. Two days later the Eastern Region seceded as the Republic of Biafra and the Nigerian civil war began. He was overthrown by another coup on 29 July 1975.

Griffiths, James (1890–1975) British politician. Born in Carmarthenshire, Wales. Became a miner. In 1908 bcame a member of Independent Labour Party. Active in, and eventually president of, the South Wales Miners' Federation. In 1936 became Labour MP for Llanelli. Minister for Social Insurance, 1945. Colonial Secretary, 1950–51. Travelled widely in the Commonwealth. Strongly supported suppression of communist insurrection in Malaya. Actively involved in new constitutions in Singapore and Nigeria. Originally supported the idea of a Central African Federation but changed his mind after African opposition at Victoria Falls Conference. Government fell in the middle of the negotiations. First Secretary of State for Wales, 1964–66.

Grivas, Colonel George (1898–1974) Greek army officer. Served in the Second World War. In 1953 he founded EOKA which aimed to force the British out of Cyprus to pave the way for *enosis*, the union of Cyprus with Greece, which was opposed by the 20 per cent of Cypriots who were of Turkish descent. EOKA waged a terrorist campaign from 1955 to 1959. Cyprus became independent in 1960. Grivas returned as Commander of the Greek Cypriot National Guard. He was recalled to Greece in 1967 but returned to Cyprus to start a new campaign for *enosis*, which played an important part in the Turkish invasion of 1975 and the partition of Cyprus into Greek and Turkish regions.

Grunitzky, Nicholas (1913–69) Togo politician. The son of a Polish father and Togolese mother, he was born in Atakpame in western Togo when Togoland was still ruled by Germany. He was brought up in the French mandated territory and went to France to gain his degree in engineering. Returned to Togo in 1937. A successful businessman, when Togo was controlled by the Vichy government during the Second World War, Grunitzky joined the resistance. He was elected to the French Chamber of Deputies as the Togolese representative in 1951 and 1956. He also formed the Togolese Progress Party which won the election after France gave Togo a new status as the Autonomous Republic of Togo in August 1955. Grunitzky became Prime Minister, but in 1958 his party was defeated by the more radical Togolese Unity Committee. He went into exile in Dahomey in 1962 but returned to lead a coalition government after an army coup in 1963. He improved relations with France but was overthrown by a new coup in 1967. Died in Paris.

Gueye, Amadou Lamine (1891–1968) Senegalese politician. A lawyer and academic, he was an advocate at the Court of Appeal in Dakar and became Mayor of St Louis (Senegal's former capital) in 1925. Mayor of Dakar, 1945–61. He failed to gain election to the French National Assembly in 1934 and 1936, but sat in the Constituent Assembly in 1945 and secured the passage of the important law, bearing his name, which abolished the distinction between citizens and subjects. He was an influential figure in the French Socialist Party and became the secretary-general of the Senegal-Mauritania branch of the Section Française de l'Internationale

Ouvrière (SFIO – French section of the Workers' International) in 1945. The SFIO persuaded Gueye (and Senghor) to stay away from the Bamako meeting (1946) which founded the RDA (Rassemblement Démocratique Africain) because they feared it would be dominated by the Communists. This created a split for twelve years in the nationalist forces in French West Africa. In the 1950s Gueye held junior ministerial office in France, and in 1956 was a French delegate to the United Nations. In 1950 he secured the passage of another important law ending the discrimination between Europeans and Africans in the French overseas service. After the passage of the *loi cadre* in 1956, Gueye played an important but tortuous role in the difficult question of whether French West Africa should remain a federation. In January 1957 he founded the MSA (Mouvement Socialiste Africain), with Bakari of Niger and Sissoko of the French Soudan. In 1958 this merged with the Convention Africaine to form the PRA (Parti du Regroupement Africain). Later that year this merged with Senghor's Bloc Populaire Sénégalais to form the UPS (Union Progressiste Sénégalaise). Senghor had favoured a federal solution but the PRA decided to allow a free vote in de Gaulle's September referendum. In January 1959 Senegal and the French Soudan joined to form the Mali Federation. In March the UPS won all the seats in Senegal and Gueye was elected President of the Senegal National Assembly, a post he held until his death in 1968. When the Mali Federation became independent in June 1960, Keita, the President of Mali, backed Gueye as President of the Federation in place of Senghor, as had been previously agreed. This contributed to the speedy break-up of the Federation in August 1960.

Hached, Ferhat (1914–52) Tunisian nationalist and trade unionist. In the 1930s was employed by the Tunisian Automobile Transport Company of the Sahel. In 1939 tried to found a trade union organisation independent of the communist CGT (Confédération Générale du Travail). In 1946 founded UGTT (Union Générale des Travailleurs Tunisiens), which worked with the Destours and Neo-Destours parties. Assassinated by a French settler terrorist organisation on 5 December 1952.

Haile Selassi, Emperor (1892–1975) Emperor of Ethiopia (Abyssinia), 1930–74 (in exile in England during Italian occupation, 1936–41). He played a leading role in setting up the Organization for African Unity (OAU), which first met in the Ethiopian capital, Addis Ababa, in 1963. He was deposed and forced into exile by a military coup in 1974.

Hailey, (William) Malcolm (Baron) (1872–1969) Public servant. Educated at Merchant Taylors' School and Oxford. Joined the Indian civil service in 1894. Served in the Punjab, where he was responsible for re-settling peasant families on newly irrigated lands, and then in Delhi. Employed in preparing Goverment of India Act of 1919 (Montagu–Chelmsford reforms). In 1922–24 had the difficult job of steering through legislation as leader of the government bloc in the Legislative Assembly created by the 1919 reforms (with 40 nominated and 103 elected mem-bers). In 1924 became Governor of the Punjab and, in 1928, of United Provinces. In both areas he hoped for smooth constitutional progress, despite communal problems. He attended the Round Table Confer-ences in London and took part in the discussions leading to the Govern-ment of India Act of 1935. He retired from the ICS in 1934. He then became director, on behalf of Chatham House, of a comprehensive survey of Africa. He travelled 22,000 miles round Africa and the monumental *An African Survey* was finally published in 1938. This was enormously influential in the early days of decolonisation. A contemporary, Philip Mason[1], records that Hailey, although discreet in print, was open in conversation that the Africans must soon take over political power. On the outbreak of war in 1939 he was asked to visit the African colonies and make recommendations on how they could be involved in the war. His recommendations for progress were more readily followed in the west than the east of the continent. He was then sent to the Belgian Congo to rally it to the support of the Free French. After the war he continued to travel and write on Africa, publishing a new *African Survey* in 1957, as well as specialist volumes on administration in the African colonies and the High Commission Territories, the last published when he was 93. Mason says of him, 'Few men contributed so much to the transition from bureaucratic rule to democracy in India; few so much to the peaceful transfer of power in Africa'.

Hama, Boubou (1906–82) Scholar and Niger politician. Trained as a teacher at the William Ponty School in Dakar, he became a headmaster. He was a prolific writer interested in the history of the African races and the contemporary debate on whether humanity originated on the African continent. His books included *Religion and Politics, Their Role in the Evolu-tion of the African Black Races* (1955) and *Study of the Foundations and Genesis of African Unity* (1966). He was a founder member of the Niger Progress Party and the right-hand man of Hamani Diori. He was the President of the Niger National Assembly from independence in 1960 until 1974 when the government was overthrown by an army coup. Hama was im-prisoned but released in 1977.

---

[1] *Dictionary of National Biography 1961–1970,* 472.

Hammarskjold, Dag (1905–61) Swedish diplomat and Secretary-General of the United Nations, 1953–61. He played an important role as mediator in the Suez crisis of 1956, which led to the setting up of the first United Nations emergency force, who went beyond being mere observers. In 1960 he visited 24 generally newly independent African nations and was impressed by their need for United Nations help. In July 1960 the Security Council entrusted him with the task of restoring order in the Congo. He set up a military force with contingents from various member states but excluding the major military powers. In September 1961 he was killed in an air crash in Northern Rhodesia, while flying to meet Moise Tshombe, the leader of the Katanga secessionist movement.

Hancock, (William) Keith (1898–1988) Australian academic. Educated at the Universities of Melbourne and Oxford. Became Fellow of All Souls, Oxford. Wrote extensively on the Commonwealth, notably the three-volume *Survey of British Commonwealth Affairs* (1937–42) Director of London University Institute of Commonwealth Studies, 1949–56. Employed on negotiations in Uganda in 1954.

Hassan II, King (b. 1929) Became King of Morocco in 1961. He was exiled with his father by the French but returned in 1955 to become Commander of the armed forces. He became Prime Minister in 1960 and succeeded his father the following year. A strong ruler, he supplied an element of stability in a turbulent country.

Hayford, J. Casely (1866–1963) Gold Coast lawyer and journalist. He was born at Cape Coast and educated at Fourah Bay College in Sierra Leone and (1893–94) Cambridge. Called to the Bar in 1896. As a lawyer, he successfully argued against measures which would have made it easier for the colonial authorities to alienate African land. As a journalist he edited or contributed to a number of newspapers including the *Gold Coast Echo*, the *Gold Coast Chronicle* and the *Gold Coast Leader*. Head of Wesleyan Boys' High School in Accra, 1891–93. He was a passionate advocate of education and argued, for example in *Ethiopia Unbound* (1911), for the establishment of an African university on the Gold Coast. His hopes were partially fulfilled when Achimota College, with which he was associated, was established in 1927. He was impressed by Du Bois's work for Pan-Africanism and worked for a federation of the British West African colonies. In March 1920 50 delegates from these colonies met in Accra to form the National Congress of British West Africa, which subsequently met in Freetown (1923), Bathurst (1925–26) and Lagos (1929) but never achieved a mass following. Hayford was himself a member of the Gold Coast Legislative Council and advocated African majorities.

Hoare, Sir Samuel John Gurney, Viscount Templewood (1880–1959) British Conservative politician. Educated at Harrow and Oxford. Conservative MP for Ipswich, 1910–44. A member of the Round Table Conference on India, 1930. Secretary of State for India in the National government, 1931. He tried, unsuccessfully, to work with Gandhi during the second session of the Round Table Conference. While giving evidence to the Joint Select Committee examining the proposals arising from the Conference, he clashed seriously with Winston Churchill, who opposed the Indian reforms. Hoare piloted the much-delayed Government of India Act through in 1935. In June 1935 the new Prime Minister, Stanley Baldwin, moved him against his own wishes to the Foreign Office. He was compelled to resign as Foreign Secretary after the leak of the so-called Hoare–Laval plan, proposing a compromise with Italy on Abyssinia.

Ho Chi-Minh (1890–1969) Born Nguyen Tat Thanh; adopted the alias Nguyen Ai Quoc (Nguyen the Patriot). Vietnamese revolutionary leader. The son of a mandarin (civil service) family, he sailed to France as a cabin boy on a steamer in 1912. In 1919 he presented a petition to the Paris Peace Conference, asking for Vietnamese independence. When this was ignored, he turned to communism and played a part in the founding of the French Communist Party at Tours in 1920. In 1923 he went to Moscow and then China. From Canton he organised a revolutionary group in Vietnam, the Thnh-Nien Hoi, which was important in a series of revolts in Vietnam in 1930–31. In 1941 he became the secretary of the Vietminh Front, organised in southern China for the liberation of Vietnam, then in Japanese occupation. It was in 1942 that he adopted the *nom de guerre* Ho Chi-Minh. In August 1945, when the Vietminh seized Hanoi and secured the abdication of the Emperor, Bao-Dai, Ho (with the apparent approval of the Americans) proclaimed the independence of the Democratic Republic of Viet-Nam. But his communist associations made him suspect in American eyes and they backed the French against him. The French withdrew after their defeat at Dien Bien Phu in 1954 and Ho became the President of North Vietnam. He led the North against the South, although he died before the final victory of the North in 1975.

Home, Alexander (Alec) Frederick Douglas- (1903–95) British politician. Educated at Eton and Oxford. Entered the Commons in 1931 but went to the Lords in 1951, on succeeding his father as 14th Earl of Home. Returned to the Commons on renouncing his peerage under new legislation in 1963. Secretary of State for Commonwealth Relations, 1955–60, and Foreign Secretary, 1960–63. Prime Minister, 1963–64. Foreign Secretary, 1970–74. Returned to the Lords again in 1974 as a Life Peer, Baron Home of the Hirsel.

Houphouët-Boigny, Félix (1905–1993) Ivory Coast politician. He descended from a line of tribal chiefs in the old Ashanti Confederation. In 1940 he became the chief of his home district and, although he had qualified in medicine in Dakar, he followed his father in becoming a successful planter. He began his political career when he founded the Ivory Coast's first Agricultural Union in 1944 and became the spokesman for the producers, demanding minimum prices for coffee and cocoa. In 1946 he co-founded the Rassemblement Démocratique Africain (RDA, African Democratic Rally), which became the most important nationalist organisation throughout French West Africa. In 1945 he had been elected to the French Constituent Assembly, which brought the Fourth Republic into existence. In April 1946 he was largely responsible for the passage of the measure, which came to bear his name, which abolished forced labour in the French territories in Africa. He was again elected the Ivory Coast representative in the French National Assembly in 1951. From 1956 to 1958 he held a ministerial post in the French government and played an important role in the 'framework law' (*loi cadre*) of 1957, which gave internal autonomy to France's overseas territories. In 1956 he became Mayor of the Ivory Coast capital, Abidjan. He became President of the Ivory Coast Territorial Assembly in 1957 and President of the Grand Council of French West Africa, 1957–58. In 1958 he became Prime Minister of the Ivory Coast and, in November, President. He was re-elected in 1965 and remained in office until his death.

Huggins, Sir Godfrey Martin, 1st Viscount Malvern (1883–1971) Prime Minister of Southern Rhodesia and of the Central African Federation. Born and educated in England. Qualified as a surgeon and went to Rhodesia in 1911 to practise medicine. Served in the First World War. Elected to the Southern Rhodesian Legislative Assembly for the governing Rhodesian Party in 1924. Left over policy difficulties and, in 1932, became leader of the Reform Party and, in 1933, Prime Minister. The two parties merged in the United Party, which won the 1934 election. Huggins remained Prime Minister until 1953. He was a moderate reformer who saw the development of the country, despite the Depression, as the most pressing issue. On racial matters he admired Field Marshal Smuts, believing in a 'parallel development' for blacks and whites. He wholeheartedly supported Britain in the Second World War and made sure that the Southern Rhodesian contribution was a large one. Economic and other changes brought about by the war convinced him that 'parallel development' was no longer viable and he now favoured 'partnership', although seeing the non-Europeans as the junior partners. He encountered strong opposition from the political right. He would have preferred a union of

Northern and Southern Rhodesia, with full Dominion status, to the Central African Federation, but when it was established in 1953, he became its first Prime Minister. He presided over a prosperous period of economic advance and resigned in 1956 on grounds of age before the problems of the Federation became serious.

Hussein, (ibn Ali) (1852–1931) Sherif of Mecca. Exiled to Constantinople. In 1908, after the Young Turk revolution, he was appointed Emir of Mecca and returned to the Hejaz. In 1914 negotiated with Lord Kitchener about the possibility of the Arabs rising against the Turks. Took lead in Arab revolt in 1916 and his sons, Abdullah and Feisal, led armies. In autumn of 1916 he was recognised as King of the Hedj. Objected to the Sykes–Picot Agreement, defining British and French spheres of influence in the Middle East, and refused to recognise peace treaties and the Mandate System. Overthrown by Ibn Saud in 1920s.

Idris I, King (1890–1983) King of Libya, 1950–69. Born Al-Sayyid Muhammad Idris al-Sannii in Cyrenaica, then still part of the Ottoman empire. In 1916 he became the leader of the Sanusiyyah, formed originally in 1837, which successively challenged the Ottomans, French and Italians in the cause of independence. In 1920 he became Amir of Cyrenaica but, blamed for disturbances, he was forced into exile in Egypt in 1922. He took advantage of the Italian defeat in the Second World War to return in 1943. When Libya was granted independence in 1950, the Libyan National Assembly proclaimed Idris King of the United Kingdom of Libya and he ascended the throne in December 1951. Libya was very poor and dependent on British and American subsidies until the discovery of oil in the 1960s. By this time Idris was too conservative for the younger men and he was overthrown by a military coup, which brought Colonel Qadafi to power in September 1969.

Irwin, Lord (Edward Frederick Linley Wood, Lord Irwin, 1925; Lord Halifax, 1934; Earl, 1944) (1881–1959) British politician. Educated at Eton and Oxford. Conservative MP for Ripon, 1910–25. Under-Secretary for the Colonies, under Winston Churchill, in 1921. In November 1925 appointed Viceroy of India, a surprising appointment, although his family had a long connection with India. He found Indian opinion deeply offended by the fact that no Indians had been invited to serve on the Simon Commission. He proposed the Round Table Conferences. The new Labour government, with Ramsay Macdonald as Prime Minister and Wedgwood Benn as Secretary of State for India, were happy to take up the suggestion but there was an outcry from the British right, which antagonised the Indian National Congress. In January 1931 Irwin released Gandhi from prison and concluded the so-called Gandhi–Irwin (Delhi) Pact, by which the Congress agreed to attend the Round Table Conference. Irwin left India in April 1931. His preference for conciliation was not always appropriate. His later career was tarnished by his association with appeasement towards Hitler. He failed to succeed Neville Chamberlain as Prime Minister in May 1940 and instead went as Ambassador to Washington.

Jinnah, Mohammed Ali (1876–1948) Indian politician, founder of Pakistan. The son of a Karachi merchant, he studied law in London, 1892–96, and subsequently practised in Bombay. He joined the Indian National Congress in 1906 and was associated with the Moderates, led by Gokhale. From 1911 until 1930 he was the Muslim representative on the Central Legislative Council. He had joined the Muslim League in 1913 and became its President in 1915. He promoted the Lucknow Pact in 1916 because at this time he believed that Muslim–Hindu cooperation was vital to secure Indian independence. He left the Congress because he disapproved of Gandhi's non-cooperation campaign of 1919–22. He became increasingly uneasy about the safeguarding of Muslim rights and, in 1928, issued a Fourteen Point Declaration advocating a federal constitution with political and social guarantees for Muslims. He tried to retire from active politics in the early 1930s but came back in 1935. He was bitterly disappointed by the refusal of Congress to cooperate with the Muslim League after the 1937 elections, which had resulted in big Congress majorities, and set about organising the League as a modern political party. He himself became the 'Qaid-i-Azam' (Supreme Leader). Many commentators have blamed Jinnah's subsequent intransigence for the partition of India and the creation of Pakistan in 1947. He was already seriously ill with cancer in 1947 and died in 1948.

Jonathan, Chief Lebua (1914–87) Lesotho politician. The son of a chief, after education at a mission school, he went to work in South Africa in the gold fields. In 1935 he returned to Basutoland (as Lesotho was then called) to an administrative post, assisting an uncle in his chiefly duties. In 1959 he founded the Basutoland National Party, which advocated cooperation with their powerful neighbour, South Africa, in opposition to the more radical and nationalist Basutoland Congress Party, led by Ntsu Mokhehle. He won the general election in 1965 and became Prime Minister, but when it was clear that he would lose the 1970 election, he suspended the constitution and placed the King, Moshoeshoe II, under house arrest. Mokhehle mounted a guerrilla campaign against him. At first he cultivated close links with the apartheid government in South Africa, but when it became clear that they regarded Lesotho as another Bantustan, he provided refuge for ANC leaders and others who fled from South Africa. South Africa retaliated with commando raids. Jonathan was deposed by an army coup in 1985.

Kasavubu, Joseph (1913–69) Politician of Congo Democratic Republic (Congo Kinshasa). Regarded by many as the father of Congolese independence. A member of the Bakongo tribe, he was born at Tshela. He was educated at Catholic mission schools and went to the seminary at Kabwe, meaning to become a priest, but he changed his mind and became first a teacher and then a civil servant. In 1955 he became the president of Abako, a cultural organisation founded in 1950 to preserve the heritage of his tribe, the Bakongo, which had at one time been an independent and powerful nation. His first ambitions were less for Congolese independence than for the reunion of the Bakongo, who were scattered between the French and Belgian Congos and Angola. But in 1959 the Belgians banned an Abako meeting and serious riots broke out in Leopoldville. Kasavubu was briefly imprisoned but then cooperated with Patrice Lumumba and his party in talks with the Belgians, which led to independence in June 1960. Kasavubu became the first President of the Congo Democratic Republic, with Lumumba as Prime Minister. General Mobutu seized power in September and overthrew both men but was compelled to reinstate Kasavubu. Kasavubu was finally ousted by Mobutu when the latter proclaimed himself President in November 1965. Kasavubu retired gracefully to his farm.

Kaunda, Kenneth (b. 1924) Zambian (Northern Rhodesian) politician. He was born at the Lubwa mission station in Northern Zambia, the son of Rev. David Kaunda, an (African) Church of Scotland missionary and teacher from Nyasaland. He qualified as a teacher and worked for a time in Tanganyika and Southern Rhodesia. Dismayed by the discrimination he encountered, in 1949 he joined the African National Congress, led by Harry Nkumbula. He organised nearly 100 provincial branches and, in 1953, the year of the formation of the Central African Federation, became the secretary-general. The following year both Kaunda and Nkumbula were gaoled. Kaunda himself believed in non-violence and was deeply attracted by Gandhian ideals. Nevertheless, in 1958, Nkumbula was prepared to accept as a first step a constitution which would have left the Africans in an inferior position. Kaunda was not. He formed the Zambia National Congress to fight it. The new party was banned and Kaunda again imprisoned. But the British were eventually compelled to concede the right of Northern Rhodesia to secede from the Federation and demand majority rule. Kaunda went to London to help to negotiate independence. He won an overwhelming victory in the ensuing elections and became Zambia's first Prime Minister in January 1964, assuming the Presidency when Zambia became independent as a republic in October 1964. His democratic reputation was somewhat damaged when he assumed autocratic powers in 1972, but his new constitution was confirmed in 1973. He played an important role when Zambia was a so-called 'frontline state' in the struggle against the regime in Rhodesia, following its Unilateral Declaration of Independence in 1965. He relinquished the presidency in 1991 but participated in politics again as President of the United Independence Party in 1995.

Keita, Madeira (b. 1917) Mali (Soudan) politician. Educated at the William Ponty School in Dakar, he became involved in politics soon after leaving. He was a founder of the Guinea Democratic Party and was its secretary-general before Sekou Touré. He was repeatedly arrested for his political activities and suspended from his job at the French Institute of Black Africa. He returned to Mali and became active in the Soudanese Union which, like the Guinea Democratic Party, was linked to the African Democratic Rally (RDA). In April 1959 he became Minister of the Interior in Soudan's pre-independence administration and kept the post during the brief period of the Mali–Senegal Federation and when Mali became an independent state in 1960.

Keita, Modibo (1915–77) The first President of independent Mali. A Malinke and a descendant of the ancient rulers of Mali, he was born at Bamako and educated in Koranic schools before training as a teacher at the William Ponty School in Dakar. He became involved in politics at the end of the Second World War. In 1945 he founded, with Mamadou Konate, the Bloc Soudanais, which the following year merged with the African Democratic Rally (RDA) and became known as the Union Soudanise–RDA. He was closely associated with Houphouët-Boigny until the two men disagreed about federating the former colonies of French West Africa. In 1946 he was arrested in Paris and, in 1950, sent to teach in a remote region of the Sahara. In 1952 he was elected to the Territorial Assembly in the Soudan, and in 1956 he was elected the Soudanese delegate to the French National Assembly. He was the first African to be elected Vice-President (a post analogous to that of Deputy Speaker in the British Parliament) of the French National Assembly. In 1957 he became Minister for France Overseas in Bourges-Manoury's government. In 1958 he campaigned for a 'Yes' vote in General de Gaulle's referendum to ratify the setting up of the French Community to replace the French Union. In December 1958 representatives of Senegal, Soudan, Upper Volta and Dahomey met in Bamako to discuss setting up the Federation of Mali, but Dahomey and Upper Volta withdrew before independence in 1960. The federation of Senegal and Soudan (Mali) lasted only a few months, the Senegalese being unhappy with Keita's wish for a strong central government. Keita became the first President of Mali. Keita continued to work for various forms of federation, preferably based on socialist principles. He signed the Casablanca Charter linking the Arab states of North Africa with the socialist states of black Africa. These were allowed to fall into abeyance with the formation of the Organisation for African Unity in Addis Ababa in 1963, in which Keita played a prominent role.

Kenyatta, Jomo (1891–1978) Kenyan politician. Born Kamau wa Muigai, 'Jomo' was a soubriquet meaning 'Burning Spear'. He was the son of a poor Kikuyu farmer from Ichaweri, educated at a Church of Scotland mission school. In 1928 he became general-secretary of the Kikuyu Central Association, originally known as the Young Kikuyu Association, a more radical body than the Kikuyu Association and which wished to reclaim the lands taken by the white settlers. Visited England in 1929 to lobby the British government without much success. He subsequently travelled and studied in Moscow. Returned to London and studied anthropology at the London School of Economics under Professor Malanowski. In 1938 he published *Facing Mount Kenya*, a pioneering work by an African studying his own people but which also had a political purpose in demonstrating how African society had been disrupted by Europeans. He remained in London during the Second World War. In 1945 he attended the Pan-African Conference which met in Manchester and founded the Pan-African Federation with George Padmore and Kwame Nkrumah. He returned to Kenya in 1946 and became president of the newly formed Kenya African Union. The weakness of the KAU was that it was predominatly a Kikuyu organisation. In 1952 the Mau Mau outbreaks began among the Kikuyu. In April 1955 Kenyatta was detained (many felt unjustly) for complicity. He was released in August 1961. While still in detention he was elected president of the new Kenya African National Union (KANU), formed in March 1960. He entered the Legislative Council in January 1962 as Leader of the Opposition against the Kenya African Democratic Union (KADU). When KANU won the 1963 elections, he became Prime Minister. In 1964, when Kenya became a republic, he became President. He remained President until his death in 1978.

Khama, Sir Seretse (1921–80) First President of Botswana (formerly Bechuanaland). A descendant of Khama the Great, who had ruled the

Bamangwato people for 50 years and repelled the Boers, before he was five he inherited the chieftainship of the Bamangwato tribe, to which more than a third of the population belonged. His uncle, Tshekedi Khama, acted as Regent. Seretse was educated at Fort Hare and the University of the Witwatersrand and Balliol College, Oxford, before studying law at the Middle Temple in London. He offended an influential group led by Tshekedi by his marriage to an English woman in 1948 and the British agreed to exile him. He was allowed to return in 1956 when he renounced the chieftainship. In 1961 he founded the Bechuanaland Democratic Party to work for a greater share of government for Africans. The party won a handsome majority in the 1962 general election. When Botswana became a republic in 1966 he became the President and held the post until his death. As a 'frontline President' he played an important role in the negotiations which eventually resolved the problems arising from Rhodesia's unilateral declaration of independence.

Kiwanuku, Benedicto (1922–72) First Prime Minister of Uganda. A law-yer, he was educated at Pius XII University College, Basutoland, 1950–52, and University College, London, 1952–56, being called to the Bar at Gray's Inn in 1956. Soon after his return to Uganda he was elected to the Uganda Legislative Council, and became Leader of the House and Government Business in 1961 and Prime Minister February–April 1962. The rise of his Democratic Party, which was sometimes regarded as the Roman Catholic party, was only made possible by the boycott of the 1960 elections in Buganda and when Milton Obote won an overwhelm-ing victory in the 1962 elections, Kiwanuku even lost his own seat. He retired from active politics. In 1971 Idi Amin appointed him Chief Just-ice but, after he had disagreed with Amin the following year, he was arrested and never seen again.

Konate, Mamadou (d. 1956) Politician of French Sudan (Mali). Led Union Soudanaise, affiliated to RDA.

Koulamallah, Ahmed (b. 1912) Chad politician. A Muslim influential in the north of the country. A socialist with links with SFIO, his support was important to Gabriel Lisette.

Kutuklui, Noe (b. 1923) Togo politician. Born into a poor family at Anecho on the east coast of Togo, but educated in Dakar and went to France, where he studied law at the University of Caen. Active in African student groups in France and became president of the Federation of Black African Students in France. He returned to the Togo capital, Lomé, in the late 1950s and joined the United Togolese Movement. In 1962 he became its deputy secretary-general. He was close to the President, Sylvanus Olympio, assassinated in January 1963. The army formed a provisional government in which Kutuklui became Minister of Labour and Social Affairs. He strongly opposed Nicholas Grunitzky's policy of cooperation with France and after the 1963 elections was imprisoned for a short time. In 1966 he led an unsuccessful coup to overthrow Grunitzky.

Lattre de Tassigny, General Jean de (1889–1952) French soldier. Sent to take command in Vietnam after serious French reverses of the autumn of 1950. Checked Giap's campaign in the Red River valley. De Lattre, the most successful French general in the Vietnam war, died in Paris of cancer in January 1952.

Le Duc Tho (b. 1911) Vietnamese nationalist. From a middle-class family, he attended French schools but became committed to the nationalist cause. He was a founder member of the Indochinese Communist Party and spent years in gaol. He was associated with Ho Chi-Minh in the foundation of the Vietminh. He was the senior Vietminh commissar for South Vietnam under the French and continued the role in the struggle with the Americans.

Lee Kuan Yew (b. 1923) Singapore politician. Educated at Cambridge and called to the Bar. One of the founders of the People's Action Party in 1954. Became first Prime Minister of Singapore in 1959. Pursued socially conservative but very successful development policy. Resigned as Prime Minister in 1990 but continued as respected elder statesman.

Lennox-Boyd, Alan T., Viscount Boyd of Merton (1904–83) British politician. Educated at Sherborne and Oxford. Conservative MP for mid-Bedfordshire, 1931–60. Junior minister at the Ministry of Aircraft Production, 1943–45, but his main interest was always in colonial and foreign affairs. Travelled widely, 1945–51, and was frequently a spokesman on colonial affairs. Minister of State at the Colonial Office under Oliver Lyttleton, 1951. Colonial Secretary, 1954–59. He saw his principal task as preparing the colonies for self-government but he envisaged a considerably longer time-scale. He recognised the crucial importance of economic preparation and this led him to advocate federations (not all of them successful) to strengthen the economic base in East and Central Africa and the West Indies. He went to the Lords in 1960. In 1979 he went on behalf of the Conservative Party, then in opposition, to observe the elections in Rhodesia under the so-called 'internal settlement'.

Leopold II (1835–1909) King of the Belgians, 1865–1909, and founder of the Congo Free State (Belgian Congo). Leopold had long cherished colonial ambitions and he employed the explorer, Henry Morton Stanley, to organise the International Association for the Exploration and Civilisation of the Congo in 1876, which led to the recognition of the Congo Free State by the Great Powers after the Berlin West Africa Conference in 1884–85. Leopold made a personal fortune but the cruelty and exploitation eventually attracted international attention and the Belgian Parliament was compelled to take responsibility and turn the Congo Free State into an ordinary colony in 1908.

Liaqat, Ali Khan (1896–1951) Pakistan politician. A prominent member of the Muslim League. He became the first Prime Minister of Pakistan after partition in 1947. After the death of Jinnah in 1948, he was the most powerful politician in Pakistan. But his resistance to extremist demands and his attempts to improve relations with India led to his assassination in 1951.

Lisette, G. (b. 1919) Chad politician. A French West Indian, born in Panama, he studied in Paris, worked as a civil servant in Chad and was active in the Free French. Formed the Parti Progressiste Tchadien, affiliated to the RDA, and was active in the RDA itself. He was elected to the French National Assembly in 1951 but intrigues, probably supported by the French administration, kept him out in 1952. He allied with Koulamallah and in 1956 became Prime Minister of a coalition government. Unlike Koulamallah, he supported an affirmative vote in the 1958 referendum to join the French Community. In 1960 he was displaced by Tombalbaye and forced into exile.

Lugard, Frederick John Dealty, 1st Baron (1858–1945) British soldier and colonial administrator. Born in India of British parents. As a soldier, served in Afghanistan (1879–80), Sudan (1885) and Burma (1886). In 1888, no longer in the army, he went to East Africa, and in 1890 was employed by the Imperial British East Africa Company, for whom he secured the territory that became Uganda. In 1894 he was employed by the Royal Niger Company and contested control of the Middle Niger with the French. In 1900 he was made Commissioner for northern Nigeria. In 1906–11 he was Governor of Hong Kong but he returned to take up the position of Governor of the whole of Nigeria, 1912–19. In Nigeria he perfected his theories, first tried out in Uganda, of 'Indirect Rule'. It worked better in the North than in the South. In 1922 he published *The Dual Mandate in British Tropical Africa,* in which he argued for a reciprocal relationship between Europeans and Africans, emphasising the European responsibility to bring good government and progress in return for material advantages, which was very influential in its time. From 1922 to 1936 he was a member of the League of Nations Mandate Commission.

Lumumba, Patrice (1925–61) Politician of Congo Democratic Republic (Congo Kinshasa), later Zaire. Unusual in being neither a teacher, nor a civil servant, but a brewery salesman. In 1958 he joined the newly formed Mouvement National Congolais (MNC, Congolese National Mouvement) which, like the Kasavubu's Abako, was originally a cultural movement but became political. But Lumumba wanted a strong central government, unlike Kasavubu who favoured a loose federation. After the Leopoldville riots in 1959, Lumumba was present at the Round Table Conference of Congolese leaders in Brussels in January–February 1960, which set the date for independence. Lumumba's MNC won a big majority in the 1960 elections and he became Prime Minister. Four days after independence, the Congolese army mutined. Lumumba asked for and got United Nations assistance in restoring order. But he suffered a fatal blow to his prestige when Katanga seceded under Moise Tshombe. In September 1960 the President, Joseph Kasavubu, dismissed Lumumba as Prime Minister. Lumumba seized the radio station and announced that he had dismissed Kasavubu. The army commander, Joseph Mobutu, then dismissed both men. Kasavubu was later reinstated but Lumumba was arrested, after an attempt either to rally his supporters or escape. He was killed in mysterious circumstances in January/February 1961. His death caused bitter recriminations, not only in the Congo, but throughout Africa.

Luthuli, Albert John Chief (1898–1967) South African leader and first African winner of the Nobel Peace Prize. Born at Solusi mission station in Southern Rhodesia, where his father was an interpreter. Educated on a Zulu 'reservation' in Natal and became a teacher. Subsequently elected chief by his people. Joined non-racial Christian Council of South Africa and visited India in 1938 and the United States in 1948. In 1946 elected to the Natives Representative Council, set up by Prime Minister Hertzog to advise the government on African affairs. Became president of Natal section of African National Congress in 1951 and, although committed to non-violence and cooperation between black and white, led the campaign there against *apartheid* legislation. The authorities deposed him as chief but he was elected president of the African National Congress. He was 'banned', i.e. placed under various restriction orders, from 1952. In 1956 he was tried for treason under the Suppression of Communism Act. The trial eventually collapsed but he was subjected to further restrictions.

Awarded Nobel Prize in 1961 and published his most famous book, his autobiography, *Let My People Go*, in 1962. He declined an offer of sanctuary in the United States.

Lyttelton, Oliver, Viscount Chandos (1893–1972) British politician. The son of Alfred Lyttleton, who had himself been Colonial Secretary in 1903–5 in Balfour's government. Educated at Eton and Oxford. Served in First World War. Went into business between the Wars. In October 1940 Churchill made him President of the Board of Trade and he became MP for Aldershot, 1940–54. He was sent to Cairo in 1941 and conducted negotiations with the Vichy regime in Syria and Lebanon, as well as intervening for military reasons in Iranian and Egyptian affairs. Colonial Secretary, 1951–54. He saw his task as arranging orderly progress towards self-government within the Commonwealth. He was confronted by both the Malayan emergency (successfully dealt with by General Templer) and the Mau Mau emergency in Kenya. He was a strong advocate of the Central African Federation and in 1953–54 played a leading role in trying to establish a satisfactory federation in Nigeria. He retired, somewhat disillusioned, to the Lords in 1954.

Macaulay, Herbert (1864–1945) Pioneer Nigerian nationalist. Born in Lagos, the son of an African missionary and teacher and the grandson of Samuel Ajayi Crowther, the first African (Anglican) Bishop of the Niger. Educated at mission schools, in 1881 he became a clerk in the Public Works Department in Lagos. In 1890–93 a government scholarship enabled him to study civil engineering in England. Surveyor of Crown lands in Lagos, 1873–78. He then resigned to be free to defend Nigerian interests against colonial encroachment. In 1922 he organised the Nigerian National Democratic Party to fight the elections under the new constitution. In 1944 this merged with Azikiwi's National Council for Nigeria and the Cameroons, of which Macaulay became the first President.

MacDonald, Malcolm (1901–80) British politician, diplomat and colonial governor. General reputation as a trouble-shooter. The son of Ramsay MacDonald, Britain's first Labour Prime Minister. Educated at Bedales and Oxford. Became a Labour MP in 1929. In 1931 became Parliamentary Under-Secretary at the Dominions Office in the National Government. Between 1935 and 1940 at various times Colonial Secretary and Dominions Secretary. He was particularly concerned with the promotion of a colonial development policy. British High Commissioner in Canada, 1941. Governor-General of the Malayan Union, as it then was, plus Singapore and later British Borneo, 1946. United Kingdom Commissioner General for South East Asia, 1948. Concerned with problems created by French Indo-China. British High Commissioner in India, 1955–60. Co-chairman and leader of British delegation to Geneva Conference on Laos, 1961–62. Last British Governor of Kenya, 1963–64. British High Commissioner in Kenya, 1964–65. Employed by Prime Minister, Harold Wilson, as special representative in Africa, dealing with the delicate situations in Rhodesia and Nigeria, 1967–69. President of the Royal Commonwealth Society, 1971. Refused knighthood and peerage, but accepted Order of Merit in 1969.

Macleod, Iain N. (1913–70) British politician. Educated at Fettes College and Cambridge. Served in Second World War. Employed in Conservative Party Research Department, 1946. Elected MP for Enfield West, 1950. A 'One Nation' Tory, mainly concerned with domestic affairs, but in 1959 became Colonial Secretary. Supported Prime Minister, Harold Macmillan, in speeding up independence for Africa. Released Hastings Banda and Jomo Kenyatta from detention. Called constitutional conferences on Kenya, Tanganyika, Nyasaland and Uganda. Strongly attacked by Lord Salisbury, who launched his 'too clever by half' jibe, which Macleod never lived down, for his alleged betrayal of the interests of white settlers. Helped to bring about southern Arabian and West Indian federations, neither of which proved durable. Left Colonial Office in 1959. Opposed the Commonwealth Immigrants Bill of 1968 as a betrayal of the Kenyan Asians. Died prematurely just after becoming Chancellor of the Exchequer in 1970.

Macmillan, Harold, 1st Earl of Stockton (1894–1986) British politician. Educated at Eton and Oxford. Served in First World War. ADC to 9th Duke of Devonshire, 1919, then to the Governor-General of Canada, whose daughter he married. MP for Stockton, 1924–29 and 1931–45, subsequently for Bromley. In the 1930s agreed with Winston Churchill on anti-appeasement policy but against him on India. In 1942 appointed Colonial Secretary but was then sent to key post as Minister Resident at Allied Headquarters in Algiers, where he had to negotiate with General Eisenhower and General de Gaulle, among others. Described at one time as the 'Viceroy of the Mediterranean'. Held various offices in Conservative government after 1951, becoming in 1955 Chancellor of the Exchequer. Was a hawk at the beginning of the Suez operation in 1956 but, when the disastrous run on sterling began, became anxious to withdraw quickly. Succeeded Anthony Eden as Prime Minister in January 1957. Against all the odds, restored his party's fortunes and won the 1959 general election. Sometimes accused of concentrating too much on foreign and colonial affairs, at the expense of domestic questions. On 3 February 1960 made his famous 'wind of change' speech in Cape Town (previously delivered in Accra, but not picked up by the press), saying that the wind of change, which had already swept through Asia, was now sweeping through Africa. Prime Minister when many British colonies in Africa finally became independent. The right-wing Monday Club was formed in protest. Resigned the premiership in 1964 on health grounds.

Macpherson, John S. (1898–1971) British colonial governor. Educated at George Watson College and Edinburgh University. Served in First World War. Joined Colonial Service in 1921 and posted to Federated Malay States. Sent to Lagos in 1937 and became chief secretary in Palestine in 1939. During Second World War served in Washington and West Indies. Governor of Nigeria, 1948–55, one of 'new generation' of governors sought by Arthur Creech Jones and Andrew Cohen to work towards orderly transfer of power. Responsible for so-called Macpherson Constitution of 1946, worked for federation and Africanisation of services. Permanent Under-Secretary at the Colonial Office, 1956–59.

Maga, Hubert (b. 1916) Dahomey's first President after independence. A teacher by profession. Represented Dahomey in the French National Assembly, 1951–58. Became Dahomey's Labour Minister in 1958 and Prime Minister in 1959. President and Prime Minister, 1960–63. Overthrown by Christophe Soglo in 1963.

Makarios, Archbishop (1913–77) Head of the Greek Orthodox Church in Cyprus. He played an active political role and supported *enosis* – the union of Cyprus with Greece – during the British period. The British regarded his relations with the terrorist leader, Colonel Grivas, as suspect and he was deported to the Seychelles in 1956. He returned to Cyprus in 1959 and became President of Cyprus in 1960 and held the office until his death, apart from a brief period in 1974–75, when he was forced out. His ambition to make Cyprus a wholly Greek island both helped to provoke and was defeated by the Turkish invasion of 1975.

Malan, Daniel (1874–1959) South African politician. Minister of Dutch Reformed Church, 1905–15. Entered politics as Nationalist MP in 1918. Opposed South African entry into Second World War against Nazi Germany. One of a group of Afrikaaners, mainly churchmen, who evolved the doctrine of *apartheid*, the complete separation of the races. Won 1948 general election on a minority of the votes and proceeded to bring in full-blooded *apartheid* policy. Subjected to intense international criticism, particularly for his refusal to accept United Nations jurisdiction over South West Africa (Namibia).

Mandela, Nelson Rolihlahla (b. 1918) South African statesman. The son of a chief of the Tembo tribe. Educated at Fort Hare University College and University of the Witwatersrand. Conducted legal practice in Johannesburg. National Organiser of African National Congress (ANC), 1952. Tried for treason but acquitted, 1959–1961. Arrested again in 1962 and, in 1964, sentenced to life imprisonment. Released in February 1990 and played a leading role in transforming South Africa from *apartheid* state to modern democracy. Elected President of democratic South Africa in May 1994.

Manley, Norman Washington (1893–1969) Jamaican politician. Born in Jamaica of mixed Negro, Irish and English descent. In 1914 went to Oxford as a Rhodes scholar, where he read law. Served in the First World War. Called to the Bar and returned to practise in Jamaica in 1922. Became the best-known lawyer in the West Indies and sometimes pleaded cases in England. In 1938 he acted as mediator in the serious labour unrest in Jamaica. He then founded the People's National Party, aiming at universal suffrage and self-government in Jamaica. He was defeated in 1944 and 1949 by Bustamente, but he won the election in 1955 and became Chief Minister. He won the 1959 elections but he supported West Indian Federation and the 1961 referendum went against him. He lost the 1962 election and was out of power when Jamaica became independent.

Margai, Sir Albert (1910–80) Sierra Leone politician. Son of a merchant, he was educated at Roman Catholic schools and qualified as a pharmacist. In 1944 he went to London to study law, returning to set up practice in Freetown in 1948. With his brother, Milton, he formed the Sierra Leone People's Party in 1951. Elected first to the Protectorate, and then to the Colony, Legislative Assembly. Appointed Minister of Local Government and Education. He was more radical than his brother and in 1958 formed the rival People's National Party, but after its ill-success in the 1959 elections he rejoined his brother. He took part in the 1960 London conference to finalise Sierra Leone independence and became Minister of Finance in 1962. He became Prime Minister on his brother's death in 1964. He was a prominent figure at later Commonwealth conferences, in particular clashing with Harold Wilson over Rhodesian independence. But he was opposed by the All Peoples' Congress, led by Siaka Stevens, which won the 1967 election. Margai used military force to overturn the result, but in 1968 Stevens became Prime Minister and Margai went into exile.

Margai, Sir Milton (1895–1964) Sierra Leone politician. Son of a merchant, he trained as a doctor in Edinburgh. In 1946 he founded the Sierra Leone Organisation Society, a body devoted to the interests of the Protectorate, which also asked for constitutional advance. In 1951 this was merged with the People's Party, based in the Colony, which wished to see unity with the Protectorate. A genuinely political party, the Sierra Leone People's Party, emerged. In 1954 he became the Chief Minister in the Protectorate. His party won the 1957 elections but the following year his brother, Albert, formed a more radical party, which did not last long. The Sierra Leone parties united to ask for full independence at the London conference in 1960. His party won a big majority in the 1962 elections. He was knighted in 1959. He died in 1964.

Maudling, Reginald (1917–79) British politician. Educated at Merchant Taylors' School and Oxford. Called to the Bar in 1940. Joined the Conservative Party research department after the Second World War and became associated with R.A. Butler. Entered Parliament, 1950. Held various ministerial appointments under Conservative governments, including that of Colonial Secretary, 1961–62. This coincided with the last days of the Central African Federation and he forced through the independence of Northern Rhodesia (Zambia) against strong right-wing opposition. He also introduced a new land settlement scheme in Kenya, which ended the European monopoly on the White Highlands in return for compensation. Later Chancellor of the Exchequer and Home Secretary and considered a potential leader of the party, but resigned in 1972 as a result of charges of financial iregularities and never fully rehabilitated.

M'ba, Leon (1902–67) Gabonese politician. Generally conservative in stance, believing in the possibility of combining French culture with African traditions, he emerged as an elder statesman among the French-speaking African leaders. Born in Libreville, he was educated in mission schools and rose to a comparatively senior position in the Gabonese civil service even though, in the late 1930s, he was transferred to Ubanghi-Shari for his political activities in Gabon. He cooperated with the Free French and was allowed to return to Gabon in 1946. He left the civil service to go into business and campaign more openly. His Gabon Democratic Bloc (BDG), originally founded in 1946, was affiliated to the moderate African Democratic Rally (RDA). He played a prominent role in 1947 in a congress called by the French administration to resolve tribal problems. In 1952 he was elected to the Gabonese Territorial Assembly and in 1957 became the Vice-President of the Government Council. In 1956 he had also become Mayor of Libreville. In the 1957 elections his BDG narrowly defeated Aubame's UDSG and at the RDA conference in Bamako the same year he supported the moderate Houphouët-Boigny against the more strident nationalism of men like Sekou Touré. He became Prime Minister of Gabon in July 1858 and supported de Gaulle's plans to transform the French Union into the French Community, but he opposed plans for a closer federation of what was then French Equatorial Africa. He hoped for closer ties with France for Gabon, which was more prosperous than its neighbours, although he did agree subsequently to join the Central African Customs and Economic Union. Gabon became independent in August 1960. M'ba was confirmed as President by a large majority in the elections of February 1961. In 1964 relations finally broke down between M'ba and his main rival, Aubame. M'ba called in French paratroopers to assist him after Aubame's supporters attempted a coup. His party won a large majority in the April 1964 elections and he remained President until his death. In 1966 he discussed with President de Gaulle the possibility of a French-speaking Commonwealth in Africa.

Mboya, Thomas Joseph Odhiambo Niengo (1930–69) Kenyan politician and trade union leader. The son of Luo parents, he trained as a sanitary engineer. In 1952 he helped to form the Kenya Local Government Workers' Union and the following year became secretary of the Kenya Federation of Labour. He was elected a member of the Legislative Council in 1957, and in 1962 became Minister for Labour. He was an ally of Jomo Kenyatta and became secretary of the Kenya African National Union on its formation in 1960. In the first government after independence he became Minister for Justice and Constitutional Affairs and, when Kenya became a republic in 1964, he became Minister for Economic Planning and Development. He was assassinated on 5 July 1969.

Mendès-France, Pierre Isaac Isadore (1907–1982) Lawyer and French radical politician. Member of Léon Blum's administration in 1938. Escaped to London during the Second World War. Financial Commissioner to Algeria, 1943. Minister of National Economy in De Gaulle's government, 1944–45. Prime Minister and Foreign Secretary, 1954–55, came to power pledged to end French involvement in Indo-China after the French defeat at Dien Bien Phu. Armistice established at the Geneva Conference. Also paved the way for Tunisian autonomy. Deputy Prime Minister to Guy Mollet in 1956 but resigned because of Mollet's intransigence on Algeria. Lost seat in National Assembly in 1958 but re-elected in 1967.

Menon, V.P. (Rao Bahadur Vapal Pangunni) (1894–1966) Indian civil servant. Reforms Commissioner to the Government of India, 1942–45. Secretary to the Governor-General, 1945–46. He played a crucial role in drafting the final measures for independence and left important accounts in *The Story of the Integration of the Indian States* (1956) and *The Transfer of Power in India* (1957).

Menon, Vengalil Khrishnan Krishna (1897–1970) Born in Kerala. Came to England in 1924. Studied at the London School of Economics (with Harold Laski), University College London, and Glasgow University. Called to the Bar. Active in the Labour Party. Secretary of the India League and lobbied for Indian independence, 1929–47. Associated with Nehru. Indian High Commissioner in London, 1947–52. Headed Indian delegation to the United Nations, 1953–62. Supported Nehru's non-alignment policy but prejudiced in his attitude to Pakistan. Played an important role in 1954 in Korean armistice and in Geneva Conference on Indo-China.

Mobutu, Joseph (Sese Seke) (1930–97) Congolese (Zairean) politician. A member of the Bengala tribe, born in Lisala in north-west Congo. Educated at mission schools, he enrolled in the army in 1949. He left the army in 1956 and became a journalist, working on *L'Avenir* and *Actualités Africaines*, eventually becoming the editor of the latter. He joined Patrice Lumumba's Congolese National Movement (MNC) and went with Lumumba to the Brussels roundtable conference of Congolese leaders in January 1960. After independence he became Army Chief-of-Staff with the rank of colonel. When the Congolese army mutined and committed atrocities, Mobutu succeeded in restoring some degree of discipline. In September 1960 he became Commander-in-Chief. Within weeks he had intervened with military force in the quarrel between the President, Kasavubu, and the Prime Minister, Patrice Lumumba. Lumumba was murdered, Kasavubu reinstated. Nominally, civilian government was restored in February 1961 but Mobutu remained the power behind the throne. He set about reorganising the army and openly seized power again in November 1965 after a new quarrel between Kasavubu and Tshombe. This time Mobutu declared himself President and assumed autocratic powers. He was overthrown in 1997 by Laurent Kabila.

Mohammed-ben-Yusuf, (Mohammed V) Sultan (1911–61) First King of independent Morocco. The French secured his succession in 1927 as a boy of sixteen, because they thought he would be malleable. In fact in the 1930s he began to collaborate secretly with Istiqlal, the Independence Party. He was loyal to the Free French during the Second World

War, but a meeting with President Roosevelt during the Casablanca Conference in 1943 alerted him to possible American sympathy. In a speech in Tangiers in 1947 he departed from his agreed text to speak with approval of the nationalists' cause. The French tried to diminish his influence and even allied with his enemies such as the traditionalist feudal chiefs. In 1953 he was deposed and exiled to Madagascar. But the Moroccans would not accept his successor, Mulay Arafa, and the French were compelled to restore Mohammed-ben-Yusuf in November 1955. When Morocco became independent on 2 March 1956 he became head of state and took the title of King. He died suddenly in February 1961 and was succeeded by his son, Hassan II.

Moi, Daniel Arap (b. 1924) Kenyan politician. Born at Baringo in northwest Kenya, he was a teacher before turning to politics and becoming a member of the Legislative Council in 1957. He was at one time a leading member of the Kenya African Democratic Union (KADU), the rival to Kenyatta's Kenya African National Union (KANU). He became Minister of Education in 1962 and, after KANU won the 1963 elections, shadow Minister of Agriculture. In 1964 he joined KANU and became Minister for Home Affairs. He was appointed Vice-President in 1967. When Kenyatta died in 1978 he succeeded him as President. He ruled a one-party state and there was an attempted coup against him in 1982.

Mollet, Guy (1905–75) French politician. A teacher, who served in the Resistance during the Second World War. Mayor of Arras, 1945. Entered Chamber of Deputies, 1945. Secretary-General of Socialist Party, 1946, and of SFIO. An intellectual Marxist but opposed to the Communist Party. Prime Minister of the longest-lasting government of the Fourth Republic (January 1956–May 1957). Tried to solve Algerian problem. Hoped for cease-fire followed by compromise, but he was not strong enough to enforce such a policy. Appointed a liberal governor, General Catroux, but had to replace him by hard-line Robert Lacoste. Forced into policy of repression and attempted military solution. Led into Suez adventure because Nasser had supported FLN in Algeria, but did not lose public support as Eden did in Britain. Supported return of de Gaulle to power in 1958 and, subsequently, his Algerian policy.

Monckton, Walter T., Viscount Monckton of Brenchley (1891–1965) British lawyer and politician. Educated at Harrow and Oxford. His Indian connections began in 1933 when he became constitutional adviser to the Nizam of Hyderabad and the Nawab of Bhopal at the time of the Round Table Conferences. He advised the Nizam to join a federal India. Played an important role as a mediator when Edward VIII abdicated in 1936.

Winston Churchill employed him on various missions during the Second World War, including that of director-general of information in Cairo. He visited India both before and after independence and again tried to persuade the Nizam that continued independence was impossible. Only after his efforts had finally failed did India occupy Hyderabad in 1948. In 1955 he became Minister of Defence and reluctantly supported the Suez intervention in 1956. In 1959 he chaired the commission appointed to review the Central African Federation. The report recommended that the states involved should have the right to secede.

Montagu, Edwin Samuel (1879–1924) British liberal politician. Entered Parliament 1906. Under-Secretary at the India Office, 1910–14. In June 1917 became Secretary of State for India. Made the historic declaration on 20 August 1917 (although the words actually were drafted by Lord Curzon) that the British goal was the 'progressive realisation of responsible government in India'. Spent November 1917 to May 1918 touring India with a small delegation of civil servants and politicians. He kept a detailed diary (edited and published by his wife in 1930 as *An Indian Diary*) because he believed that they must produce a major report which would bear comparison with Lord Durham's famous 1839 Report on Canada and this duly appeared as 'The Report on Indian Constitutional Reforms'. But the resulting measure, the Government of India Act of 1919, disappointed the Indians, who had expected more. Montagu resigned in March 1922 after a quarrel with Lloyd George, who objected to his allowing the Indian government to protest about the treatment of Turkey.

Moshoeshoe II, King (Paramount Chief Motlotlehi Moshoeshoe) (1938–96) King of Lesotho (Basutoland). A descendant of Moshesh, the founder of the Basuto nation, he was born Prince Constantine Bereng Seeiso. He succeeded his father, Chief Simeon Seeiso Griffith, at the age of two. His stepmother, Princess Mantsebo Seeiso, became Regent while he was educated, first in Basutoland and then in England, at Ampleforth (a Roman Catholic public school) and the University of Oxford. He insisted on returning home in 1960 to take personal charge. He disliked the new constitution when Basutoland became independent in 1966 and wished to revive the powers of his predecessor, Moshoeshoe I. An insurrection in December 1966, after which Moshoeshoe was placed under house arrest for a short period, compelled him to agree to govern constitutionally.

Mossadeq, Mohammed (1880–1967) Iranian politician. Foreign Minister, 1922–24, after which he withdrew from politics, but returned to Parliament in 1942. Headed campaign against Anglo-Iranian Oil Company.

Became Prime Minister in 1951 and carried through threatened nationalisation, despite strong opposition from Britain. The Company did not prosper after nationalisation and Mossadeq was unable to deliver promised social and economic reforms. Overthrown by coup in 1953, probably engineered by the CIA and with tacit support of his Head of State, the Shah. Arrested and sentenced to three years imprisonment for treason. Remained under house arrest until his death.

Mountbatten, Louis, 1st Earl Mountbatten of Burma (1900–79) Admiral of the Fleet, Allied Commander South East Asia and last Viceroy of British India. Born Prince Louis of Battenberg at Windsor, he was closely related to the British royal family, a direct descendant on his mother's side of Queen Victoria. The First World War compelled his father to resign as First Sea Lord and led to the family changing its name. Louis entered the navy and served in both World Wars. In April 1942 appointed Chief of Combined Operations. In August 1943 named as Allied Supreme Commander in South East Asia. When he arrived the Allied forces had been worsted almost everywhere by the Japanese. During the next two years, the tide began to turn, notably in Burma, but the war in the east was ended by the atomic bomb. Mountbatten then had to deal with the post-war situation, notably in Indo-China and the Dutch East Indies. He doubted whether the pre-war colonial situation could ever be restored and, for example, in Burma made terms with Aung San, who had cooperated with the Japanese up to a late date. His apparent acceptance of the necessity for decolonisation may have played a part in Clement Attlee's invitation to him in December 1946 to become Viceroy of India. Mountbatten was able to negotiate a very free hand for himself and was responsible for key decisions, such as the setting of independence in 1948 and then advancing it to 1947. He came to accept the necessity of partition, although he disliked the Muslim leader, Jinnah. He hoped that some degree of cooperation and coherence between India and Pakistan would continue but this perished in the communal violence of the autumn of 1947. Mountbatten's handling of the transfer of power remains acutely controversial. His critics maintain that such precipitate withdrawal, with boundaries unsettled, leading to massive refugee problems and thousand of casualties, could have been avoided by more patient negotiation; his defenders claim that speedy action prevented even greater violence and loss of life. He left India in June 1948 to resume his naval career. From 1959 to 1965 he was Chief of Defence Staff. He was assassinated by the IRA at Mullaghmore on 27 August 1979.

Moyne, Lord (Walter Edward Guiness) (1880–1944) British politician and traveller. Born in Dublin. Served in both the South Africa War

(1899–1902) and the First World War. Became a Conservative MP in 1907. Travelled very extensively, particularly in the Middle East. Chairman of the West Indian Royal Commission, 1938–39. Colonial Secretary, 1941. Sent to Cairo, 1942, and, in June 1944, became Minister-Resident in the Middle East. On 6 November 1944 he was assassinated in Cairo by the Stern Gang.

Mugabe, Robert Gabriel (b. 1924) Rhodesian (Zimbabwean) politician. Largely self-educated, he became a teacher in 1942 and worked in Ghana, where he was influenced by Nkrumah. He became deputy secretary-general of the Zimbabwe African People's Union (ZAPU) in 1961. He was arrested in 1962 and fled to Tanganyika, where he formed the Zimbabwe African National Union (ZANU) with Ndabiningi Sithole in 1963. He was detained in Rhodesia from 1964 to 1974; after which he spent five years in Mozambique. In 1976 ZANU and ZAPU, led by Joshua Nkomo, cooperated to form the Patriotic Front and carried on guerrilla activities against the regime in Rhodesia. In 1979 he attended the Lancaster House Conference, called to discuss the granting of legal independence to Rhodesia. In 1980 he defeated Nkomo and Muzorewa in the first post-independence elections and became Prime Minister. Himself a member of the majority Shona peoples, he was accused of creating a one-party state and discriminating against the second-largest group, the Matabele. When ZANU and ZAPU merged in 1987, he became 'Executive President' with extended powers.

Munongo, Godefroid (b. 1925). Katangan (Congo) politician. Descended from the rulers of Katanga before the Belgian colonisation, he was a founder member of the Confédération des Associations Ethniques de Katanga (CONAKAT) and was Moise Tshombe's chief lieutenant when he formed his secessionist government in July 1960. He denied accusations of complicity in Lumumba's murder. When Tshombe became President of the Congo in June 1964, Munongo became Minister for the Interior. He lost power after Mobutu's coup in 1965.

Mutesa, Sir Edward (Kabaka Mutesa II) (1924–69) Kabaka (King) of Buganda. He was the son of Sir Daudi Chwa II, 24th Kabaka of Buganda, the largest of the political units which made up Uganda. He succeeded his father in 1939 at the age of fifteen but was not crowned until 1942. He was educated at King's College, Budo, and Makerere College (later the University), and at Magdalene College, Cambridge. He served briefly in the Brigade of Guards. He played a leading part in demanding independence for his country and refused to allow it to be joined in a federation with neighbouring Kenya and Tanganyika. In 1953 the British

Governor, Sir Andrew Cohen, exiled him to London, where he established himself as a popular character, whom the newspapers called 'King Freddie' (Frederick was the third of his seven Christian names). He was allowed to return in 1955. After independence in 1962, his continued defence of the special position of Buganda and its Kabaka led him into conflict with the President, Milton Obote. In May 1966 Ugandan government troops attacked his palace and he was forced into exile in Britain again.

Muzorewa, Bishop Abel (b. 1925) Bishop of the United Methodist Church and Rhodesian (Zimbabwean) politician. He led the opposition to the proposals put foward in 1971 by Sir Alec Douglas-Home and Iain Smith to end the illegal regime in Rhodesia. He led the African National Congress delegation at the Victoria Falls talks in 1975 and again represented them in Geneva in 1976. He was exiled to Lusaka but returned to Rhodesia in 1977. Less hard-line than some of his colleagues, he signed the internal Rhodesian settlement of 1978, which did not receive international acceptance. He was a member of the transitional government, 1978–80, but was heavily defeated by the more uncompromising Robert Mugabe in the 1980 elections.

Nasser, Colonel Gamal Abdel (1918–70). Soldier and Egyptian politician. Educated at the Royal Military Academy at Sandhurst. Fought in the 1948 Arab-Israeli war. The officer corps blamed the King, Farouk, for their defeat and Nasser was the principal founder of the Free Officers movement, which compelled Farouk to abdicate in 1952, although the first titular leader was the more senior Colonel Neguib. Nasser displaced Neguib in 1954 to become Prime Minister and the Chairman of the Revolutionary Council, which governed Egypt at this time. Nasser was determined to build the Aswan High Dam, which he was convinced was essential for the Egyptian economy. When the West withdrew its financial support because of his dealings with Eastern bloc countries, Nasser nationalised the Suez Canal. This provoked armed intervention from Britain, France and Israel. On this occasion world opinion saved Nasser. He brought about a rather artificial union with Syria in 1958 which lasted until 1961. In 1967 he closed the Gulf of Aqaba to Israeli shipping. In the ensuing Six Day War Israel comprehensively defeated Egypt, Syria and Jordan. His prestige was damaged but he remained President until his death.

Neguib, Mohammed (1901–84) Egyptian soldier and politician. He was a founder and the first leader of the Free Officers movement, formed by soldiers who blamed King Farouk for their humiliation at the hands of the Israelis. Farouk was deposed in 1952 and Neguib became President of Egypt but he was overthrown in 1954 by his younger colleague, Nasser.

Nehru, Jawaharlal (Pandit Nehru) (1889–1964) Indian nationalist and first Prime Minister of independent India. Born in Allahabad, the son of a wealthy and westernised Brahmin family of Kashmiri origins. Educated at Harrow and Cambridge where, unusually, he read science. Read for the Bar at the Inner Temple, 1910–12. On his return to India he worked with his father, Motilal, who was already involved in the Indian National Congress. According to his own account, the Amritsar massacre in 1919 altered his thinking and he was drawn into Gandhi's non-cooperation campaign in 1920. He was arrested in 1921 and was imprisoned intermittently between then and 1945, spending a total of nearly nine years in gaol, a time which he employed reading and writing. Unlike Gandhi, he was never a mystic or a religious leader. Much more modern in outlook and welcoming economic advance, he first became acquainted with peasant poverty in the 1920s. In some ways he took a harder line than Gandhi, demanding independence, rather than Dominion status. In 1926–27, he travelled in Europe and visited the Soviet Union, but, while wanting a secular and socialist state, he was not attracted by communism. He first became President of the Indian National Congress in 1929. Imprisoned again during the Second World War, he was invited to join the Viceroy's Council in September 1944, becoming Vice-President and responsible for external affairs. Mountbatten regarded him as the most important Indian leader with whom he had to negotiate after the war. After Gandhi's assassination in 1948, he stood alone as India's leader. The first general election after India's new republican constitution came into force in 1950 gave the Congress party an overwhelming victory. He set about a vigorous campaign to modernise his country and deal with the problem of poverty by a series of five-year plans. He became an important international leader, preaching that the nations of Africa and Asia must remain 'non-aligned' and not be drawn into the confrontation between America and the Soviet Union. His critics felt that his high moral tone on international politics accorded badly with his willingness to seize Hyderabad in 1948 and Goa in 1961. He undoubtedly had a blind spot on Kashmir, where the majority population was Muslim, but which he wished to keep in India. A brief war with Pakistan in 1947 led to a *de facto*, and unsatisfactory, partition of the province.

Nehru, Motilal (1861–1931) Indian lawyer and moderate nationalist leader. The father of Jawaharlal Nehru. Of Kashmiri Brahmin descent, he was born in Allahabad. He travelled widely in Europe and at first hoped that his son would join the elite Indian civil service. Became President of Indian National Congress in 1919. He became rather more radical in his views during the First World War and was briefly imprisoned for his activities in 1921. In 1922 he was one of the founders of the Swaraj (Freedom) party. Brought up in the United Provinces, a Hindu (of rather relaxed observance), his mother tongue was Urdu, and he hoped for Muslim–Hindu unity, which he believed to be entirely attainable.

Neto, Agostino (1922–79) Angolan politician. Nationalist leader against the Portuguese. Frequently imprisoned, 1952–62. President of the People's Movement for the Liberation of Angola (MPLA), 1962–74, and led the guerrilla movement against the Portuguese. Became President of Angola on independence in 1975. Called in Cubans to help him defeat South African-backed rivals.

Ne Win, U (b. 1911) Burmese politician. Was Chief of Staff of the collaborationist army in Japanese-occupied Burma, 1942–44, but changed sides and led a pro-Allied guerrilla force against the Japanese in 1944. Became second-in-command of the army when Burma became independent in 1948. Caretaker Prime Minister, 1958–60. Seized power in a coup in 1962. President of one-party state, 1974–81.

Ngo Dinh Diem, (1901–1963) Vietnamese politician. Catholic and anti-communist. Served as provincial governor under the French in 1929–32 but turned against the French and founded the National Union Front in 1947. Exiled to the United States. Returned in 1954 after Geneva Agreements to become Prime Minister to the Emperor, Bao Dai. Ousted Bao Dai and became President of South Vietnam in 1955 following a rigged referendum. His regime was unpopular and he was assassinated in November 1963 by army officers with probable CIA connivance.

Nkomo, Joshua (b. 1917) Zimbabwean nationalist leader. Born in Matabeleland, although himself a member of a minority tribe. Became politically active in 1950s. President of Zimbabwe African People's Union (ZAPU) in 1961. At first prepared to accept 1961 constitution, which would have given Africans a minority of seats, as a first step, but then rejected it and boycotted elections. Placed under government restrictions. Quarrelled with fellow nationalist, Sithole, in 1963. Tried, unsuccessfully, to reach compromise with Prime Minister, Ian Smith, in 1975. In 1976 formed Patriotic Front with Mugabe's ZANU to work for black majority rule in an independent Zimbabwe. Given a cabinet post by Mugabe after independence in 1980 but dismissed in 1982.

Nkrumah, Dr Kwame (1909–72) Ghanaian (Gold Coast) politician. Born Francis Nwia Kofi, the son of a goldsmith from the western part of the Gold Coast, he was educated at Catholic mission schools and considered becoming a priest but instead trained as a teacher at Achimota. Influenced by Aggrey and wished to go to America. Went to America by way of London in 1935. Studied at Lincoln University and the University of Pennsylvania. As he recounted in his *Autobiography*, he studied 'revolutionaries and their methods'. In London, 1945–47. Attended 5th Pan-African Conference in Manchester in 1945 and remained committed to Pan-African cause. Became secretary of West African National Secretariat in Gray's Inn Road, which became meeting place for African students. Also belonged to inner group, 'The Circle', with clearly revolutionary aims. In 1946 Danquah invited him to return to organise the United Gold Coast Convention, not realising how much more radical Nkrumah's view were. Nkrumah was arrested following riots in Accra. In 1949 founded Convention People's Party. Arrested again after organising strikes and boycotts but released after his party won the 1951 elections. Arden-Clarke invited him to become 'Leader of Government Business', in effect Prime Minister. Before the 1956 election Britain promised to set a date for independence if a majority wished for it. Date set for 6 March 1957. In post-independence Ghana, as it was now called, Nkrumah created a one-party state. Gained virtually dictatorial powers in 1960. In foreign affairs aligned himself with the Communist Powers. Had made many enemies at home and the army and police carried out a successful coup against him when he was visiting Pekin (Beijing) in 1966. He died in exile in Conakry.

Nkumbula, Harry (1916–83) Zambian (Northern Rhodesian) politician. The son of a chief, he qualified as a teacher in 1934 and took a job on the Copperbelt. He was awarded a scholarship to Makerere College in Uganda and later to the London School of Economics. He was already interested in politics and, in Northern Rhodesia, had joined the Kitwe African Society. In London he was associated with Jomo Kenyatta and Kwame Nkrumah in the Africa Committee, whose agenda was independence for the African colonies. In 1950 his scholarship was withdrawn because he was suspected of subversive activities and he returned home. He turned down an offer of a government job and became a trader. In 1951 he turned full-time to politics and became president of the Northern Rhodesia African National Congress, which led the opposition to the Central African Federation. He gathered a group of young men round him, of whom the most important was Kenneth Kaunda, the future leader of an independent Zambia. He was imprisoned for a short time in 1955 for possessing subversive literature, but the younger men regarded him as insufficiently radical, and in 1958 Kaunda and others left him to form the Zambia National Congress. The 1962 elections did not produce a clear majority and Nkumbula took part in a coalition as Minister of African Education. But the 1964 elections, after the dissolution of the Central African Federation, almost wiped out Nkumbula's party in favour of Kaunda's.

Nuri es Said, General (1888–1958) Soldier and Iraqi politician. The son of an official of the Ottoman empire, he first came into contact with Arab nationalism before 1914 and joined the secret al-Adh (Covenant) Society. In 1916 he joined the Arab revolt and worked with Feisal. Joined Feisal in Iraq in 1921. Became Minister of Defence in 1922 and Prime Minister in 1930. Signed Anglo-Iraqi treaty of 30 June 1930. Ousted from power by opponents in 1936–38 and 1940–41. Pro-British and caused Iraq to declare war on the Axis Powers during the Second World War. Joined in the war against Israel, 1948–49. Active in establishing the Arab League in 1954. Joined Baghdad Pact in 1955 but the following year supported Gamal Nasser in his nationalisation of the Suez Canal. Died in the Baghdad rising with King Feisal II on 14 July 1958.

Nyerere, Julius Kambarage (b. 1922) Tanzanian (Tanganyikan) politician. He was the son of a chief but his childhood was spent in poverty. Educated at a Roman Catholic boarding school near Musoma and the Government Secondary School in Tabora. In 1943 he went to Makerere College in Uganda and returned to teach in a Roman Catholic school in Tabora, 1945–49. The Church sponsored him to go to the University of Edinburgh. After graduating, he returned to Tanganyika to teach in 1952. In 1953 he became president of the Tanganyika African Association. The following year he transformed this from a mainly social to a political organisation, the Tanganyika Africa National Union (TANU). In 1955 he testified before the United Nations Trusteeship Council. In 1957 he became a nominated member of the Legislative Council but resigned after four months. He worked full-time for TANU in 1958 and 1959 and the party won 70 of the 71 elected seats in the 1960 elections. Nyerere became Chief Minister. He resigned a month before independence in December 1961 to concentrate on building up TANU. In the 1962 elections he gained 97 per cent of the vote and became President when Tanganyika became a republic. He survived an army mutiny in January 1964 with the aid of British troops. The mutiny coincided with the revolution in neighbouring Zanzibar when the Arab-dominated government was overthrown. In April 1964 he announced the formation of a union between Tanganyika and the Zanzibar People's Republic, which later took the name of Tanzania. He created a one-party state in Tanzania. During the Cold War, the West suspected him of communist leanings, although his avowed policy was non-alignment and even his critics conceded that he energetically tackled Tanzania's social and economic problems.

Obote, Milton, (b. 1925) Ugandan politician. The son of a chief in northern Uganda. He spent some time at Makerere College but left in 1950 without graduating. He wished to study in either the United States or Britain but failed to obtain the necessary finances. He worked for a time as a labourer in Kenya, first in a sugar works and then with a construction company. In Kenya he became interested in trade unionism and in politics. He was an active member of Jomo Kenyatta's Kenya African Union until it was banned at the time of the Mau Mau emergency. He subsequently took part in organising the social clubs which took the place of the banned political parties. He returned to Uganda in 1957 and became a member of the Uganda Legislative Council. In the elections of October 1958 he was returned as a Uganda National Congress member but, in 1960, he split from the UNC and founded his own party, the Uganda People's Congress. The 1960 elections were boycotted in Buganda, the largest of the four kingdoms which made up Uganda. In the confused politics which followed, Obote led the opposition but his most important work was to make an alliance with the Buganda party, the Kabaka Yekka, and persuade Buganda to join in the negotiations for Ugandan independence. In the April 1962 elections the UPC-Kabaka Yekka coalition won 68 of the 92 seats. Obote became Prime Minister and the Kabaka, Mutesa II, President, but the coalition did not last and in April 1966 Obote engineered a coup, by which he became Executive President. A new consitution destroyed the autonomy of Buganda. In 1971 Obote himself was deposed by Idi Amin while attending a Commonwealth Conference in Singapore. He went into exile in Tanzania. Ugandan dissidents and the Tanzanian army invaded Uganda in 1979 to depose Idi Amin. Obote was elected President in 1980 but again deposed in 1985.

Odinga, Ajuma Oginga (1912–1994) Kenyan politician. Educated at Makerere College, Uganda, he taught for a time before turning to politics and business. When Jomo Kenyatta organised the Kenya African Union in 1946, it was mainly a Kikuyu movement but Odinga brought in members of his own tribe, the Luo. When Kenya became independent in December 1963, Odinga became Minister of Home Affairs, one of several Luos in the Cabinet. A year later, when Kenya became a republic, he became Vice-President but he resigned in April 1966, accusing his colleagues of conspiring against him. He then formed his own party, the Kenya People's Union, with a more radical land programme, but it had little electoral success.

Ojukwu, Lt Col. C.O. (b. 1933) Nigerian soldier and Biafran politician. Born in northern Nigeria but of Ibo descent. His father, Sir Odumegwu-Ojukwu, was one of the wealthiest men in Nigeria. He was educated in Lagos and then at Epsom College, Surrey, before going to Lincoln College, Oxford, 1952–55, where he read history. Returned to Nigeria and worked in the civil service in eastern Nigeria before again going to Britain to train as a soldier. Taught officer cadets in Ghana before again returning to Nigeria. Served in the Congo with the United Nations peace-keeping force. He was promoted rapidly. In 1964 he was appointed to command the 5th Battalion in Kano in northern Nigeria. After the military coup of January 1966 he became Military Governor of Eastern Nigeria. The following year he announced the secession of the Eastern States as the independent Republic of Biafra. He became the President of Biafra. When Biafra was finally defeated in the ensuing civil war he fled, in January 1970, to the Ivory Coast.

Olympio, Sylvanus Epiphanio, (1902–63) Togo politician. Born in Lomi, when still under German rule. Educated at the University of Vienna and the London School of Economics. Returned to West Africa in 1926 and was employed by United Africa Company, reaching the highest post then held by an African in a multinational company. Leader of Ewe movement, which wished to unite the part of Togoland which had been mandated to France with that mandated to Britain and obtain independence. The French administration succeeded in keeping Olympio out of power for some years but he used Togoland's continued status as a trust territory to appeal to the United Nations. Won 1958 elections, supervised by the United Nations. As Prime Minister went to Paris with Ahmadou Ahidjo of the Cameroons (also a trust territory) and secured independence in 1960. Became President in 1962. Assassinated during military coup on 13 January 1963.

Ormsby-Gore, William George Arthur, 4th Baron Harlech (1885–1964) British politician. Educated at Eton and Oxford. Served in Egypt during the First World War and in 1916 joined the Arab Bureau as an intelligence officer. In March 1917 he became parliamentary private secretary to Lord Milner. He was impressed by Zionism and formed a friendship with Chaim Weizmann. Appointed the British liaison officer with the Zionist mission sent out to Palestine in March 1918. A member of the British delegation at the Paris Peace Conference in 1919 and the first British member of the League of Nations Mandate Commission, 1921–22. Under-Secretary at the Colonial Office, 1922–29, apart from the period of the Labour government in 1924, when he was chairman of the all-party commission which visited East and Central Africa. He advised against federating the territories but secured a £10 million loan for developments, which was the forerunner of the 1929 Colonial Development Act. Colonial Secretary, 1936–38. The most pressing problem was Palestine, where the Arabs were demanding an end to Jewish immigration. A Royal Commission reported that the Mandate was becoming unworkable and recommended partition and the creation of a small Jewish state. Ormsby-Gore persuaded the government, but not Parliament, of the merits of this idea. He also disapproved of the government's appeasement policy and took the opportunity of his succession to the title in May 1938 to resign. He was British High Commissioner to South Africa, 1941–44, and Chairman of the Bank of British West Africa, 1951–61.

Padmore, George (Malcolm Ivan Meredith Nurse) (1902–1959) West Indian politician and writer. Born and educated in Trinidad. Went to USA in 1924 and studied at Columbia University, New York University Law School and elsewhere. Joined Communist Party in 1927. 1929, went to USSR and became head of Negro Bureau of the Red Institute of Labour Unions. In 1931 went to Germany to head the International Trade Union Committee of Negro Workers. Edited *Negro Worker* and published *Life and Struggles of Negro Toilers.* Quarrelled with the Communist Party and was formally expelled in 1934. Moved to England. 1937, Published *Africa and World Peace* and became associated with the Pan-Africanist cause. Active in organising the 5th Pan-African Conference in Manchester in 1946 and formed a friendship with Kwame Nkrumah. Published *The Gold Coast Revolution* (1953) and *Pan-Africanism and Communism* (1956). Moved to Ghana in 1957 as an adviser to Nkrumah but died unexpectedly in 1959.

Pétain, Henri Philippe (Marshal) (1856–1951) French soldier and politician. A hero of the First World War. Led the campaign against the rebels in Morocco, 1925–26. Minister of War, 1934. Became Prime Minister in June 1940 as the German armies swept through France. Negotiated the Armistice with Germany. Headed what became known as the Vichy regime. Tried for treason after the war and sentenced to death but reprieved by General de Gaulle.

Pethick-Lawrence, Frederick William, Baron (1871–1965) British Labour politician. Educated at Eton and Oxford. Called to the Bar, 1899. Moved by the conditions in the East End of London. Strong supporter of women's suffrage. Entered Parliament in 1923 as a Labour MP. Member of Round Table Conference on India, 1931. Secretary of State for India, 1945. In 1946 led the 'Cabinet Mission' to try to persuade the Indian National Congress and Muslim League to compromise and save the unity of India, and came near to success. On 20 February 1947 made the announcement that Britain would leave India not later than June 1948. Resigned in April 1947 because of failing health.

Pol Pot, (Pseudonym) Saloth Sar (1928–98) Kampuchean (Cambodian) leader. Joined underground Communist Party in 1946. Student in Paris, 1950–53. Became secretary of Kampuchean Communist Party in 1963 and organised Khmer Rouge guerrillas, who captured capital, Phnom Penh, in 1975. Prime Minister, 1976–79. Attempted to destroy western influence and recreate wholly agricultural society. Responsible for three or four million deaths among his own people in one of most brutal twentieth-century regimes. Overthrown by Vietnamese army in 1979 but continued guerrilla activities.

Powell, J. Enoch (1912–98) British politician and scholar. Educated at King Edward School, Birmingham, and Cambridge. Professor of Greek, Sydney, Australia, 1937–39. Served in the Second World War. Entered Parliament in 1950 and held various offices under Conservative governments but regarded as a maverick. In 1959 denounced Kenyan government for death of eleven Africans in Hola Camp. Became notorious in the 1960s for strong attacks on Commonwealth immigration, which was affecting his Birmingham constituency. Partly responsible for the 1968 Commonwealth Immigration Act, which restricted entry of Kenyan Asians expelled by Idi Amin. Left Conservative Party in 1974 because he disagreed with European policy, but sat in Parliament as Ulster Unionist, 1974–92.

Rabemananjara, Jacques (b. 1913). Malagasy poet and politician. He joined the French administration in 1939 and, being in Paris at the time of the fall of France, was unable to leave. Became well-known as a writer and poet. Returning to Madagascar, in 1946 he was elected to the French National Assembly. He became the first secretary-general of the Democratic Movement for Malagasy Revival and campaigned for self-government. He was imprisoned in France after the 1947 rising but returned to Madagascar when it became independent in 1960 to become Economics Minister.

Radcliffe, Cyril John, Viscount Radcliffe (1899–1977) Lawyer. Born in Wales. Educated at Haileybury and New College, Oxford. Called to the Bar in 1924. Director General of Ministry of Information, 1941. Lord of Appeal in Ordinary, 1949. Chaired many commissions and committees of enquiry including, in 1947, the two Boundary Commissions which attempted to determine the frontiers of India and Pakistan before the partition of the country became operative under the Government of India Act.

Rahman, Tunku Abdul (b. 1903) Malayan politician. First Prime Minister and Minister of External Affairs in Malay Federation in 1957 and first Prime Minister of Malaysia when it was formed in 1963. Resigned in 1970 after public unrest.

Ravoahangy, Andrianavalona, Joseph (b. 1893) As a medical student in 1916 he was deported to the Comores Islands by the French for campaigning for Malagasy home rule. He returned to complete his studies and practised as a doctor. He founded medical and dental trade unions. In 1945 he represented Madagascar in the French Constituent Assembly, which drew up the constitution of the Fourth Republic. He established the Democratic Movement for National Revival (MDRN) to work for independence. He was arrested and exiled after the 1947 uprising. He returned after independence in 1960 to become Minister of Health.

Richards, Arthur Frederick, 1st Baron Milverton (1885–1978) British colonial governor. Educated at Clifton College and Oxford. Entered colonial service in 1908 and was posted to Malaya. Under-Secretary to the government of the Federated Malay States, 1926. Governor of North Borneo, 1930, still under Chartered Company administration. Governor of the Gambia, 1933. Governor of Fiji and High Commissioner for the Western Pacific, 1936. Governor of Jamaica, 1938, at a time of serious disorder. Governor of Nigeria, 1943–47. His name is particularly associated with the 1946 constitution. The constitution was not popular with the Nigerians, who complained he had consulted too little. Richards maintained that consultations would have been fruitless because of the deep divisions and he had tried to keep a balance between a unified and a federal structure. After his retirement he was, at various times, a director of the Colonial Development Corporation, the Bank of West Africa and the West Indian Sugar Company.

Roosevelt, Franklin Delano (1882–1945) American President. Democrat. Became President in 1933 and instituted the 'New Deal' to combat the effects of the Depression. Although he could not at first overcome the isolationism of his countrymen, he supported Britain in 1940–41 by Lend-Lease arrangements, 'lending' wartime supplies in return for the lease of bases. Had close relations with Winston Churchill but he was not sympathetic to the continuation of the European empire. At the Casablanca Conference in 1943 encouraged Moroccans to seek independence. At the Yalta Conference in February 1945 (when he may already have been seriously ill) pursued rather contradictory policy, half-believing the British empire was too powerful and must be checked, half-believing that Britain was no longer a truly Great Power and that he must seek agreements with the Soviet Union. Died suddenly in April 1945.

Sadat, Anwar al- (1919–81) Egyptian politician. Joined Free Officers in 1950 after the humiliation of the war with Israel. Participated in 1952 coup, which overthrew the monarchy. Was Vice-President at the time of Nasser's death in 1970 and was elected as his successor. Attempted to reach a settlement with Israel and signed Camp David treaty in 1978. He was assassinated by the army in 1981.

Salazar, Antonio de Oliveira (1889–1970) Portuguese dictator. Prime Minister, 1932–68. Main architect of fascist-style constitution of 1933. He maintained Portuguese neutrality during the Second World War. He was determined to keep the Portuguese empire intact and made few or no concessions to the new post-war situation.

Salisbury, 5th Marquess of, (Robert Arthur James Gascoyne-Cecil, courtesy title before succeeded to Marquisate, Lord Cranborne) (1893–1972) British politician. Educated at Eton and Oxford. Served in the First World War. Entered Parliament as a Conservative, 1929. Mainly concerned with foreign policy and was associated with Winston Churchill in opposition to both appeasement in Europe and reform in India. Helped to delay the passage of the Government of India Act of 1935. In Churchill's wartime government became Dominion Secretary, 1940–41. Went to the Lords in January 1941 to act as spokesman there on foreign affairs. In February 1942 became Colonial Secretary, and Dominion Secretary again in September 1943. In 1943 declined offer to become Viceroy of India. In 1952 became Secretary for Commonwealth Relations. Strongly supported Eden on Suez intervention in 1956. Did not get on well with Eden's successor, Harold Macmillan, and in March 1957 resigned over the release of Archbishop Makarios. Thereafter strongly opposed decolonisation in Africa, culminating in his attack on Iain Macleod. He admitted that Rhodesian Unilateral Declaration of Independence was unconstitutional in 1965 but made it clear he sympathised with it.

Schuman, Robert (1886–1963) French politician. Prime Minister from November 1947 to July 1948 but, more importantly, Foreign Minister under ten successive governments, 1948–1953. Author of the 'Schuman Plan' and responsible for setting up the European Coal and Iron Community, the forerunner of the European Economic Community.

Selwyn-Lloyd, John Selwyn Brooke, Baron Selwyn-Lloyd (1904–78) British politician. Educated at Fettes College and Cambridge. Lawyer. Served in the Second World War. Entered Parliament as a Conservative in 1945. In 1951 became Under-Secretary at the Foreign Office; in 1954, Minister of Defence; and in December 1955, Foreign Secretary. Played leading role in the Suez intervention in 1956 but, unlike Eden, remained in office after it. Chancellor of the Exchequer, 1960–62. Speaker of the House of Commons, 1971.

Senghor, Leopold Sedar (b. 1906) Senegalese poet and politician. In 1962 he was a strong contender for the Nobel Prize for Literature. He was educated mainly in France, including the University of the Sorbonne. He obtained the *Agrégé de Grammaire*, the highest French academic qualification. He taught at the Descartes Lycée at Tours, 1935–38, and at the Marcellin Bertholet Lycée in Paris, 1938–44. He was a member of both French Constituent Assemblies at the end of the Second World War, that of October 1945–June 1946 and that of June–October 1946. From November 1946 until November 1958 he represented Senegal as a Deputy in the French National Assembly. During Faure's ministry, 1955–56, he served in the Prime Minister's Office and from July 1959 to July 1960 he was Minister-Counsellor for Cultural Affairs, Education and Justice. He also represented France at UNESCO (United Nations Economic, Social and Cultural Organisation). While a member of Faure's government he played an important role in the negotiations which led to Tunisian independence and, despite his apparent integration into French metropolitan affairs, he was one of the first western-educated Africans to state clearly that Africans must be given the right of self-determination. In 1948 he organised the Indépendants d' Outre Mer, a rival organisation to Houphouët-Boigny's Rassemblement Démocratique Africain, as well as the Bloc Démocratique Sénégalais. Neither his long absence in Europe, nor the fact that he was a Roman Catholic in an overwhelmingly Muslim country and a member of a minority tribe, damaged his high prestige in Senegal. When the country became independent in August 1960, he became its President. He defeated an attempted coup by his Prime Minister, Mamadou Dia, in December 1962, even though the latter had some army backing. While respecting French culture, Senghor was an early exponent of the idea of *négritude*, stressing the value and autonomy of African culture. He was largely responsible for the first World Festival of Negro Arts, held in the Senegalese capital, Dakar, in 1966. He wished to see cooperation between the former French colonies in West Africa and explored the possibility of creating a link between all French-speaking countries, which would roughly parallel the British Commonwealth, but he rejected Nkrumah's ideas of the political unification of Africa.

Sihanouk, Prince Norodom (b. 1922) Cambodian leader. Elected Head of State following his father's death in 1960.

Simon, Sir John Allsebrook, 1st Viscount Simon (1873–1954) Lawyer and British Liberal politician. Called to the Bar, 1899. Liberal MP, 1906–18, 1922–40. As a lawyer he specialised in cases from the Dominions. In 1927 appointed chairman of the statutory committee set up to review the workings of the Government of India Act of 1919. The committee reported in 1930 but it had been resented by the Indians because it was a parliamentary committee with no Indian representation and its proposals were overtaken by events, Lord Irwin's suggestion of a Round Table Conference and the 1929 Labour government's sympathy with the idea. Simon subsequently held a variety of offices, including Foreign Secretary, Home Secretary and Lord Chancellor.

Sithole, Revd Ndabaningi (b. 1920) Zimbabwean (Rhodesian) churchman and politician. A Congregational minister, he was the Chairman of the Zimbabwe African People's Union (ZAPU), but when he split from Nkomo in 1963, he became the leader of the Zimbabwe African National Union (ZANU). He was imprisoned in 1963 and when he was released in 1974 he went to Zambia and was associated with Bishop Muzorewa and the African National Council. In 1976 he broke with Muzorewa and attended the Geneva Conference. Leadership of ZANU was at this time in dispute between Sithole and Mugabe. He returned to Rhodesia in July 1977 and again allied with Muzorewa. In March 1978 he became a party to the internal Rhodesian agreement, which led to the formation of a transitional government.

Smith, Ian Douglas (b. 1919) White Rhodesian leader. Born in Rhodesia and educated there and at Rhodes University in South Africa. Served with distinction as a fighter pilot in the Second World War. Entered Rhodesian politics in 1948. In 1953–61 a member of the ruling United

Federal Party. In 1961 became a founder member of the Rhodesian Front, which wanted immediate independence for Rhodesia, without African majority rule. Became Prime Minister in April 1964. Issued illegal Unilateral Declaration of Independence in November 1965. After Britain applied sanctions, he met British Prime Minister, Harold Wilson, in unsuccessful negotiations on HMS *Tiger* in 1966 and on HMS *Fearless* in 1968. In 1977 reached internal agreement on majority rule and Bishop Muzorewa formed a government in which Smith became minister without portfolio. In 1980 he became a MP in the elections after official independence.

Smuts, Jan Christian (1870–1950) South African soldier and politician. Of Boer descent, he fought against the British in the South African War of 1899–1902 but subsequently became an elder statesman of the British Commonwealth. Prime Minister of the Union of South Africa, 1919–24 and 1939–48. Many Afrikaaners saw him as too pro-British and too liberal on racial questions. In the 1948 election he was narrowly defeated by the hard-line and pro-*apartheid* Daniel Malan.

Soglo, Gen Christophe (1909–83) Soldier and Dahomey politician. Born in Abomey, he joined the French army in 1931. He distinguished himself in the Second World War, serving in France and Morocco, and took part with the Allied forces in the landings in Corsica, Elba and the south of France. After the war he was appointed to the Colonial Forces general staff and in 1947 became military adviser to the Minister for Overseas France. He served in the Indo-China war and was awarded the Croix de Guerre (1956). He served in Senegal, 1956–60, before becoming military adviser to the President in the newly established Dahomey Republic. The following year he became Chief of Staff. He staged an army coup in October 1963, when the country was crippled by a general strike, but re-established civil government the following year. He staged another coup in November 1965 and this time retained power until overthrown by army coup in 1967.

Soulbury, Lord (1887–1971) British politician. Educated at Uppingham and Oxford. Called to the Bar, 1911. Conservative MP, 1929–41. Held various offices in the National government after 1931. In November 1944 became chairman of the Commission on Constitutional Reform in Ceylon, which reported in October 1945, recommending internal self-government as a step towards Dominion status. His proposals were accepted. After Ceylon became independent, he was Governor-General, 1949–54.

Souphanouvong, Prince (1912–95) Leader of Pathet Lao, resistance movement against the French, which later made common cause with the Vietminh. President of Laos, 1975–86.

Stanley, Oliver Frederick George (1869–1950) British Conservative politician. Served in the First World War and called to the Bar in 1919. Became a Conservative MP in 1924. Colonial Secretary during the Second World War, 1942–45. Put in train some developments which only took effect after the war.

Stevens, Siaka (1905–88) Sierra Leone trade union leader and politician. In 1943 he was one of the founders of the United Mineworkers' Union and in 1945 was nominated to the Protectorate Assembly to represent workers' interests. He subsequently studied at Ruskin College, Oxford. He was at this time a member of Milton Margai's Sierra Leone People's Party and in 1951 he became Minister of Lands, Mines and Labour. But, after losing his seat in the Legislative Assembly in 1957, he joined Albert Margai's People's National Party. He attended the 1960 London conference to discuss independence but quarrelled with other delegates and eventually formed his own All-People's Congress Party (APC). Mayor of Freetown, 1964–65. The APC won the 1967 elections, but this result was temporarily overturned by the army. Became President in 1971 and introduced a one-party state in 1978. He alienated the trade unions and there was a general strike in 1981. Retired 1985.

Suharto, General Mohamed (b. 1921) Indonesian general and politician. Officer in Japanese-sponsored Indonesian army, 1943. Chief of Army Staff, 1965–68. Assumed emergency powers in March 1966. Prime Minister, 1967. President, 1968.

Sukarno, Ahmed (1901–70) Indonesian nationalist leader. Graduated in engineering and seemed destined for a career in Dutch service, but studied Indian nationalism and came to admire Gandhi. In 1929 founded the National Party. Imprisoned in 1929 and again in 1937. He was exiled from Java when the Japanese invaded. The Japanese released him in 1942 and he worked with them. On 17 August 1945, with Dr Hatta, proclaimed the independence of Indonesia. President of Indonesia. Suharto effectively took power from him in March 1966.

Swinton, 1st Earl (Philip Cunliffe-Lister) (1884–1972) British politician. Educated at Winchester and Oxford. Called to the Bar, 1908. Served in the First World War. Conservative MP, 1918–35, after which he went to the Lords. Colonial Secretary, 1931, undertook economic survey of the colonies and re-organised the colonial service. Minister Resident in West Africa, 1942–44, where he organised the war effort, both economic and military from Accra. Secretary of State for Commonwealth Relations, 1952.

Telli, El-Hadj Boubacar Diallo (1925–77) Guinean civil servant and first secretary-general of the Organisation of African Unity. A member of the Foulah tribe, he attended the Dakar Lycée and studied at the Paris Faculty of Law, where he took his doctorate. In 1951 he was the first black African admitted to the École de la France d'Outre-mer, the training ground for senior colonial administrators. In 1957 he became secretary-general of the Grand Council of French West Africa. After Guinea refused to join the French Community in 1958, he became, in 1959, Guinean representative in the United Nations and Ambassador to the United States. In 1963 he was Vice-President of the UN General Assembly and chaired the committees on decolonisation and on South African *apartheid.* In 1964–72 he became the first secretary-general of the new Organisation of African Unity. Returned to Guinea and became Minister of Justice. In July 1976 arrested for supposed implication in a plot to overthrow the government. There is circumstantial evidence that he was tortured and then starved to death, dying 25 February 1977.

Templer, Gerald W.R. (1898–1979) British soldier. Educated at Wellington College and Sandhurst. Regular army. Served in both World Wars and between the wars in Persia, Iraq, Egypt and Palestine. Vice Chief of the Imperial General Staff, 1948–50. In 1951, when Sir Henry Gurney, the High Commissioner in Malaya, was assassinated, Templer was sent out to head both military and civil operations. Successfully put down the communist insurgency; almost unique in this period in defeating guerrillas but the explanation was probably that the rebels were Chinese and did not have the support of the local Malayan population. In 1955 became Chief of the Imperial General Staff.

Thatcher, (Hilda) Margaret (Baroness Thatcher) (b. 1925) British Prime Minister. Became Conservative MP, 1959. Leader of Conservative Party, 1975. Prime Minister, 1979–91. Prime Minister at the time of the Falklands War with Argentina in 1982. Opposed the use of sanctions against South Africa.

Tilak, Bal Gangadhar (Lakamanya, that is 'revered one') (1856–1920) Indian nationalist leader. A Brahmin, born in Maharashtra. Educated at Deccan College and Elphinstone College but turned against western education. Wished to uphold Hindu caste system and all traditional values. Defended child marriage and opposed education for women and vaccination against smallpox. Unlike his rival, Gokhale, he was prepared to advocate violence and even political assassinations. Differences came to a head over the partition of Bengal. Gokhale was regarded as the leader of the 'Moderate' party in the Indian National Congress, Tilak of the 'Extremists'.

Todd, Reginald Stephen Garfield (b. 1908) White Southern Rhodesian politician. The son of a missionary, he was regarded as being on the liberal side of white politics. He became Prime Minister of Southern Rhodesia in 1953, when the Central African Federation was formed with Northern Rhodesia and Nyasaland. His party, the United Federal Party, rejected him as too liberal in 1958, and after the Unilateral Declaration of Independence he was subject to government restriction orders in 1965–66 and 1972–76. He attended the Geneva talks in 1976 and acted as an adviser to Joshua Nkomo.

Tombalbaye, François (Ngartha) (1918–75) First President of the Chad Republic. A teacher by profession, he was a founder of the Chad Progressive Party (PPT), led by Gabriel Lisette, which was affiliated to the RDA. In 1957 he became a member, and subsequently Vice-President, of the Grand Council of French Equatorial Africa. His relations with Lisette became strained and in May 1959 he replaced him as Prime Minister of Chad. When Chad became independent in 1960 he became President. In1968 he called in French forces to help fight guerrillas of FROLINAT, northerners who had opposed him since 1966. In 1972 Colonel Qadaffi of Libya, who had previously supported the northerners, changed his policy and aided Tombalbaye but the war did not end. In 1973 Tombalbaye inauguarated a cultural revolution to restore Chad customs and changed his own name from François to Ngartha. He was assassinated in a coup on 13 April 1975.

Touré, Ahmed Sekou (1922–84) One of the most radical leaders of French-speaking Africa during the independence struggle. President of Guinea for 26 years. The son of a peasant farming family in Faranah, a village on the Niger, he claimed descent from Samory Touré, who had fought the French until his capture in 1898. At the age of fifteen he was expelled from technical college for leading a strike. He became a post office clerk and soon became a trade union leader. Forged links with the GCT (Confédération Générale du Travail), the French equivalent of the TUC, which was Communist-dominated, and in 1950 became Guinean secretary-general of the GCT's coordinating committee for French West Africa. But in 1957 he broke with the French Communist Party and became the first secretary-general of UGTAN (General Union of Workers of Black Africa). In 1946 he had been a founder member of Houphouët Boigny's RDA (African Democratic Rally), and in 1952 became the secretary-general of the PDG (Guinean Democratic Party), the Guinean branch of the RDA. He was elected mayor of Conakry in 1955 and the deputy representing Guinea in the French National Assembly, 1956–58. In 1957 he became Vice-President (virtually Prime Minister) of the Government Council of Guinea. He was strongly opposed to General de Gaulle's concept of the French Community, although, in opposition to Houphouët-Boigny, he wished to keep a West African federation in being. His was the only territory to vote 'No' in the 1958 referendum. Guinea left the French Union and Touré became Head of State in October 1958. This caused a quarrel with his previous ally, Houphouët Boigny, who favoured a 'Yes' vote. France immediately cut off all aid, although some technical cooperation was resumed after 1959. His attempts to 'go it alone' had mixed success. He attempted, unsuccessfully, to bring about a union with Ghana and Mali. He sought aid from both the United States and the Eastern bloc. Unfortunately, he saw plots everywhere and in 1966 arrested the American Ambassador and expelled the (American) Peace Corps. But he again turned to France and the United States for aid in the 1980s. The army took over after his death.

Truman, Harry S. (1884–1972) American President. Democrat. As Vice-President, he succeeded to the presidency on Roosevelt's unexpected death in April 1945. Elected in his own right in 1948. Pursued vigorous anti-communist policy. In 1947 enunciated 'Truman Doctrine', spelling out US determination to contain the communist advance. Closely associated with the creation of NATO. Assisted European nations to overcome economic crisis at the end of the Second World War by the 'Marshall Plan', named after the Secretary of State, George C. Marshall. The United States provided $17 billion worth of aid. Prepared to withhold aid to force compliance with American views. Some contradictions began to emerge between American anti-colonialism and anti-communism, especially in South East Asia, but this became more obvious after Truman left office in 1953.

Tshombe, Moise Kapenda (1919–69) Congolese politician. Born at Musumba in Katanga, the son of a wealthy businessman, he descended from the royal family of the Lunda tribe, which had an extensive empire in medieval times. He was educated at an American mission school. He went into the family business, but after failing badly at that he turned to politics. In 1956 he became the president of the Confederation of Mutual Associations of the Lunda Empire which, although originally a non-political body, became in 1959 the basis of the political Confédération des Associations du Katanga (CONAKAT). In January 1960 he attended the Brussels Conference called to decide the future of the Congo. His plans for a loose federation lost out to Patrice Lumumba's plans for a strong unitary state. On 11 July 1960, eleven days after the Congo became independent, he declared Katanga an independent republic and on 8 August the Katanga Assembly elected him Head of State. Katanga was extremely rich in mineral wealth and he had the financial backing of the Belgian-controlled Union Minière du Haut Katanga. He also had the support of neighbouring Northern Rhodesia and tacit sympathy from France and Belgium. His action was, however, strongly condemned by most African leaders, who feared similar secessionist tendencies in their own countries. The murder of Lumumba on Katangan soil completed his international disgrace. United Nations troops entered Katanga in August 1961 but Katanga's secession only finally came to an end in June 1963. Tshombe went into exile but was recalled by President Kasavubu to become Prime Minister of the whole Congo in July 1964. He crushed subsequent rebellion with the aid of white mercenaries and, in November 1964, Belgian paratroopers. Kasavubu, fearing that Tshombe meant to seize the presidency, forced him to resign in October 1965. When Mobutu seized power, Tshombe was forced into exile. He was sentenced to death in absentia but his plane was hijacked to Algeria, where he remained under house arrest until his death.

Tsiranana, Philibert (1912–78) First President of the Malagasy Republic. From a peasant family, a teacher by original profession, he was partly educated in France at Montpellier. In 1952 he was elected to the Madagascar Representative Assembly and in 1956 to represent Madagascar in the French National Assembly. In 1956 he founded the Social Democratic Party (PSD). In October 1958 when Madagascar became internally self-governing, he became head of the provisional government. In May 1959 he was elected President and proclaimed the independence of the Malagasy Republic in June 1960. He was re-elected in 1965 and January 1972, but in May 1972 was compelled to surrender power to the army.

Turnbull, Richard (b. 1909) British civil servant. District officer in Kenya, 1931; Chief Secretary there, 1955. Governor of Tanganyika, 1958. High Commissioner, Aden and Protectorate of Southern Arabia, 1965.

Twining, Edward Francis, Baron Twining (1899–1967) British colonial governor. Joined regular army but, after two tours of duty in Uganda, transferred in 1928 to the colonial service. Served in Uganda, 1929–39; Mauritius, 1939–43; St Lucia, 1943–46; Governor of North Borneo, 1946–49 and Governor of Tanganyika, 1949–58. In North Borneo he had to deal with the aftermath of the Japanese occupation and the transfer of administration from the Chartered Company to the Colonial Office. In Tanganyika, he achieved some personal popularity by touring the country but had little sympathy with the political changes and could not establish a relationship with Nyerere.

Wavell, Archibald Percival, Field Marshal, 1st Earl (1893–1950) British soldier and Viceroy of India. Was in command in Palestine and Transjordan in 1937–38 during serious disturbances. Became Commander-in-Chief in the Middle East in July 1939 just before the outbreak of the Second World War. He offended Winston Churchill by ordering a British withdrawal from Somaliland but launched a successful campaign in the Western Desert, which reached Tobruk, although the British were later compelled to retreat. Crete was lost but Syria deserted Vichy France. In July Wavell was replaced by Auchinlek and sent as Commander-in-chief to India. In December 1941 he was made Supreme Commander in the South West Pacific but could not save Singapore. In June 1943 he was made Viceroy of India. He agreed no constitutional progress could be made during the war and was confronted by the Bengal famine and the presence of the Japanese in Burma. In 1945 he ordered the release of the Congress leaders from gaol so that negotiations could begin. The Cabinet Mission failed and Wavell told the Prime Minister, Clement Attlee, in despair that Britain must either resign herself to remaining in India for another decade or hand over the government to the only functioning authorities, the provincial governments. Attlee rejected the advice and replaced Wavell by Mountbatten in February 1947.

Weizmann, Chaim, (1874–1952) Zionist and first President of Israel. Born in Russia. Studied at University in Berlin. Chose to settle in Britain as the country most likely to sympathise with Zionist aspirations. Research chemist at Manchester University. Became leader of Zionist pressure group. Had particular influence with the British government during the First World War because of the importance of his scientific work to the war effort and had direct influence on Balfour Declaration of 1917. Principal Zionist speaker at the Paris Peace Conference in 1919. Head of World Zionist movement after 1920. During the Second World War he exerted his main efforts in the United States. President of Israel, 1948–52.

Williams, Eric (1911–81) First Prime Minister of independent Trinidad and Tobago, 1962–81. Born and received early education in Trinidad. Went to the University of Oxford where he graduated BA in 1932 and D.Phil. in 1938. In 1939 went to the USA and joined the faculty of Howard University. While there he served on the Caribbean Commission to co-ordinate the economic development of the region. Returned to Trinidad in 1955 and founded the People's National Movement. His party won a landslide election in 1961 when the Federation of the West Indies was breaking up and he became Prime Minister. The author of numerous books, including *Capitalism and Slavery.*

Wilson, (James) Harold (1919–96) Lord Wilson of Rievaulx. British politician. Entered Parliament in 1945 and was elected Leader of the Labour Party in 1963. A cabinet minister, 1947–51, and Prime Minister, 1964–70 and 1974–76. The main phase of British decolonisation was over before he became Prime Minister but he tried unsuccessfully to resolve the dilemma created by Rhodesia's Unilateral Declaration of Independence in 1965.

Wilson, Thomas Woodrow (1856–1924) President of the United States. He brought the United States into the First World War, having originally tried to maintain a position of neutrality. He was determined to inject a new morality into international affairs. He supported the creation of the League of Nations and issued his Fourteen Points, supplemented by other statements such as the Four Principles, which he hoped would provide the basis for the post-war world. He suffered a serious stroke in 1919 and was unable to persuade his country to join the League of Nations.

Yameogo, Maurice (b. 1921) Upper Volta politician. Born in Koudougou, a member of the dominant Mossi tribe. He was educated at a seminary and then became a clerk in the French West African administration. In 1946 he became a member of the Grand Council of French West Africa, representing first the Ivory Coast and then Upper Volta. He was an active trade unionist and a founding member of the RDA (African Democratic Rally). He later founded his own political party, the Voltaic Democratic Movement. Although it came second to the RDA in the 1957 elections, Yameogo became Minister of Agriculture. The coalition later broke up and Yameogo rejoined the RDA, becoming Minister of the Interior. He succeeded Ouezzin Coulibaly as Prime Minister in 1958. When Upper Volta became independent in 1960, he became President. He declined to merge with either Mali or Ghana, preferring a loose grouping of French-speaking West African states. Personal extravagance made him unpopular and he was overthrown by the army in January 1966.

Yembit, Paul-Marie (b. 1917) Gabonese politician. Educated at a Roman Catholic mission school and in Lambarene, he first went into business. From 1952 to 1957 he served on Gabon's Territorial Council. In 1957 he became Minister of Agriculture and subsequently of Labour and the Civil Service. At independence in 1960 he was deputy secretary-general of the Gabon Democratic Bloc (BDG) and second in command to Leon M'ba. From 1961 to 1966 he was Vice-President of the National Assembly.

Youlou, Abbé Fulbert (1917–72) Priest and politician of Congo Republic (formerly part of French West Africa). Educated at a seminary in Brazzaville and subsequently in Gabon and Cameroun, he was ordained in the Roman Catholic Church but suspended from the priesthood in 1956. He continued to use the title 'Abbé' and wear ecclesiastical dress. He entered politics in 1955. In 1956 he founded the Union Démocratique pour la Défense des Intérêts Africains (UDDIA) and was elected mayor of Brazzaville. In 1957 his party won half the seats in the Territorial Assembly. The Assembly proclaimed the Congo Republic in November 1958 and he became Prime Minister. In 1959 the UDDIA gained a large electoral victory and in November he was elected President. He organised a conference in Brazzaville in 1960 from which emerged the 'Brazzaville Bloc' of twelve countries, all moderate and pro-western. He supported Tshombe's secession in Katanga. He came to be regarded with suspicion by more radical politicians and was overthrown in August 1963, despite calling in the assistance of French troops. He was detained but escaped in March 1965 and went into exile.

Zinsou, Dr Emile-Derlin (b. 1918) Dahomey politician. The son of a teacher, he studied at the William Ponty school and the Medical College in Dakar. Qualified as a doctor in France. He was a councillor of the Assembly of the French Union, 1947–53, and in 1948 headed the Assembly's enquiry into the bloodshed in Madagascar. A founder member of the African Democratic Rally (RDA) and of Dahomey's first mass political party, the Dahomey Progressive Union (UPD). He was an enthusiastic supporter of African unity and prominent in the African Federation Party (PFA). He was defeated in the 1953 elections and returned to medical practice but in 1955 was elected a member of the French senate and joined Leopold Senghor's Overseas Independents Party (IOM). He held various ministries in Dahomey, both before and after independence, including that of Minister for Foreign Affairs, 1960–63 and 1965–66.

Glossary

Achimota College. Established near Accra on the Gold Coast in 1924. Prepared students for London University examinations and provided training for primary teachers. Kwame Nkrumah was among its alumni. The Asquith Commission, appointed by the British government in 1943 to advise on the development of higher education in the British colonies after the war, recommended that Achimota develop towards university status, as did Walter Elliott's Commission of 1945. It became the University College of the Gold Coast linked to the University of London on 11 August 1948, and a university in 1961.

Action Group. Nigerian political party, led by Chief Awolowo and particularly associated with the Western Region.

African Democratic Rally. Anglicisation, sometimes used in the press, of Rassemblement Démocratique Africain.

African National Congress (ANC). Founded at a meeting in Bloemfontein in 1912 as the South African Native National Congress. Like the Indian National Congress, in its early days it was a predominantly middle-class and socially conservative body formed to protest at the continued exclusion of most non-Europeans from the franchise after the Union of South Africa Act of 1909 and the introduction of segregationist legislation by the new government. It changed its name to African National Congress in 1923 but did not become a mass movement or exercise much political influence until the *apartheid* era. The Sharpeville shootings of peaceful demonstrators in 1960 galvanised it. Nelson Mandela and others formed Umkhonto we Sizwe (Spear of the Nation) to begin an armed struggle. Mandela was arrested and the ANC 'banned', that is declared illegal. The ANC established bases in Zambia but could not mount an effective guerrilla campaign until white rule collapsed in Angola, Mozambique and Rhodesia. In 1990 the South African government began a process of conciliation by 'unbanning' the ANC and releasing Nelson Mandela. The ANC's claim to represent all Africans in South Africa was challenged, but unsuccessfully, by Inkatha, a Zulu-based movement. The ANC won an overwhelming victory at the 1994 elections.

Afro-Asian bloc. Name given to a grouping of African and Asian Powers at the United Nations, which increased in size and importance as more and more European colonies became independent.

Afro-Shirazi Party (ASP). Zanzibar political party, formed by Africans to counter Arab dominance.

Ahimsa. The principle, particularly associated with the Jain religion, of doing no harm to any living creature. Linked to the ideas of Mahatma Gandhi.

AKEL. Cypriot Communist Party.

Algérie Française. Slogan of the French settlers in Algeria and their supporters affirming their belief that Algeria was French.

All People's Congress. Sierra Leone political party, led by Shika Stevens.

Alliance des Bakongo (ABOKO). Originally a social and cultural group among the Bakongo tribe in the (Belgian) Congo, organised into a political party by Joseph Kasavubu in 1955.

Amritsar massacre. 10 April 1919. Following unrest in the Punjab, the British Commander, General Dyer, forbade public meetings. Nevertheless a crowd gathered in the Jalianwala Bagh in Amritsar (some for the annual horse fair, unaware of the prohibition, some for political reasons). Dyer ordered his men to open fire, unaware that locked gates prevented the crowd from dispersing. At least 329 people were killed. Dyer was censured by the Hunter enquiry committee and retired from active service, but the tragedy permanently damaged Anglo-Indian relations at a critical moment just before the 1919 Government of India Act.

Ansar. Sudanese political party, which wanted the Sudan to be independent of Egypt as well as of Britain.

Anti-Fascist People's Freedom League. Burmese coalition, led by Aung San, which negotiated independence with Britain in 1946–47.

Apartheid Literally 'apartness' (Afrikaans). A quasi-theological doctrine of racial separation evolved by Afrikaans thinkers in the 1930s and put into practice in South Africa by Daniel Malan's government after 1948. In theory it allowed for the 'separate but equal' development of Africans, notably in the Bantustans, or 'Homelands' set up in 1959. In practice it meant discrimination on grounds of race in employment, housing and social life (for example in the petty *apartheid,* which forbade Africans or those of mixed race to use the same hotels or sporting facilities as whites). It was increasingly condemned in the United Nations, as more ex-colonies joined the organisation, but action was difficult because of the prohibition on intervention in the internal affairs of member states, although South Africa's irregular position in South West Africa (Namibia) after 1946 opened a door.

Arab League. Established by Egypt, Lebanon, Iraq, Syria, Transjordan, Yemen and Saudi Arabia in March 1945 to encourage Arab cooperation and unity. Subsequently joined by other Arab states. Has generally supported Palestinians in their struggles with Israel. Has been dominated by Egypt throughout most of its history but Egypt was excluded from membership, 1979–89, following the conclusion of the Egyptian Peace Treaty with Israel and the headquarters of the League were moved from Cairo to Tunis.

Ashanti. Powerful confederation of tribes resident in the Gold Coast (Ghana).

Ashiqqa. Sudanese party, which favoured union with Egypt.

Ashram. Literally, hermitage. Particularly used of Mahatma Gandhi's home at Ahmedebad, where he lived a very simple life, surrounded by his disciples.

Assimilation. The ideal on which the French empire was built. Believing that the principles of the great revolution of 1789, founded on the writings of the French philosophers of the eighteenth century on how human society should be governed, were of universal application, the French had no inhibitions in interfering in other people's societies (unlike the British – see Burke). They hoped that the inhabitants of their colonies would become 'assimilated' to French culture and would be content to be governed from Paris, where their representatives would take part in government. It broke down in the nineteenth century, partly because of the vast numbers of colonial subjects suddenly acquired, partly because some cultures (particularly in Algeria and Indo-China) proved unexpectedly resistant to French ideas. It was replaced in part by the idea of *association.*

Association. After the French ideal of *assimilation* had broken down in the nineteenth century, the idea of *association* was substituted. This meant the more modest objective of cooperation between France and its colonies and protectorates without fully assimilating their inhabitants to French culture and political practices.

Axis. Term for the alliance of Germany, Italy and Japan during the Second World War.

Baghdad Pact. (Later the Central Treaty Organisation.) Designed to combat Soviet influence in the Middle East. It was signed by Turkey and

Iraq in February 1955, by Britain in April, by Pakistan in September and by Iran in November. The United States became associated with it by a number of bilateral agreements in 1959. It was strained by the Anglo-French intervention in Suez in 1956.

Balfour Declaration. Statement made by the British Foreign Secretary, A.J. Balfour, promising a 'national home' for the Jews in Palestine after the war, provided it did not prejudice the civil and religious rights of non-Jews resident there. The promise was made in a letter to Lord Rothschild (2 November 1917) and subsequently published.

Balfour Report. Report of the Inter-imperial Relations Committee, chaired by Lord Balfour (A.J. Balfour), accepted by the 1926 Imperial Conference. This became the classical definition of the British Common-wealth and, more particularly, of the status of the Dominions within it. It read, in part,

> The Committee are of opinion that nothing would be gained by attempting to lay down a Constitution for the British Empire . . . it defies classification and bears no real resemblance to any other political organization which now exists or has ever been tried . . . [Britain and the Dominions] are autonomous communities . . . equal in status, in no way subordinate one to another in any aspect of their domestic or external affairs, though united by a common allegiance to the Crown, and freely associated as members of the British Commonwealth of Nations . . . The British Empire depends . . . on positive ideals. Free institutions are its life-blood. Free co-operation is its instrument.

Bamako Conference. Meeting of political leaders from French West and Equatorial Africa in the Ivory Coast capital in 1946, which led to the estab-lishment of the RDA (Rassemblement Démocratique Africain, African Democratic Rally), which became the most important nationalist grouping in French Africa, with affiliated parties all over West and Equatorial Africa. The moving spirit was Félix Houphouët-Boigny and it had links with the French Communist Party. Its main weakness was that some leading politicians, notably Leopold Senghor of Senegal, had not been in Bamako and came to form a rival grouping.

Bantu. Strictly a linguistic term denoting a family of African languages and the people who speak them. Has fallen into some disrepute because used during the *apartheid* era in South Africa to mean a black African with few rights.

Bataka. A Ugandan political party, principally supported by the peasant farmers.

Berlin West Africa Conference, 1884–85. An international conference, called after other nations had protested about a bi-lateral Anglo-Portuguese agreement on the Congo. It laid down the ground rules for recognising European territorial claims in Africa and led directly to the Scramble for Africa as each country hastened to establish its claims.

Biafra, Republic of. The name given to the Eastern Region of Nigeria, which broke away to form a separate state in May 1967. The secession was not accepted by the rest of Nigeria and a civil war began in July 1967 which lasted until January 1970, when the Biafran army surrendered and Nigeria was reconstituted.

Black Consciousness. Similar to the French idea of *négritude*. A sense that the black races of the world are in no way inferior to the white races but have their own history and identity. An early exponent of the idea was Edward Blyden. It was important in encouraging Africans to assert their rights against the Europeans. A later exponent was Steve Biko, whose death in police custody in South Africa helped to unite world opinion against *apartheid*.

Black Power. A more political concept than Black Consciousness. Particularly associated with the radical black movement in the United States in the late 1960s and 1970s, but had resonances in the colonial or ex-colonial world.

Boer War, 1899–1902. Also called the Anglo-Boer War or the South African War. A war between Britain and the autonomous Boer Republics, the Transvaal and the Orange Free State. Although Britain won the war, it deeply divided British opinion, and the peace made many concessions to the Boers, particularly on the matter of the franchise, which helped them later to establish the *apartheid* regime.

Brahmin. The highest of the four Hindus castes; the priestly caste. Both Gokhale and Tilak belonged to it. (Gandhi did not.)

Brazzaville Conference. Conference which met 30 January–8 February 1944, attended by senior administrators from French West and Equatorial Africa, to discuss what should be done after the war. General de Gaulle was also present. Although the deliberations were partly intended to win American support for the Free French, the emphasis was more on assimilation and a greater say for the colonies in decision-making, than on decolonisation as it was later understood.

Briggs Plan. The strategy during the Malayan Emergency of bringing Chinese civilians into 'protected' villages, where they could neither supply, nor be intimidated by, the guerrillas. It worked largely because the indigenous Malay population did not sympathise with the guerrillas. It failed in other countries where it was tried, whenever there was natural sympathy between the general population and the guerrillas.

British India. Term used during the British Raj to mean that part of India which was under direct British rule (about half the sub-continent), as distinct from the Princely States, which Britain controlled more indirectly through the Indian rulers.

British South Africa Company. Chartered Company, founded by Cecil John Rhodes in 1889, which ruled Northern and Southern Rhodesia until 1923/24.

Buganda. The largest and most important of the four political units which made up the British colony of Uganda. Owed allegiance to its own Kabaka or King and often wished to assert its own separate identity.

Burghers. People of mixed Dutch and Singalese descent, resident in Ceylon (Sri Lanka).

Burns Constitution. 1946 constitution in the Gold Coast, called after the Governor, Sir Alan Burns. Regarded as very advanced at the time because it provided for an elected African majority in the Legislative Council.

Cabinet Mission. Mission of three cabinet ministers, Lord Pethick-Lawrence, A.V. Alexander and Sir Stafford Cripps, sent to India by the new Labour government in 1946 to seek agreement on the transfer of power. They proposed a form of federation but eventually both the Indian National Congress and the Muslim League rejected it.

Casablanca Conference, January 1943. Wartime conference of Allied leaders in Morocco. Important in a colonial context because Moroccans realised that Americans sympathised with their desire for independence after the war.

Central African Federation. Federation of Northern and Southern Rhodesia and Nyasaland, set up in 1953.

Chama Cha Mapinduzi Party (CCM) (Revolutionary Party). Formed in 1977 by merger of Tanganyika African National Union and Afro-Shirazi Party.

Chamber of Deputies. Elected Lower House of French Parliament under the Third Republic.

Church of Scotland. Presbyterian church 'established', i.e. part of the constitution, in Scotland. Had important educational role in many parts of Africa, especially Nyasaland (Malawi).

CIA. (American) Central Intelligence Agency. Sometimes took an active role in supporting or destablising regimes, according to whether they were regarded as being in the United States' interest.

Citizens. Normally those with full civil rights, including the franchise, but for full discussion see under Subjects.

Civilisados/cidados. Terms used in the Portuguese empire meaning citizens, those who had full political and civil rights.

Cold War. The international tension between the United States and its allies on one side and the Soviet Union and its allies on the other, which began in 1947 and lasted until after the changes in Eastern Europe in 1989. It frequently had a direct effect on the colonial situation. Ideologically the communist Powers sympathised with the Third World in its struggles with the 'imperialist' Western Powers, but rarely had either the resources or the inclination to intervene directly. The United States also historically sympathised with independence movements but its actions were often checked by a desire to keep out left-wing, potentially pro-Soviet governments.

Colonists' Association. Pressure group of British settlers in Kenya, founded in 1903.

Colons. French colonists or settlers, especially those in Algeria.

Colour bar. Discrimination in employment, franchise or housing based on an individual's race or skin colour.

Colour blind. Colloquial term applied mainly to British colonial constitutions, denoting that the franchise (or access to office) was not dependent on race.

Comité Révolutionnaire d'Unité et d'Action (CRUA). Revolutionary committee which masterminded the Algerian rising against the French in November 1954.

Communal electorates. Franchise arrangements by which particular communities, usually ethnic or religious communities, vote separately and/or have a certain number of seats reserved for them in the Legislature.

Condominium. Joint rule by two Powers, particularly applied to the Anglo-French government of the New Hebrides and the Anglo-Egyptian government of the Sudan.

Confédération des Associations Tribales du Katanga (CONAKAT). Congolese grouping, led by Moise Tshombe, based in Katanga, the mineral-rich province, which tried to secede in 1960.

Convention of Associations. Often colloquially called the Settlers' Parliament. An organisation of European settlers, formed in 1911, which lobbied, ultimately unsuccessfully, for Dominion status for a 'white' Kenya.

Convention People's Party (CPP). Party founded by Kwame Nkrumah in the Gold Coast in 1949 after he had broken with the United Gold Coast Convention of J.B. Danquah.

Copper Belt. The area of Northern Rhodesia (Zambia) which was rich in copper ore and became the main industrial region.

Coussey Committee. Committee, chaired by an African judge, Mr Justice Coussey, which took evidence and made recommendations on the progress achieved under the Burns Constitution in the Gold Coast. Reported it was already obsolete.

Cripps Offer. The British government proposal, which Sir Stafford Cripps took to India in March 1942, promising that Britain would accept the conclusions of an Indian Constituent Assembly at the end of the war, subject to some safeguards for minorities. Rejected by the Indian National Congress.

Crown Colony. A British colony, which had not yet reached the stage of self-government, although it might have some degree of representative government.

Deir Yassin. A village which was the scene of a particularly brutal massacre of Arab civilians during the 1948 Arab-Israeli war, arousing fears that it was a terror tactic to compel Arabs to flee the country.

Democratic Party. Ugandan political party, initiated by the Roman Catholic bishops and predominantly Catholic in membership.

Destour Party. Literally Constitution Party. Formed in 1912 to demand a modern constitutional state in Tunisia.

Devonshire White Paper, 1923. A very important statement issued by the British government, when the Duke of Devonshire was Colonial Secretary, affirming that Kenya was primarily an African territory and that, if African interests conflicted with those of the immigrant races, European or Indian, African interests must prevail.

Dien Bien Phu, battle of, March–May 1954. Dien Bien Phu was of little strategic significance but the French had committed so much force and prestige to its defence that its loss marked the end of French power in Indo-China.

Dominion. Term used in the British empire to denote a former colony which had achieved internal self-government and, by 1931, full control of its foreign policy. The word was used in the British North America Act of 1867, establishing the Canadian confederation, to avoid offending American susceptibilities by using the word 'Kingdom', which would have been technically correct. The classic definition is in the Balfour Report of 1926.

Dominion status. For definition see Balfour Report. Many colonies aspired to Dominion status as a step to complete independence.

Donoughmore Commission/Constitution. A Commission, chaired by Lord Donoughmore, which enquired into the constitutional position in Ceylon in 1927–28 and resulted in a new constitution in 1931, which was regarded as a model of its kind.

Dual Mandate. The title of a book published by Lord Lugard in 1922 which argued that Europeans had a right to open up the African continent but also a duty to educate the existing inhabitants so that they could share in the benefits of modern civilisation. The phrase came into general use.

Dyarchy. A term particularly associated with India from the Government of India Act of 1919 onwards but occasionally used in other contexts, meaning the division of administration into 'transferred subjects' such as health and education, now the responsibility of the Indians, and 're-served subjects', such as defence and external relations, still under the control of the British.

East African Protectorate. Kenya and, originally, the Eastern Province of Uganda.

Eastern bloc. Term used during the Cold War period to mean the Soviet Union and its satellites.

East India Company. Strictly the English East India Company (to distinguish it from the Dutch and French companies). Incorporated under royal charter on 31 December 1600. It opened up India to British trade, governed Bengal for the Mogul Emperor from 1765, and governed British India in partnership with the British Crown, 1884–58. It surrendered its charter in 1858 and its powers passed to the British Crown.

East of Suez policy. The name given to the contention that Britain must retain a military presence in Asia and the Far East. Some regarded it as untenable after the Suez crisis of 1956, but it lingered on until the late 1960s and, arguably, until the return of Hong Kong to China in 1997.

Elysée Agreement, 1949. The French President, Vincent Auriol, and the Vietnamese Emperor, Bao Dai, agreed that Vietnam should be an 'Associated State' of the French empire.

Enosis. Literal meaning: 'union'. The policy of the Greek Cypriots who wished to unite Cyprus with Greece.

Ethniki Organosis Kypriakou Agonos (EOKA) (National Organisation of Cypriot Struggle). A Cypriot terrorist organisation led by Colonel Grivas, which wanted union with Greece. Most active 1955–59.

Evian Conferences. Discussions in 1961–62 between General de Gaulle and the Algerian Provisional Government which led to an Agreement on 18 March 1962 by which the French accepted Algerian independence.

Evolués. Educated and 'assimilated' Asians or Africans in France's colonies, who were considered to have 'evolved' far enough to be treated as French citizens. Often took important civil service or political roles.

Fabians. Group of British Socialist thinkers, including Sidney Webb, who, in contrast to the Marxists who believed in revolution, believed in the gradual achievement of socialist ideals by democratic processes. Interested in colonial issues and sometimes very influential.

Fashoda. Serious Anglo-French crisis in 1898 when Kitchener's victorious army found a small French detachment under Captain Marchand camped at Fashoda and claiming the Upper Nile for France. Led to demarcation of frontiers and, in part, to Anglo-Egyptian Condominium Agreement on the Sudan in 1899.

Four Principles. War aims of American President, Woodrow Wilson, supplementing the Fourteen Points. It was the Four Principles which specifically enunciated the right to self-determination.

Fourah Bay College. Established in Freetown, now part of the University of Sierra Leone. It was the oldest institution in British Africa providing post-secondary education, mainly teachers' training, linked to the University of Durham in 1876. The most famous member of staff was James Aggrey, the first African Vice-Principal, who influenced a whole generation of African reformers.

Fourteen Points. The war aims of the American President, Woodrow Wilson, to which the other Allied Powers subscribed. They were mainly concerned with the post-war settlement in Europe but the new high standards in the conduct of international relations which were implicit in them were quickly seized on by colonial peoples.

Free French. The French who supported General de Gaulle in carrying on the war against Germany after the French government had surrendered in June 1940.

Free Officers. A group of Egyptian army officers, including Colonel Nasser, angered by King Farouk's incompetent leadership, who finally overthrew him in July 1952.

French Community. The looser organisation of what had previously been the French Union set up after the Fifth Republic replaced the Fourth in 1958.

French Union. The organisation of the French empire set up in 1946 as part of the constitution of the Fourth Republic.

Frente de Libertacão de Mocambique (FRELIMO). (Front for the Liberation of Mozambique), most important liberation movement in Mozambique, founded in 1962.

Frente Nacionalde Libertacão de Angola (FLNA). One of the main liberation movements in Angola.

FRETILIN. Marxist liberation movement in East Timor. Gained independence from Portugal but since 1976 has been engaged in guerrilla struggle with Indonesians who seized territory in December 1975.

Front de Libération Nationale (FLN). A coalition of the main nationalist movements in Algeria, which came together in 1954 and launched an, ultimately successful, war against the French.

Geneva Conference, 1954. Meeting to discuss the Indo-China problem, attended by United States, France, Britain, the Soviet Union, China and representatives of Cambodia, Laos and North and South Vietnam. Agreement in July called for cessation of all hostilities in Vietnam, Cambodia and Laos, and fixed a demarcation line on the 17th parallel in Vietnam, pending elections. The United States expressed reservations and South Vietnam denounced the arrangement. The elections were never held.

Ghana. The name of a West African empire which flourished from the eighth to the eleventh century. It lay to the north of the later British colony of the Gold Coast, but when the Gold Coast became independent in 1957 it took the name Ghana, contending that its peoples were descended from the peoples of the old empire. The precedent of assuming a historic name was widely followed in th ex-colonial world.

GPRA. The Algerian Provisional [Nationalist] Government which met in Tunis in the last days of French rule in Algeria.

Haganah. Jewish Defence Force, set up in 1929, to defend Jews in Palestine at the time of street violence between Jews and Arabs. Played an important role in the 1948 war.

Harijans. Literally 'People of God', a term coined by Mahatma Gandhi to replace the description 'Untouchable'.

Hartal. Strike.

Hindustan. Term coined (but which never came into general use) to describe India after Pakistan had become a separate country.

Hola Camp massacre. Incident in Kenya in 1959 when a number of Kikuyu held on suspicion of involvement in Mau Mau refused to work and were beaten by guards. Eleven died. There was an outcry in Britain.

Hutu. The majority tribe in Ruanda-Burundi but one which has historically been subordinate to the smaller Tutsi tribe.

Imperial British East Africa Company (IBEAC). The British chartered company which opened up Kenya and Uganda. It was always undercapitalised and surrendered its powers to the British government in 1895.

Indépendants d'Outre Mer (IOM). Sengalese political party, founded in 1948 by Leopold Senghor.

Indian Civil Service (ICS). The elite service which administered British India. It was the most prestigious service in the British empire and until after the First World War had no difficulty in attracting high-quality recruits. It set new standards of public probity. Indians were not debarred from it and a few like R.C. Dutt joined it, but recruitment procedures were heavily weighted in favour of Europeans. More Indian recruitment to the ICS was one of the main demands in the early days of the Indian National Congress.

Indian National Conference. This, a purely Indian creation, met in Calcutta for the first time in 1883, attended by delegates from all over India. In 1886 it, in effect, merged with the Indian National Congress, which, because it at that time enjoyed British patronage, was recognised as being likely to have more political influence.

Indian National Congress (INC). By far the most important Indian nationalist organisation, which provided a model for similar organisations throughout the world. It first met in Bombay in 1885. The initiative in calling it had been taken by a retired British official, Alan Octavian Hume, the son of the radical, Joseph Hume. (This was sometimes denied by Indian nationalists, who disliked the idea that the Congress was founded by a Scotsman. It is true that it also had Indian antecedents, especially in the Indian National Conference.) It was at first a very conservative body (although critical of British rule), made up of professional men who had had a western-style education. Muslims were always under-represented and eventually formed their own organisation, the Muslim League. It became a mass organisation in the twentieth century, led by Mahatma Gandhi and Jawaharlal Nehru. As the Congress Party it remained the dominant political force in post-independence India and did not lose a general election until 1977.

Indigenas. Portuguese term meaning 'natives'; those who did not have full civil rights in distinction from the *civilisados* who did.

Indigènes. French term meaning 'natives'; much the same as *sujets.*

Indirect Rule. A term, particularly associated with Lord Lugard, by which in the British empire the administration was left as far as possible in the hands of the existing non-European authorities. It had always been used in Protected States but a constitutional historian, E.A. Walker, wrote in 1943, 'Indirect rule, as it is understood today [is] different. Its fundamental principle is that British Resident and native ruler, District Officer and district or village headman shall all be parts of a single administration, one and indivisible'[1]. It encouraged devolution of responsibility and so, in some ways, made decolonisation easier, but it also tended to strengthen the traditional authorities and so made the accommodation of emerging western-educated elites more difficult.

Irgun. Irgun Zvai Leumi, National Military Organisation. Jewish terrorist organisation founded in 1937 by David Raziel. Its most important leader was Menachem Begin. Responsible for many of the most serious terrorist incidents after 1945, including the blowing up of the King David Hotel and the massacre at Deir Yassin.

Irian Jaya. Formerly Dutch New Guinea.

Istiqlal. Moroccan independence party, formed in 1944.

Jains. Indian religious group. Although the Gandhis were orthodox Hindus, Mahatma Gandhi's mother was deeply influenced by the Jains and, through her, Gandhi may have become acquainted with Jain doctrines such as *ahimsa.*

---

[1] *The British Empire: Its Structure and Spirit,* p. 105.

Jewish Agency. Organisation set up in 1929 to aid Jewish immigration into Palestine. Until the government of Israel was established in 1948, it negotiated with Britain and international organisations on Jewish questions.

Kabaka. Title of the ruler of Buganda.

Kenya African Democratic Union (KADU). One of Kenya's two main political parties prior to independence, favoured a federal structure and was supported by the Masai, but lost influence to the Kenya African National Union.

Kenya African National Union (KANU). One of Kenya's two main political parties prior to independence, led by Jomo Kenyatta, favoured a centralised government and was supported by the Kikuyu. Became the ruling party after independence.

Khadi. Hand-spun and hand-woven cloth. Used as symbol by Indian nationalists.

Kikuyu. Kenyan tribe, predominantly farmers, the group most disturbed by European settlement.

Kikuyu Central Association. Nationalist movement in Kenya founded as Young Kikuyu Association in 1921. More radical than Kikuyu Association founded the previous year. Jomo Kenyatta became its secretary-general in 1929.

Linggadjati Agreement. Agreement which would have divided Indonesia into an Indonesian Republic, exercising jurisdiction over Java, Madura and Sumatra, and the State of Eastern Indonesia with jurisdiction over most of the rest. Signed on 25 March 1947 but Dutch public opinion turned hostile and it never became operative.

Loi cadre. Outline or skeleton law. Law passed by Guy Mollet's government in June 1956. Marked the abandonment of centralisation and *assimilation* in the French empire. Opened the way for the establishment of the French Community.

Loi fondamentale Fundamental law passed in May 1960 setting up a federal state of six provinces in the Belgian Congo.

Mahatma. Literally 'Great Soul'. Title often bestowed on M.K. Gandhi.

Majlis. Iranian Parliament.

Makerere College, now Makerere University, near Kampala in Uganda. Founded as a technical college in 1922, it added teachers' training in 1924. It drew students from the whole of British East Africa and was an important training ground for future leaders.

Manifesto (Algerian). Manifesto drawn up by Ferhat Abbas in 1943 demanding an autonomous Algeria in a federal relationship with France.

Marshall Plan. American plan for the economic reconstruction of Europe after the Second World War, called after the American Secretary of State, George Marshall. Between 1948 and 1952, the United States provided $17 billion in aid, which was vital to the recipient countries and gave the United States considerable influence over their policies, including their colonial policies.

Masai. Kenyan tribe. Nomadic pastoral people. Would have preferred a more decentralised political system to that favoured by the Kikuyu.

Mashona. See Shona people.

Massacre Plot. A supposed plot to murder Europeans in Nyasaland in 1959. Completely discredited by the Report of Mr Justice Devlin who was sent out to investigate.

Matabele. Important but minority group in Zimbabwe. An offshoot of the Zulu people, they had established a dominant position in what became Southern Rhodesia. Their king, Lobengula, signed the agreement which allowed Cecil Rhodes's British South African Company to move into the region.

Mau Mau. Terrorist organisation in Kenya in the 1950s. Confined to the Kikuyu people and probably reflecting the disruption of their life by European settlement. Committed serious atrocities but victims were more often fellow Africans than Europeans.

Mesopotamia. Literally 'between two rivers', the Tigris and the Euphrates, the old name for Iraq.

MI6 Military Intelligence, Section 6. The British intelligence agency concerned with overseas operations, as distinct from MI5, concerned with counter-intelligence at home.

MNRM. Mozambique political party which opposed FRELIMO, 1976–92, with at first South African and Rhodesian support.

Monckton Commission. Commission chaired by Walter Monckton appointed by the British government in 1959 to report on the progress of the Central African Federation. Its report of 1960, stating that each territory should have the right to secede, led to the dissolution of the Federation in 1963.

Montagu–Chelmsford Reforms. The Government of India Act of 1919, named after Lord Montagu, the Secretary of State for India, and Lord Chelmsford, the Viceroy. Its terms disappointed the Indians, who had hoped for more after their support for Britain during the First World War.

Montego Bay Conference, 1947. Conference which led to the setting up of the short-lived federation of British West Indian islands.

Morley–Minto reforms. The Indian Councils Act of 1909, called after John Morley, the Secretary of State for India, and Lord Minto, the Viceroy. Although it provided for only a very modest advance in Indian self-government, it was welcomed at the time in India.

Moslem Association Party (MAP). Small Ghanaian party in the 1950s.

Mouvement Démocratique de la Révolution Malgache (MDRM). Democratic Movement for Malagasy Revival/Revolution.

Mouvement National Congolais (MNC). Congolese National Movement, founded in 1958 by Patrice Lumumba and others.

Mouvement pour l'Evolution Sociale de l'Afrique Noire (MESAN). Movement for the Social Development of Black Africa, led by Barthélemy Boganda.

Mouvement pour le Triomphe des Libertés Démocratiques (MTLD). Coalition of Ferhat Abbas's UDMA and Messali Haj's Algerian People's Party, which contested Algerian elections, 1947–54.

Movimento Popular de Libertacão Angola (MPLA). Popular movement for the Liberation of Angola, founded in 1956, communist in sympathy.

Muslim Brotherhood. A fundamentalist organisation, founded in Egypt in 1928, which wished to establish an Islamic state and shari'a law. It organised demonstrations and helped to compel King Farouk to join in the Arab-Israeli war in 1948, but did not attempt to fight elections as a political party. It was banned by Farouk's government, 1948–51, and by the Free Officers in 1954. Responsible for an attempt to assassinate Colonel Nasser in 1954.

Muslim League. Founded in 1906 by Indian Muslims, who feared that the Indian National Congress was too dominated by the Hindus and who had been alarmed by B.G. Tilak's Hindu fundamentalism. Although there were rapprochements, as in the Lucknow Pact of 1916, relations were frequently strained between the League and the Congress, which continued to assert that it represented all Indians. Relations deteriorated after the 1937 elections and the League committed itself to the establishment of a separate state for Muslim-majority provinces, Pakistan.

National Congress of West Africa. An organisation founded in Accra by J.E. Casely Hayford in 1918 to bring the British colonies in West Africa together and work for more democratic government.

National Council of Nigeria and the Cameroons (NCNC). A party founded in 1942 by Nmande Azikiwe to transcend tribal divisions. In 1944 it merged with the Nigerian Democratic Party but retained its original name.

National Indonesian Party. Party founded in the Dutch East Indies in 1927 by Ahmed Sukarno.

National Liberation Army. The army formed by Algerian nationalists in August 1956, which even 200,000 French troops were unable to defeat.

National Liberation Front. Established in Hanoi in December 1960 to bring together the opposition to Ngo Dinh Diem's government in South Vietnam.

National Liberation Movement. Political party in the Gold Coast in the 1950s, which drew its strength from the Ashanti region.

National Party. Afrikaans-dominated South Africa party. The original National Party had been led by General Hertzog but Daniel Malan broke away in 1934 to form the so-called 'Purified' National Party. It was Malan's party which won the 1948 elections and introduced the policy of *apartheid.*

NATO. North Atlantic Treaty Organisation. A military alliance set up in 1949 by Britain, France, Italy, the United States, Canada, Belgium, Luxembourg, the Netherlands, Norway, Denmark, Portugal and Iceland to combat the perceived threat from the Soviet Union. Greece, Turkey and Western Germany later joined. France left in 1966. Arguably the strongest single grouping in the post-war world.

Négritude. Term in use among French speakers, meaning much the same as Black Consciousness among English speakers. Conscious pride in being black.

Neo-Destours Party. Successor to Destours Party in Tunisia. Founded by Henri Bourguiba in 1934.

Nigerian National Democratic Party. Founded by Herbert Macaulay in 1922 to fight elections under 1922 constitution. Later merged with National Council of Nigeria and the Cameroons.

Northern People's Congress (NPC). Nigerian political party, led by Ahmadu Bello, the Sardauna of Sokoto.

Northern People's Party (NPP). Gold Coast party in the 1950s, representing the traditional chiefs.

Organisation Armée Secrète (OAS). Secret Army Organisation. Terrorist organisation formed by French settlers in Algeria, aided by some elements in the army, in 1961 to resist at all costs the handing of Algeria to the Arab nationalists. Thwarted by General de Gaulle, whom they tried to assassinate.

Organisation of African Unity (OAU). Organisation set up after a meeting in Addis Ababa in 1963, including almost all the then independent black African states. It brought together both the Casablanca group of radical states, including Algeria, Ghana, Guinea, Mali, Morocco and Egypt, and the more pro-western Monrovia group. At its first meeting its members agreed to accept the inherited colonial boundaries, artificial though they were, and so prevented many, although not all, subsequent border disputes. The Organisation has mediated between member states and has been an important pressure group against *apartheid* in South Africa and in securing a settlement in Namibia.

Ottoman empire. Turkish empire, with its capital at Constantinople (now Istanbul), which had ruled most of the Middle East and North Africa and a large part of the Balkans. It began to disintegrate in the nineteenth century. Most of the Balkans had broken away before 1914. Britain, France and Italy had gained control of North Africa. The Arabs threw off Turkish rule during the First World War. At the end of that war Turkey emerged as a much smaller state. The Sultan, the religious leader of millions of Muslims, disappeared. The new Turkey was a secular state, re-organised by Kemal Ataturk along the lines advocated by the Young Turks who had tried to reform Turkey in 1908.

Pakistan A name coined by C. Rahmat Ali in 1933 from **P**unjab, **A**fghan (i.e. North West Frontier Province), **K**ashmir and Baluchi**stan** to signify the Muslim majority areas of North West India. The creation of a separate Islamic state became increasingly attractive to the Muslim League in the late 1930s and was adopted as its official policy in 1940. When Pakistan was created in 1947 it consisted of West Pakistan (Baluchistan, Sind and western Punjab) and East Pakistan (East Bengal and Sylhet, previously part of Assam). East Pakistan broke away in 1971 to become the separate state of Bangladesh.

Pan-African Conferences/Congresses. A series of important, although entirely unofficial, meetings of prominent Africans to discuss matters of common interest. The first such meeting took place in London in 1900. Another, usually regarded as the first in the regular series, took place in Paris in 1919, organised by W.E.B. Dubois. It tried to influence the deliberations of the Peace Conference, not only in relation to the fate of the former German colonies, but also in the direction of setting standards for all colonial powers in Africa. They gained only polite platitudes. Further meetings were held in 1921, 1923 and 1927. The meeting in Manchester in 1945 was of a different order from the others. It was much larger with over 700 delegates. It included many of the most important first-generation nationalist leaders, such as Kwame Nkrumah and Jomo Kenyatta, and politically it was much more radical.

Pan-Africanism. A desire to transcend colonial divisions and both establish cooperation between African countries and allow Africa to speak with one voice. It took a concrete form in the Pan-African Conferences but some African politicians were more enthusiastic than others and it never really bridged the gap between the Anglophone English colonies and the Francophone French colonies as it wished to do. The creation of the Organisation of African Unity in 1963 achieved some of its objectives.

Pandit. Properly, 'one learned in Sanskrit' but became a term of respect bestowed on distinguished Hindus, hence Pandit Nehru (Jawaharlal Nehru).

Paris Peace Conference, 1919. The conference which met to settle the peace after the First World War. Although it included all the Allied nations and the 'friendly neutrals', it was dominated by the Great Powers, Britain, France and the United States. The British Dominions, Canada, Australia, New Zealand and South Africa, gained separate representation, thus recognising their coming of age as national states. Many groups, including the Indian National Congress, tried to lobby the delegates but without much success. The former German colonies were allocated to various Allied Powers, but the introduction of the Mandate System was very important in setting new standards.

Parti de Regroupement Africain (PRA). Party formed in 1958 by Leopold Senghor. Strongly committed to the idea of maintaining some kind of federal structure in the former French West Africa after independence. Included most of the parties not committed to the Rassemblement Démocratique Africain.

Parti National du Progrès (PNP). National Progress Party. Congo party led by Godefroid Munongo.

Parti Populaire Algérien. Algerian People's Party. Founded in 1937 by Messali Haj.

Partido Africano da Independeñcia da Guiné a Cabo Verde (PAIGG). African party for the Independence of Guinea and Cape Verde Islands. Founded by Amilcar Cabral in 1956.

Partnership. Idea popular among liberal whites in Kenya and Southern Rhodesia in the 1950s and early 1960s that there could be a 'partnership' between the races in which each would play its part, sometimes associated with communal electorates. The policy of Michael Blundell and his United Country Party in Kenya. Generally overtaken by more hard-line figures on both right and left.

Patriotic Front. In October 1976 Joshua Nkomo's ZAPU and Robert Mugabe's ZANU formed the Patriotic Front to wage guerrilla warfare against Ian Smith's regime in Rhodesia.

Permufakaten Perhimpunam Poltiek Kebangsaan Indonesia (PPPKII). Union of Indonesian Political Associations. A coalition of nationalist groups brought about by Ahmed Sukarno in 1928.

Pieds noirs. Literally 'black feet'. Nickname for French settlers in Algeria.

Polisario. Movement formed in 1973 with Algerian support to gain independence for the Western Sahara. In 1975 Spain withdrew and control was divided between Morocco and Mauritania. In 1976 Polisario proclaimed an independent Saharan Arab Democratic Republic.

Popular Front. Left-wing coalition government in office in France 1936–37 and briefly in 1938, with Leon Blum as Prime Minister. Initiated various advances in relations between France and its colonies though these were not followed up by subsequent governments.

Princely States. Term used in India during the British Raj to mean states (about half the subcontinent) which remained under their former rulers but whose defence and external relations were controlled by Britain. The British also intervened to a variable extent in their internal policies through 'Residents' or 'Advisers'.

Progress Party. Ghanaian political party led by Dr Busia, which won the 1970 election when civilian government was temporarily restored.

Progressive Liberal Party. Political party in the Bahamas which won the 1972 election on an independence programme and achieved independence in 1973.

Progressive Party. A Ugandan political party founded in 1955, mainly Protestant in membership.

Radcliffe Award. Decision on borders between India and Pakistan announced the day after Indian independence in August 1947, made by Cyril Radcliffe.

Raj. Hindu term meaning kingdom or rule. The period when the British governed India is often referred to as the British Raj (or, in English usage, simply as the Raj).

Rassemblement Démocratique Africain (RDA). African Democratic Rally. The most important nationalist grouping in French Africa, with affiliated parties throughout French West and Equatorial Africa. Founded in Bamako in 1946. Its most important leader was Félix Houphouët-Boigny. Sometimes in conflict with Leopold Sengor and the Parti de Regroupement Africain.

Rassemblement du Peuple Français (RPF). Rally of the French people. The supporters of General de Gaulle after 1946.

Renville Line. Line agreed aboard USS *Renville* in January 1948 separating Sukarno's Indonesian Republic from territories of Malino group still in close relationship with the Dutch.

Representative government. Term important in the constitutional evolution of the British colonies. An important stage was regarded as having been reached when the Legislative Council (or its equivalent) began to include elected or nominated representatives of the inhabitants of the colony. In time elected representatives would become the majority and gain control of the Executive (see responsible government).

Responsible government. Term important in the constitutional evolution of the British colonies. A stage reached in Canada in the 1840s, in the Australian colonies in the 1850s and subsequently in other colonies of settlement and in the twentieth century in other parts of the empire. The Executive government in the colony became responsible (answerable) to the elected Legislature. At first this would apply only to local matters, with defence, external relations etc. remaining the responsibility of the Governor, answerable to the British government. This system was institutionalised in India between the wars under the name Dyarchy. Foreign policy too gradually passed to the control of the local government. The Statute of Westminster of 1931 made clear that the Governor-General in a Dominion no longer had a political role and was not the representative of the British government. Virtually all British colonies evolved through this process, although after 1945 it was more often described as the achievement of ministerial (or occasionally, cabinet) government, rather than the old term, responsible government.

Rhodesian Front. Right-wing European party in [Southern] Rhodesia, led by Winston Field and then Ian Smith, which issued the Unilateral Declaration of Independence in 1965.

Richards Constitution. Nigerian constitution of 1947, called after the Governor, Sir Arthur Richards. Although it represented a constitutional advance, it was open to criticisms of having institutionalised regional divisions.

Round Table Conferences, 1930–32. Meetings held in London between representatives of the main British political parties and of the main groups in India to discuss constitutional advance. They revealed deep divisions between different communities in India.

Round Table Conference, 1949. Meeting in The Hague, at which the Netherlands agreed to Indonesian independence.

Royal Niger Company. British Chartered Company which opened up and administered most of what became Nigeria, 1886–99. In 1899 it surrendered its political and administrative powers to the British government.

San Remo Conference, 1920. An international conference which finalised most of the details of the Mandate System.

Satyagraha. Literally 'truth-force'. Term coined by Mahatma Gandhi to describe his methods of non-violent resistance, which he insisted was not a passive but a dynamic reaction to injustice.

Scheduled castes. Official title, adopted between the Wars, for the Untouchables.

Scramble for Africa. Popular name, coined by *The Times* newspaper, for the partition of Africa between the European powers, 1884–98.

Section Française de l'Internationale Ouvrière (SFIO). French Section of Workers' International. A socialist, as distinct from communist, network to which some parties in French West Africa affiliated.

Senatus consultus. French law of 1895 which made it possible for Algerians to become French citizens and subject to French, not Islamic, law. Not attractive to most Algerians because they saw it as abjuring their religion.

Shona. Majority people of Zimbabwe (Southern Rhodesia).

Sidky–Bevin Agreement, 1946. Agreement between the Egyptian Prime Minister and British Foreign Secretary, by which British forces would have been progressively withdrawn from Egypt. Not ratified.

Sierra Leone People's Party. Party formed in 1951 by Milton Margai to work in the interests of both the Colony and the Protectorate.

Social Darwinism. Philosophy popular in late nineteenth and early twentieth centuries, which purported to extend Charles Darwin's scientific work on the evolution of species to human societies. Justified imperialism on the grounds that the laws of nature determined that the fittest (usually misinterpreted to mean the most aggressive) would survive.

South West African People's Organisation (SWAPO). Founded in 1960. Conducted guerrilla activities, partly from Angola, in the 1970s.

Statute of Westminster, 1931. Important British statute which in effect confirmed the British Dominions as independent nations. The Governor-General ceased to have any political functions or to represent the British government. Britain surrendered all control over Dominion legislation (except over the British North American Act of 1867, the Canadian constitution, which was made an exception at the Canadians' request).

Sterling Area. Set up in 1931, this included all countries that used sterling as the medium of exchange in trade and kept their reserves in London. It included most of the British empire (Canada was a conspicuous exception) and some other countries.

Stern Gang. Terrorist organisation, set up in 1940 by Abraham Stern, who disapproved of Irgun's decision, later rescinded, not to attack the British during the war. Responsible for a number of atrocities, including involvement in Deir Yassin massacre.

Subjects. English and French usage differs. In English usage an individual is properly a citizen of a republic but a subject of a monarchy. To be a 'subject' of Queen Victoria did not imply an inferior condition. On the contrary it conferred rights, as in Queen Victoria's Proclamation of 1 November 1858 promising equality of treatment for all her subjects, English or Indian. (In late twentieth-century English, however, 'citizen' is often substituted for 'subject'.)

In French usage there was a clear distinction between citizen and subject (*sujet*). A citizen had full civil rights. A subject did not and might even be compelled to provide labour services. Most 'natives' in the French colonies were subjects, although citizenship might be acquired by more or less complicated procedures. The distinction between citizens and subjects was abolished by the Lamine Gueye Act of 7 May 1946.

Suez Canal Zone. The area of the Suez Canal. Although it never ceased to be Egyptian territory, it was a very important British base. British troops withdrew there from the rest of Egypt after 1946 and finally evacuated it by agreement with the Egyptians in March 1956. Britain retained rights (effectually cancelled after the Suez crisis later in 1956) to return in the event of an international crisis.

Suez crisis, 1956. The international crisis consequent on Colonel Nasser's nationalisation of the Suez Canal and the Anglo-French military intervention.

Swadeshi. Literally 'of one's own country'. Slogan of an Indian movement beginning in Bengal in 1905 to boycott foreign goods but which leading members of the Indian National Congress such as Gokhale insisted was not merely a negative boycott but a positive re-affirmation of Indian values (see also Khadi).

Swarajya. Self-government. Indian aspiration between the Wars which could, however, be interpreted to mean either Dominion status or complete independence.

Sykes–Picot Agreement, 1916. Anglo-French agreement on their respective spheres of influence in the Middle East after the First World War. The French sphere included Syria, the British sphere included Iraq and Palestine. This largely determined the distribution of the mandates at the end of the war. Italy was angry at being left out. Although it was carefully worded so as not to conflict directly with promises concurrently being made to the Arabs, it led to serious confrontations immediately after the war.

Tamil Tigers. Terrorist movement among minority Tamil population in Sri Lanka in response to what they regard as oppression by the majority Sinhalese population.

Tanganyika African National Union (TANU). Nationalist party founded by Julius Nyerere in 1954, which was to dominate Tanganyikan politics before and after independence.

Third World. Term coined after the Second World War to describe nations which did not belong to either the prosperous Western bloc of the United States and its allies (the First World) or to the Soviet bloc. Included most of Africa and Asia. More or less synonomous with 'undeveloped' (later 'developing') nations.

Thirty comrades. Burmese nationalist leaders, including Aung San, who planned to take advantage of the Second World War to drive the British from Burma with Japanese help.

Trucial States. Now United Arab Emirates.

Tutsi. Minority but traditionally dominant tribe in Ruanda-Burundi.

UDT. Party in East Timor, which opposed FRETILIN.

Uganda National Congress. Founded in 1952, mainly Ganda in membership.

Uganda People's Union. Founded in 1958 mainly to combat Buganda separatism.

Ulama. Founded by Ben Badis in 1931. Intent on asserting Algeria's identity as an Arabic, Islamic nation.

Umma. Sudanese party which wanted independence from Egypt as well as Britain.

Uniho Nacional Par a Independencia Total de Angola (UNITA). Union for Angolan Independence. Nationalist group opposed to communist MPLA. In control of southern Angola at time of independence in 1975. Received support from South Africa. MPLA received support from Cuba. State of civil war continued until 1994 (with break in 1989–93).

Unilateral Declaration of Independence. The illegal declaration of Rhodesian independence by Ian Smith's government in November 1965. Rhodesia finally became legally independent as Zimbabwe in 1980.

Union Démocratique du Manifeste Algérien (UDMA). Founded in 1946 by Ferhat Abbas.

Union of Angolan Peoples (UPA). Nationalist organisation established by Holden Roberto in 1950s to work for Angolan independence.

Union of Soviet Socialist Republics (USSR). Formally ceased to exist on 26 December 1991. Replaced by the Russian Federation of 89 territories, some autonomous. The Baltic States (Latvia, Estonia and Lithuania), Belarus (formerly Byelorussia) and Ukraine became independent nations in 1991.

United Gold Coast Convention. Political party founded by J.B. Danquah in 1947 to work for further constitutional advance. Nkrumah returned to become its general secretary.

United Malays National Organisation (UMNO). Formed in 1946.

United National Independence Party. Founded in 1960 by Kenneth Kaunda and others who felt that Harry Nkumbula's Northern Rhodesian African National Congress was not radical enough.

United Nations Commission to Indonesia (UNCI). The more formal successor to the UN Good Offices Committee, established in January 1949.

United Nations Special Committee on Palestine (UNSCOP). Set up in 1947.

Unofficials. Convenient short-hand term to describe elected or nominated members of Legislative (or less often Executive) Councils in British colonies to distinguish them from the 'official' members, who were there by reason of their job. As a colony grew in maturity, the proportion of unofficial to official members increased (as did the proportion of elected members).

Untouchables. The most oppressed class of Hindus, who fell outside the four Hindu castes. They were usually poor, confined to the worst types of employment, and suffered serious social discrimination. Gandhi championed their cause and called them Harijans (Children of God), but they distrusted the Indian National Congress as being dominated by the caste Hindus and looked for representation of their own. Their case was strongly argued by Dr Ambedkar at the Round Table Conferences in 1930–32.

Vanua'aku Party (VP). Nationalist party in New Hebrides.

Vichy government. Provisional government set up after French surrender to Germany in 1940. The Vichy government and the Free French contended for the loyalty of the French colonies.

Vietcong. The military face of the National Liberation Front. Highly efficient communist guerrillas who operated in South Vietnam, 1961–75.

Vietminh. Originally called Viet Nam Doc Lap Dong Minh, the Vietnam Independence League, founded by Ho Chi Minh in 1941, to work for Vietnamese independence.

Wafd. Literally 'Delegation'. The main Egyptian nationalist party. Organised by Saad Zaghlul in 1918 to demand a voice at the Paris Peace Conference. The British exiled its leaders in 1919, but after the Protectorate ended in 1922 the Wafd was organised as a political party which swept to victory in the 1924 elections on a programme of constitutional government and Egyptian control of both the Suez Canal and the Sudan. Nahas Pasha, who had succeeded Zaghlul as leader, became Prime Minister for the first time in 1928. Nahas negotiated the 1936 Treaty with Britain but the new king, Farouk, dismissed him in 1937. Nahas supported the Allies against the Axis Powers and the British compelled his return in 1942. After the war the Wafd took the lead in demanding the abrogation of the 1936 Treaty and British withdrawal. The party was, however, losing support, partly on suspicions of corruption and after the Free Officers' revolution, the Revolutionary Command Council disbanded the Wafd.

Westminster model. The British system of parliamentary democracy, which the British hoped would be an enduring legacy to all their former colonies. In fact it seldom survived in Africa where independence was almost always followed sooner or later by military coups. It did survive in India, which is the largest parliamentary democracy in the world.

ZANLA. The military wing of the Zimbabawe African National Union which conducted a guerrilla war against Ian Smith's regime, 1966–79.

Zanzibar Nationalist Party. Predominantly Arab in membership and at odds with the the African Afro-Shirazi Party. A radical party with links with Egyptian nationalists.

Zimbabwe. An important culture of South Central Africa, associated with the ruins of Great Zimbabwe. The name chosen for the successor state of colonial Southern Rhodesia, for much the same reason as Ghana became the name of what had been the Gold Coast.

Zimbabwe African National Union (ZANU). African political party formed in Southern Rhodesia in 1963 by Robert Mugabe and Ndabaningi Sithole when they split from Joshua Nkomo's Zimbabwe African People's Union (ZAPU). Cooperated with ZAPU in the Patriotic Front in the struggle against Ian Smith's regime. Now fights elections as ZANU-PF and draws most of its strength from the Shona people.

Zimbabwe African People's Union (ZAPU). African party founded by Joshua Nkomo in Southern Rhodesia in 1961 after his National Democratic Party, which had replaced the moribund Southern Rhodesian African National Congres, was banned by the government. Weakened when ZANU split from it in 1963 but cooperated in the Patriotic Front, 1976–79. Became associated with non-Shona peoples, including Matabele, and did not do well in elections after independence.

Zionism. The movement for the re-establishment of a Jewish state in Palestine. It gained momentum from the persecution of Jews in Russia and Russian-controlled Poland in the late nineteenth century. Theodor Herzl published *Der Judenstaat* in 1896 and organised the first Zionist conference in Basle in 1897. Both Herzl and Chaim Weizmann looked to Britain as the country most likely to be sympathetic to their aspirations, although Weizmann later turned to the United States for support. Britain, as the Mandatory Power in Palestine after the First World War, experienced great difficulty in reconciling its sympathy with Jewish aspirations for a 'homeland' with its promises to protect the interests of the Arabs resident in Palestine. The Holocaust and American pressure after the Second World War led to the setting up of the state of Israel.

ZIPRA. The military wing of the Zimbabwe African People's Union which conducted a guerrilla warfare against Ian Smith's regime, 1966–79.

SECTION SIX

Bibliography

Reference Works

Statesman's Yearbook (Annual)
Whitaker's Almanack (Annual)
Yearbook of the United Nations (Annual)

For the British empire and Commonwealth, *Commonwealth Yearbook* (Annual): first published in 1862 as *Colonial Office List*; *Dominion and Colonial Office List*, 1926–40 (publication suspended during the Second World War); *Commonwealth Relations Office List*, 1951–66; *Commonwealth Office Yearbook*, 1967.

Nothing strictly comparable exists for other European empires but for France there is the *Annuaire statistique de la France d'Outre-Mer* from 1946, and for Portugal *Anuarion Estatistico do Ultramer* from 1943 (available in French translation).

European decolonisation involved practically the whole world and needs to be set in a broader context. Two useful background books are the *Longman Handbook of World History since 1914* by C. Cook and J. Stevenson (1991) and the *Longman Companion to the Middle East since 1914* by R. Ovendale (1992).

Theories of Decolonisation

The most obvious explanation of the European loss of empire after 1945 is that two internecine 'civil wars' in the heart of the European continent had destroyed the economic and political supremacy which had allowed the European nations to conquer the rest of the world in the first place. Two superpowers emerged after the Second World War, the United States of America and the Soviet Union, neither of which was ideologically sympathetic to the idea of empire – although both had large land-based empires themselves, based on the conquest of alien peoples, and, in the case of the United States, had for a time joined in the acquisition of overseas empire in the late nineteenth century. But few historians have been satisfied with the general proposition that decolonisation was simply the result of the two World Wars. Most would agree with John Darwin, *End of Empire: The Historical Debate* (1991) that decolonisation, like the acquisition of empire, must have been multicausal.

Until 1989 Marxist explanations confronted non-Marxist ones, although decolonisation was always an embarrassment to Marxist historians. On a straightforward reading of the key text, *Imperialism: The Highest Stage of Capitalism* (1916), Lenin had diagnosed the acquisition of empire as an important symptom of over-ripe capitalism, which was about to collapse. No satisfactory Marxist theory of decolonisation ever evolved. Nor, so far, has a comprehensive or generally accepted non-Marxist one. Decol-onisation is still a recent phenonenon. Archives are only just being opened to scholars. Some of the best early studies were by journalists, which are likely to have a continuing value because, in many cases, they were eye-witnesses of the events. Among these are John Hatch, *History of Post-war Africa* (1965) and Colin Cross, *The Fall of the British Empire* (1968). *The New Africans: Reuter's Guide to the Contemporary History of Emergent Africa and its Leaders* (1967) is also very useful. In a slightly different category but also drawing on journalistic expertise and interviews with participants is Brian Lapping, *End of Empire* (1985), written to accompany the television series. It considers only the British empire but includes Iran, Palestine and Aden.

Books have begun to pour out with the opening of the archives. Some merge into international histories, others are straight national histories of former colonies. In the following section, the focus is on works which concentrate on the decolonisation process. A fundamental question which must underlie many studies is the relative importance of the pressure of anti-colonial nationalism, changing international relations and the domestic politics and calculations of national interest on the part of the former colonial powers.

General Studies of European Decolonisation

Early in the field was Henri Grimal, *La Décolonisation* (1965) which, translated by Stephan de Vos, became available in English in 1978 as *Decolonization: The British, French, Dutch and Belgian Empires, 1919–1963*; it includes a selection of documents. Franz Ansprenger, *The Dissolution of the Colonial Empires* (1989, first published in German in 1981) is another useful introduction to the subject. R. von Albertini, *Decolonization: The Administration and Future of the Colonies, 1919–1960* (English translation, 1971) is a weighty work. V. Kiernan, *European Empires from Conquest to Collapse, 1815–1960* (1982) takes a now-unfashionable Marxist line but is stimulating and shrewd. Tony Smith, *The Pattern of Imperialism: The United States, Great Britain, and the Late-Industrializing World since 1815* (1981) is also thought-provoking. M. Kahler, *Decolonization in Britain and France: The Domestic Consequences of International Relations* (1984) is a comparative study. R.F. Holland, *European Decolonization, 1918–1981: An Introductory Survey* (1985) is, in fact, a great deal more than a survey. M.E. Chamberlain, *Decolonization: The End of the European Empires* (1985) is a short introduction.

The complexity of the subject has given rise to a number of collective works. Among the best are three edited by P. Gifford and W.R. Louis,

France and Britain in Africa: Imperial Rivalry and Colonial Rule (1971); *The Transfer of Power in Africa: Decolonization, 1940–1960* (1982); and *Decolonization and African Independence: The Transfer of Power, 1960–1980* (1988). Still useful is L.H. Gann and P. Duignan (eds), *Colonialism in Africa, 1870–1960*, 5 vols (1969–75). More recent are W.H. Morris-Jones and G. Fischer (eds), *Decolonization and After: The British and French Experience* (1980); and W.J. Mommsen and J. Osterhammel (eds), *Imperialism and After* (1986).

H. Baudet, 'The Dutch Retreat from Empire' and A.J. Hanna, 'The British Retreat from Empire' in J.S. Bromley and E.H. Kossman (eds), *Britain and the Netherlands in Europe and Asia* (1968) make some interesting comparisons, as does John Kent, *The Internationalization of Colonialism: Britain, France and Black Africa, 1939–1956* (1992).

Other works cover a wide canvas, for example, H. Tinker, *Men Who Overturned Empires* (1987), which looks at nationalist leaders. J.F. Cady, *The History of Post-War South East Asia* (1974) is a useful introduction and see also J.M. Phivias, *South-East Asia from Colonialism to Independence* (1974). John Keay, *Last Post: The End of Empire in the Far East* (1997) considers the Americans in the Philippines, as well as the British, French and Dutch empires, and hints at revisionist views in asking whether the colonial experience was not actually stimulating to nations which have gone on to become the tiger economies of the late twentieth century.

David Birmingham, *The Decolonization of Africa* (1995) is a good short introduction to one continent, as is Henry S. Wilson, *African Decolonization* (1994). Basil Davidson's many books are always interesting. *The Black Man's Burden: Africa and the Curse of the Nation State* (1992) was one of his last.

For the role of the United Nations see E. Luard, *The History of the United Nations*, Vol. 2, *The Age of Decolonization, 1955–1965* (1988).

The British Empire

General

D. Judd, *Empire: The British Imperial Experience from 1765 to the Present* (1996) provides a bird's eye view and, unlike older general histories, devotes a great deal of space to decolonization.

The official archives are now open and the massive publication of 'British Documents on the End of Empire' is now under way, although only a few volumes have yet appeared. The first of Series A to appear was Vol. 2, *The Labour Government and the End of Empire*, edited by R. Hyam (1992). The first of Series B was Vol. 1, *Ghana*, edited by R. Rathbone (1992). They have now been followed by David Goldsworthy (ed.), *The Conservative Government and the End of Empire, 1951–1957* (Series A, Vol. 3,

1994) and A.J. Stockwell (ed.) *Malaya* (Series B, Vol. 3, 1995). A multi-volume *History of the British Empire* to replace the old *Cambridge History of the British Empire* is also in train.

Before the archives became open, popular accounts already abounded, some of them good and stimulating such as J. Morris, *Farewell the Trumpets: An Imperial Retreat* (pbk. 1979). Among older books, A.P. Thornton, *The Imperial Idea and its Enemies* (1957) and J. Strachey, *The End of Empire* (1959) are still well worth reading. B. Porter, *The Lion's Share: A Short History of British Imperialism, 1870–1983* (3rd edn, 1996) is broad-brush but a useful introduction. G. Woodcock, *Who Killed the British Empire?* (1974) has stood the test of time as an interesting analysis.

The best single-volume study to date is probably J. Darwin, *Britain and Decolonization: The Retreat from Empire in the Post-war World* (1987). His *End of Empire* (1991) deals with the political debate within Britain as well as with general theories of decolonisation. J. Gallagher, *The Decline, Revival and Fall of the British Empire* (1982) takes a longer perspective, as does P.M. Kennedy, *The Rise and Fall of British Naval Mastery* (1976). Also concerned with defence issues are C.J. Bartlett, *The Long Retreat: A Short History of British Defence Policy, 1945–1970* (1972); P. Darby, *British Defence Policy East of Suez, 1947–1968* (1973); and R. Neillands, *A Fighting Retreat: The British Empire, 1947–1997* (1996). Michael Howard, *The Continental Commitment* (1974) looks at the tension between the defence of empire and Britain's European commitments.

Decolonisation is so closely connected with the decline of Britain as a world power that many studies of the causes of British decline could be cited, but D. Dilkes, *Retreat from Power*, 2 vols (1981) must be mentioned. An important article by W.R. Louis and R. Robinson, 'The Imperialism of Decolonization' is in the *Journal of Imperial and Commonwealth History*, 22 (1994). John Kent, *British Imperial Strategy and the Origins of the Cold War, 1944–1949* (1993) is also interesting. A particular aspect, Britain's dependence on an unsympathetic America at the end of the Second World War, is closely analysed in W.R. Louis, *Imperialism at Bay: The United States and the Decolonization of the British Empire, 1941–1945* (1977, pbk. 1986) See also his 'American Anti-Colonialism and the Dissolution of the British Empire' in *International Affairs*, 61 (1985).

Many works on British politics since 1945 give essential background, as do the memoirs of the politicians, but of immediate relevance are P.S. Gupta, *Imperialism and the British Labour Movement, 1914–1964* (1975); D. Goldsworthy, *Colonial Issues in British Politics, 1945–1961* (1971); Stephen Howe, *Anticolonialism in British Politics: The Left and the End of Empire, 1918–1964* (1993); and P. Murphy, *Party Politics and Decolonization: The Conservative Party and British Colonial Policy in Tropical Africa, 1951–1964*

(1995). Older but with some useful points is J.M. Lee, *Colonial Development and Good Government: A Study of the Ideas Expressed by the British Official Classes in Planning Decolonization* (1967). See also A. Cohen, *British Policy in Changing Africa* (1959) and L.H. Gann and P. Diugnan, *African Proconsuls* (1978). Essential memoirs include A. Eden, *Full Circle* (1960) and H. Macmillan, *Riding the Storm* (1970) and *Pointing the Way, 1959–1961* (1972). Some of the Proconsuls have now been studied, including J.W. Cell, *Hailey: A Study in British Imperialism, 1872–1969* (1992) and Clyde Sanger, *Malcolm MacDonald: Bringing an Empire to an End* (1995).

Other studies important for an understanding of British policy are P.J. Cain and A.G. Hopkins, *British Imperialism*, Vol. 2, *Crisis and Deconstruction, 1914–1990* (1993), although the discussion of decolonisation is brief; and D.K. Fieldhouse, *Unilever Overseas: The Anatomy of a Multi-National* (1978) and his *Merchant Capitalism and Economic Decolonization: The United African Company, 1929–1987* (1994). Marjory Perham, *The Colonial Reckoning* (1962, the Reith Lectures); A. Creech-Jones, *The Labour Party and Colonial Policy* (New Fabian Colonial Essays, 1959); and G.C. Carrington, *The Liquidation of the British Empire* (1960) still have value. New ground is broken in S.L. Carruthers, *Winning Hearts and Minds: British Governments, the Media and Colonial Counter-Insurgency, 1944–1960* (1995) and T.R. Mackaitis, *British Counterinsurgency in the Post-Imperial Era* (1995).

C. Bayly, *Atlas of the British Empire: A New Perspective on the British Empire from 1500 to the Present* (1989) includes a good deal of text. A.N. Porter and A.J. Stockwell, *British Imperial Policy and Decolonization, 1938–1964*, 2 vols (1987, 1989) provides a good selection of documents with a substantial introduction.

N. Mansergh, *The Commonwealth Experience*, Vol. 2, *From British to Multi-racial Commonwealth* (1982 edn) still provides a good introduction to the idea of the Commonwealth, but see also D. Judd and P. Slinn, *The Evolution of the Modern Commonwealth, 1902–1980* (1982) and W.D. McIntyre, *The Significance of the Commonwealth, 1965–1990* (1991).

India

Because of its pivotal importance, there is far more literature on Indian independence than on the transfer of power in any other part of the British empire. *The New Cambridge History of India* will provide a standard work of reference when completed, but so far few modern volumes have appeared. B.R. Tomlinson, *The Economy of Modern India, 1860–1970* (1993), which considers the state of the Indian economy in 1947, is an exception. An excellent introduction is provided by Judith Brown's *Modern India: The Origins of an Asian Democracy* (1985) and the 4th edition of S. Wolpert's *New History of India* (1993) now takes the story up to 1992.

Important background books include Anil Seal, *The Emergence of Indian Nationalism* (1968); P. Hardy, *The Muslims of India* (1972); and S. Joshi, *The Struggle for Hegemony in India, 1920–1947: The Colonial State, the Left and the National Movement* (1992). The last examines the relations between the Indian Communist Party and the Congress.

The standard documentary study of the end of British rule is the massive *India: The Transfer of Power*, ed. N. Mansergh, 12 vols (1970–83). A useful single volume of documents covering the whole period of the British Raj is C.H. Philips, *Select Documents on the History of India and Pakistan*, Vol. IV, *The Evolution of India and Pakistan* (1962).

Mahatma Gandhi was a world figure, not just an Indian one, and there are many biographies of him. Among the best is Judith Brown, *Gandhi, Prisoner of Hope* (1989) and Louis Fischer, *The Life of Mahatma Gandhi* (pbk., 1982). A useful short introduction is A. Copley, *Gandhi: Against the Tide* (1987). Indispensible to any understanding of Gandhi is his own autobiography, although it covers only his early years. First published as *My Experiments with Truth*, it was reissued under the title *Gandhi: An Autobiography* in 1966. There is a three-volume selection from his works, edited by R.N. Iyer, *The Moral and Political Writings of Mahatma Gandhi* (1986–87). Among important or thought-provoking studies are R.N. Iyer, *The Moral and Political Thought of Mahatma Gandhi* (1978); M. Chatterjee, *Gandhi's Religious Thought* (1983); G. Richard, *The Philosophy of Gandhi: A Study of his Basic Ideas* (1982); E. Erikson, *Gandhi's Truth: On the Origins of Militant Nonviolence* (1970); J.V. Bondurant, *Conquest of Violence: The Gandhian Philosophy of Conflict* (rev. edn, 1969); and D. Dalton, *Mahatma Gandhi: Nonviolent Power in Action* (1993).

Nehru too left a partial autobiography, *Autobiography: Towards Freedom* (1942) and there is also his *The Discovery of India* (3rd edn, 1951). There are important biographies by M. Brecher, *Nehru: A Political Biography* (1959); S. Gopal, *Jawaharlal Nehru: A Biography*, 3 vols (1979); and A.J. Akbar, *Nehru: The Making of India* (1988).

Two studies of M.A. Jinnah are S. Wolpert, *Jinnah of Pakistan* (1984) and A. Jalal, *The Sole Spokesman: Jinnah, the Muslim League and the Demand for Pakistan*. Akbar S. Ahmed offers a new and more sympathetic portrait of Jinnah in *Jinnah, Pakistan and Islamic Identity* (1997). See also I. Talbot, *Provincial Politics and the Pakistan Movement, 1937–1947* (1985).

The British can be studied in P. Woodruff (Philip Mason), *The Men Who Ruled India* (pbk. 1963), which gives an anecdotal but vivid picture. For Lord Curzon, there is David Dilks, *Curzon in India*, 2 vols (1970) and David Gilmour, *Curzon* (1994). For the two Viceroys most immediately concerned with the transfer of power there are P. Moon (ed.), *Wavell: The Viceroy's Journal* (1973) and P. Ziegler, *Mountbatten: The Official Biography*

(1985). There is further first-hand information in V.P. Menon, *The Transfer of Power in India* (1957) and Alan Campbell-Johnson, *Mission with Mountbatten* (1951). For a highly critical account of Mountbatten see A. Roberts, *Eminent Churchillians* (1994).

Among the many studies of the transfer of power and of partition, there are the following, which between them represent most of the major approaches: B.N. Pandey *The Break Up of British India* (1969), which takes a long perspective; H.V. Hodson, *The Great Divide: Britain, India, Pakistan* (1969); C.H. Philips and D. Wainwright, *Partition of India: Politics and Perspectives* (1970); B.R. Tomlinson, *The Indian National Congress and the Raj: The Penultimate Phase* (1976); R.J. Moore, *Churchill, Cripps and India* (1979) and *Escape from India: The Attlee Government and the Indian Problem* (1983); and *India's Partition: Process, Strategy and Mobilization*, edited by M. Hasan (Themes in Indian History Series, Delhi, 1993). The last, although intended mainly for undergraduate use, includes documents and discussion of controversial issues. Patrick French, *Liberty or Death: India's Journey to Independence and Division* (1997) uses recently declassified British intelligence documents.

Less mainstream but giving particular viewpoints on related questions are P.W. Fay, *The Forgotten War: India's Armed Struggle for Independence, 1942–1945* (1993), the history of the Indian National Army, formed by the Japanese, and R. Kumar, *The History of Doing: Illustrated Accounts of Movements for Women's Rights and Feminism in India, 1800–1990* (1993).

For events after independence including the break-up of Pakistan see W.J. Barnds, *India, Pakistan and the Great Powers* (1972); L. Binder, *Religion and Politics in Pakistan* (1963); K. Siddiqui, *Conflict, Crisis and War in Pakistan* (1972); D. Gilmartin, *Empire and Islam: Punjab and the Making of Pakistan*; R. Chowdhurry, *The Genesis of Bangladesh*; and W. Wilcox, *The Emergence of Bangladesh* (1973).

Asia other than India

Hugh Tinker edited the documents on the independence of Burma, comparable to the Indian series, *Burma: The Struggle for Independence, 1944–1948* (1993–94). J.F. Cady, *A History of Modern Burma* (1958) is a straightforward account. Sri Lanka is considered in S. Arasaratnam, *Ceylon* (1964) and C.R. De Silva, *Sri Lanka: A History* (1991), and modern Sri Lanka is dealt with in A.J. Wilson, *Politics in Sri Lanka, 1947–1979* (1979). On Malaya there is G.P. Means, *Malaysian Politics* (1970) and A.J. Stockwell, *British Policy and Malay Politics during the Malayan Union Experiment, 1942–1948* (1979) and his 'British Imperial Policy and Decolonisation in Malaya, 1942–1952', *Journal of Imperial and Commonwealth History*, 13 (1984). There is a biography of Tunku Abdul Rahman by H. Miller, *Prince and Premier*

(1959). The Malayan emergency has been analysed from very different standpoints, for example, H. Miller, *The Communist Menace in Malaya* (1954); R. Clutterbuck, *The Long, Long War* (1966); V. Purcell, *Malaya: Communist or Free?* (1954); and A. Short, *The Communist Insurrection in Malaya, 1848–1960* (1975). Two accounts of Singapore are C.M. Turnbull, *A History of Singapore, 1819–1975* (1977) and E.C.T. Chew, *A History of Singapore* (1992). Other aspects of South East Asia are dealt with in S. Runciman, *The White Rajahs* (1960); G. Saunders, *History of Brunei* (1996); and J.D. Waiko, *A Short History of Papua New Guinea* (1993).

Africa (also see under General sections)
W.M. (Lord) Hailey, *African Survey* (1957) ranks as a primary source of the first importance. A good overall view is provided by John Hargreaves, *Decolonization in Africa* (1988).

Works important for understanding the background of African nationalism include P.D. Curtin (ed.) *Africa and the West: Intellectual Responses to European Culture* (1972); R.W. July, *The Origins of Modern African Thought* (1968); J. Ayo Langley, *Ideologies of Liberation in Black Africa, 1856–1970: Documents on Modern African Political Thought from Colonial Times to the Present* (1979); Henry S. Wilson, *Origins of West African Nationalism* (1969); and G. Padmore, *Colonial and Coloured Unity: History of the Pan-African Congress* (2nd edn, 1963). Pan-Africanism is also covered in C. Legum, *Pan-Africanism* (1962) and I. Geiss, *Pan-Africanism* (1974). P.C. Lloyd, *The New Elites of Tropical Africa* (1966) is interesting, as is E. Ashby, *African Universities and Western Tradition* (1966).

The writings of the nationalist leaders themselves, sometimes autobiographical, are also important. They include O. Awolowo, *Path to Nigerian Freedom* (1947) and *Awo: Autobiography* (1960); K. Nkrumah, *Autobiography* (1957); J.K. Nyerere, *'Ujaman', the Basis of African Socialism* (1962); Tom Mboya, *Freedom and After* (1963); Oginga Odinga, *Not Yet Uhuru* (1967); K. Kaunda, *Zambia Shall Be Free* (1962); N. Sithole, *African Nationalism* (1959); and Joshua Nkomo, *The Story of my Life* (1984). An analysis by a Briton closely involved with Africa is Thomas Hodgkin, *Nationalism in Colonial Africa* (1956).

The evolution of British policy can be traced in R.D. Pearce, *The Turning Point in Africa: British Colonial Policy, 1938–1948* (1982); A. Cohen, *British Policy in Changing Africa* (1959); J. Lee and M. Petter, *The Colonial Office, War and Development Policy* (1982); and Y. Baugura, *Britain and Commonwealth Africa* (1983). See also a number of articles, D.K. Fieldhouse, 'The Labour Government and the Empire-Commonwealth' in R. Ovendale (ed.) *The Foreign Policy of the British Labour Governments, 1945–1951* (1984); John Flint, 'Planned Decolonization and its Failure in Africa', *African Affairs* 82 (1983); and R. Pearce, 'The Colonial Office and Planned Decolonization in Africa', *African Affairs* 83 (1984).

Books on events after decolonisation, which often throw light on earlier decisions, include R. Harris, *Independence and After: Revolution in Under-Developed Countries* (1962); J. Hatch, *Africa Emergent: African Problems since Independence* (1974); A.H.M. Kirk-Greene, *Stand by Your Radios* (a brief analysis of post-independence military coups, 1981); S. Decalo *Coups and Army Rule in Africa* (1976); and D.K. Fieldhouse, *Black Africa, 1945–1980* (1986).

Studies of individual areas include the following:

West Africa: A.J.F. Ajayi and M. Crowder, *History of West Africa*, Vol. 2 (1974); A.G. Hopkins, *An Economic History of West Africa* (1973); D. Austin, *Politics in Ghana* (1964); D. Birmingham, *Kwame Nkrumah* (1990); Y. Petchenkine, *Ghana in Search of Stability, 1957–1992* (1992); A. Burns, *History of Nigeria* (interesting as being the account of a later British colonial governor, 1929, rev. edn, 1963); K. Post, *The Nigerian Federal Election of 1959* (1963); K.W.J. Post and F.D. Jenkins, *The Price of Liberty: Personality and Politics in Colonial Nigeria* (1973); A.H.M. Kirk-Green, *Crisis and Coflict in Nigeria* (1971); John de St Jorre *The Nigerian Civil War* (1972); and S.E. Oyovbaine, *Federation in Nigeria* (1985). The standard work on Sierra Leone is C. Fyfe, *History of Sierra Leone* (1962). For the Gambia there is A. Hughes and D. Perfect, *Political History of the Gambia, 1816–1892* (1993).

East Africa: G. Bennett, *Kenya: A Political History* (1963) is still the best introduction. E. Huxley and M. Perham, *Race and Politics in Kenya* (1957) is enlightening, as is E. Huxley, *White Man's Country* (1953). For a later study see G. Wasserman, *Politics of Decolonization: Kenyan Europeans and the Land Issue, 1960–1965* (1976). Mau Mau attracted much discussion including, from very different standpoints, F.D. Corfield, *The Origins and Growth of Mau Mau* (1960); C.G. Rosberg and J. Nottingham, *The Myth of Mau Mau* (1966); D.L. Barnett and K. Njama, *Mau Mau from Within* (1966); and D. Throup, *The Economic and Social Origins of Mau Mau, 1945–1953,* (1987). On Uganda, K. Ingham, *The Making of Modern Uganda* (1958) is a good introduction, while D.A. Low, *Buganda in Modern History* (1971) deals with a key aspect. J. Hatch, *Tanzania* (1972) and I.N. Kimombo and A.J. Temu, *A History of Tanzania* (1969) set the scene. A.G. Maguire, *Towards 'Uhuru' in Tanzania: The Politics of Participation* (1969) and C. Pratt, *The Critical Phase in Tanzania, 1945–1968: Nyerere and the Emergence of a Socialist Strategy* (1976) deal with particular aspects in more detail.

The Rhodesias: Two very different viewpoints are presented in R. Blake, *A History of Rhodesia* (1979) and T.O. Ranger, *Peasant Consciousness and Guerrilla War in Zimbabwe* (1974) or M. Lomey *White Racism and Imperial*

Response (1974). See also A. Roberts, *A History of Zambia* (1976); Philip Mason, *The Birth of a Dilemma* (1958) and *Year of Decision; Rhodesia and Nyasaland in 1960* (1960); Patrick Keatley, *The Politics of Partnership* (1963); R.C. Good, *UDI: The Internal Politics of the Rhodesian Rebellion* (1973); and W.H. Morris-Jones (ed.) *From Rhodesia to Zimbabwe* (1980). For two of the personalities involved see P. Short, *Banda* (1974) and R. Welensky, *4000 Days* (1964).

South Africa: The standard works are still M. Wilson and L. Thompson (eds), *Oxford History of South Africa*, 2 vols (1970) or T.R.H. Davenport, *South Africa: A Modern History* (4th edn, 1991). To bring the story up to date see the excellent summary in N. Worden, *The Making of Modern South Africa: Conquest, Segregation and Apartheid* (1994). Specifically on Namibia there are P.H. Katjavivi, *A History of Resistance in Namibia* (1988) and V. Gupta, *Independent Namibia: Problems and Prospects* (1990). On Botswana, Lesotho and Swaziland see J.E. Spence, *Lesotho: The Politics of Dependence* (1968); J. Parson, *Botswana: Liberal Democracy and Labour Reserves in Southern Africa* (1984); and A. Booth, *Swaziland: Tradition and Change in a South African Kingdom* (1984).

Caribbean

J.H. Parry and Philip Sherlock, *A Short History of the West Indies* (1971) is still a useful introduction. See also J. Mordecai, *The West Indies: The Federal Negotiations* (1968); M. Manley, *Jamaica: The Struggle in the Periphery* (1983); A.J. Payne, *Politics in Jamaica* (1988); F.A. Hoyes, *Tom Adams: A Biography* (1988); C.A. Hughes, *Race and Politics in the Bahamas* (1981); and C.H. Grant, *The Making of Modern Belize* (1976).

The Middle East

The best overall study is W.R. Louis, *The British Empire in the Middle East, 1945–1951* (1984). To set the scene see J. Darwin, *Britain, Egypt and the Middle East: Imperial Policy in the Aftermath of War, 1918–1922* (1980).

On Egypt, P. Mansfield, *The British in Egypt* (1971) and John Marlowe, *Anglo-Egyptian Relations, 1800–1956* (1965) remain useful introductions. There is also A. Sattin, *Lifting the Veil: The British in Egypt, 1800–1956* (1988). Carrying the story further forward is D. Hopwood, *Egypt: Politics and Society, 1945–1990* (3rd edn, 1992); R. Stephens, *Nasser* (1971); and J. Berque, *Egypt: Imperialism and Revolution* (1972). An enormous amount has been written on the Suez crisis of 1956. A number of participants have left accounts including Anthony Eden, *Full Circle* (1960) and Anthony Nutting, *No End of a Lesson* (1967). A variety of approaches can be studied in W.R. Louis and R. Owen (eds), *Suez 1956: The Crisis and its*

Consequences (1989). It is also worth reading T. Robertson, *Crisis: The Inside Story of the Suez Conspiracy* (1964); L. Epstein, *British Politics in the Suez Crisis* (1964); and J. Eayrs, *The Commonwealth and Suez: A Documentary Survey* (1964).

P.M. Holt, *A Modern History of the Sudan* (3rd edn, 1979) still provides a good introduction. See also P. Woodward, *Sudan, 1898–1989: The Unstable State* (1991).

For the British mandate in Palestine and Jordan there is D. Horowitz and M. Lissak, *Palestine Under the Mandate* (2nd edn, 1979); M.J. Cohen, *Palestine: Retreat from the Mandate* (1978) and *Palestine and the Great Powers, 1945–1948* (1982). See also R.B. Satloff, *From Abdullah to Hussein: Jordan in Transition* (1994). (For a fuller bibliography see R. Ovendale, *Longman Companion to the Middle East since 1914* (1992)).

F. Heard-Bey, *From Trucial States to United Arab Emirates* (1982) is useful. On Aden see R.J. Gavin, *Aden Under British Rule* (1975) for the background. For various aspects of the crisis see W.P. Kirkman, *Unscrambling an Empire* (1966) and David Ledger, *Shifting Sands* (1983) – the first is a journalist, the second is a soldier. H. Trevelyan, *The Middle East in Revolution* (1970) is the last British governor's account.

Although Iran was not formally part of the British empire, its role was important. For the political background see E. Abrahamian, *Iran Between Two Revolutions* (1982). For the extraordinary story of the abortive intervention against Mossadeq see C.M. Woodhouse, *Something Ventured* (1982) and Kermit Roosevelt, *Counter-coup: The Struggle for the Control of Iran* (1979).

A great deal has been published on Cyprus and *enosis*. Try RIIA, *The Dispute and the Settlement* (1959); G. Grivas, *Memoirs* (1964); R.H. Stevens, *Cyprus: A Place of Arms* (1966); P.N. Vanezic, *Makarios: Faith and Power* (1972); N. Crawshaw, *The Cyprus Revolt* (1978); S. Mayes, *Makarios: A Biography* (1981); and G.H. Kelling *Count Down to Rebellion: British Policy in Cyprus, 1939–1955* (1990). Sir Hugh Foot, Britain's last governor, also gave his account in *A Start in Freedom* (1964).

Oceania

For a recent dispute see B. Gough, *The Falkland Islands/Malvinas: The Contest for Empire in the South Atlantic* (1992), and for another difficult problem, B.J. Lal, *Broken Waves: A History of the Fiji Islands in the Twentieth Century* (1992). For an older problem, J.J. Cremona, *The Constitutional Development of Malta Under British Rule* (1963). See also B. Macdonald, *Trusteeship and Independence in Nauru* (1988). For an interesting exercise in looking forward there is Hungdah, Chiu et al. (eds), *The Future of Hong Kong: Towards 1997 and Beyond* (1987).

The French Empire

The amount of material available in English for the study of the French empire is limited. R. Betts, *France and Decolonization* (1982) and C.M. Andrew, *France Overseas* (1981) provide general studies; M. Kahler, *Decolonization in Britain and France* (1984) and J. Kent, *The Internationalization of Colonialism: Britain, France and Black Africa* (1992) comparative ones. A. Clayton, *The Wars of French Decolonization* (1994) does not confine itself to military matters. To bring the story up to date see R. Aldrich and J. Connell, *France's Overseas Frontier* (1992). D. Bruce Marshall, *The French Colonial Myth and Constitution-making in the Fourth Republic* (1973) and Paul C. Sarum, *Intellectuals and Decolonization in France* (1977) look at particular aspects.

General studies relating to France and Africa include W.B. Cohen, *Rulers of Empire: The French Colonial service in Africa* (1971); V. Thompson and R. Adloff *French West Africa* (1957) and *The Emerging States of French Equatorial Africa* (1960); T. Hodgkin and R. Schachter Morgenthau, *French-Speaking West Africa in Transition* (1960); P. Neres, *French-Speaking West Africa* (1962); R.S. Morgenthau, *Political Parties in French-Speaking Africa* (1964); E.H. Lewis (ed.), *French-Speaking Africa: The Search for Identity* (1965); and E. Mortimer, *France and the Africans, 1944–1960* (1969). Specifically relating to the role of General de Gaulle is Dorothy Shipley White, *Black Africa and De Gaulle: From the French Empire to Independence* (1979). There is a study of the Black Governor-General who brought Equatorial Africa into the Second World War on de Gaulle's side, B. Weinstein, *Eboué* (1972). On particular countries there is M.A. Saint Paul, *Gabon: The Development of a Nation* (1989); F. Fugelstad, *A History of Niger, 1850–1960* (1984); and M.W. DeLancey, *Cameroon: Dependence and Independence* (1989).

Classic works on Algeria include A. Horne, *A Savage War of Peace* (rev. edn, 1988) and F. Fanon, *Studies in a Dying Colonialism* (1955) and *The Wretched of the Earth* (1965). There is also E. O'Balance, *The Algerian Insurrection, 1954–1962* (1967); T. Smith, *The French Stake in Algeria, 1945–1962* (1978); and W.B. Quandt, *Revolution and Political Leadership: Algeria 1954–1969* (1969). On Tunis there is C.A. Micaud, *Tunis: The Politics of Modernization* (1964) and N. Salem, *Habib Bourguiba, Islam and the Creation of Tunisia* (1984), and on Morocco, D. Ashford, *Political Change in Morocco* (1961).

On the Middle East see P.S. Khoury, *Syria and the French Mandate* (1986); H. Cobban, *The Making of Modern Lebanon* (1985); and J.F. Devlin, *State and Society in Syria and Lebanon* (1994).

An enormous amount has been published on the Vietnam war. Many accounts of the war look back to the French period. One such is S. Karnow,

Vietnam: A History, the First Complete Account of Vietnam at War (1983). See also R. Smith, *Vietnam and the West* (1968) and A. Short, *The Origins of the Vietnam War* (1989). More specifically concerned with the French period are: D.G. Marr, *Vietnamese Anti-Colonialism, 1885–1925* (1971); D.J. Duiker, *The Rise of Nationalism in Vietnam, 1900–1941* (1976); and E.J. Hammer, *The Struggle for Indo-China, 1940–1955* (1966). J. Buttinger, *Vietnam: A Dragon Embattled*, Vol. 1, *From Colonialism to the Vietminh* (1967) also deals with this period. For the battle of Dien Bien Phu see Jules Roy, *The Battle of Dien Bien Phu* (trans. R. Baldick, 1966) and Vo Nguyen Giap, *Dien Bien Phu* (1962). There are several lives of Ho Chi Minh, among them J. Lacouture, *Ho Chi Minh: A Political Biography* (trans. P. Wiles, 1968) and Charles Fenn, *Ho Chi Minh: A Biographical Introduction* (1973). On the other French possessions in Indo-China there are M.E. Osborne, *The French Presence in Cochin China and Cambodia* (1969) and D.P. Chandler, *The Tragedy of Cambodian History: Power, War and Revolution since 1945* (1992).

The Dutch Empire

Most accounts are concerned with the former Dutch East Indies (modern Indonesia). They include G.McT. Kahin, *Nationalism and Revolution in Indonesia* (1952); L. Palmier, *Indonesia and the Dutch* (1962); and A. Arthur Schiller, *The Formation of Federal Indonesia, 1945–1949* (1955). There are several studies of General Sukarno, among them G.D. Legge, *Sukarno: A Political Biography* (1972).

The Portuguese Empire

The long-drawn-out death of the Portuguese empire gave rise to a number of studies. Some date back to the Penguin African Library such as B. Davidson, *In the Eye of the Storm: Angola's People* (1975). General studies include G. Clarence Smith, *The Third Portuguese Empire, 1825–1975: A Study in Economic Imperialism* (1985) and Norrie MacQueen, *Decolonization of Portuguese Africa: Metropolitan Revolution and the Dissolution of Empire* (1997). On Angola there is G.J. Bender, *Angola under the Portuguese: The Myth and the Reality* (1978); J.A. Marcum, *The Angolan Revolution*, 2 vols (1969, 1978); and W.M. James, *Political History of the War in Angola* (1991). On Mozambique, there is E. Mondlane, *The Struggle for Mozambique* (1969); A. and B. Isaacnau, *Mozambique from Colonialism to Revolution, 1900–1982* (1984); and W.A. Finnegan, *A Complicated War: The Harrowing of Mozambique* (1992). There are some works on Portugal's smaller possessions, for example R. Fegley, *Equatorial Guinea: An African Tragedy* (1989). There is a biography of Amilcar Cabral by P. Chabal (1983) and a collection of his works, *Unity and Struggle: Speeches and Writings Selected by the PAIGG* (1980).

The Spanish Empire

Works on the twentieth-century dissolution of the Spanish empire relate mainly to the problems of the Western Sahara such as V. Thompson and R. Adloff, *The Western Saharans: Background to Conflict* (1980) and T. Hodges, *The Western Sahara: The Roots of a Desert War* (1984).

The Belgian Empire

The tragic legacy of the Belgian empire in the Congo has given rise to a number of studies. These include R. Lemarchand, *Political Awakening in the Congo* (1964); Conor Cruise O'Brien, *To Katanga and Back* (1962); C. Hoskyns, *The Congo since Independence* (1965); C. Young, *Politics in the Congo, Decolonization and Independence* (1965); J. Gerard-Libois, *Katanga Secession* (1966); T. Kanza, *Conflict in the Congo: The Rise and Fall of Lumumba* (1972); and C. Young and T. Turner, *The Rise and Decline of the Zairian State* (1985). R. Anstey, *King Leopold's Legacy: The Congo under Belgian Rule, 1908–1960* (1966) is still useful to set the scene, as is R. Slade, *The Belgian Congo* (1980). The neighbouring trust territory can be studied in R. Lemarchand, *Rwanda and Burundi* (1970).

The Italian Empire

This collapsed before the end of the Second World War but its legacy in parts of Africa is dealt with in G.H. Becker, *The Disposition of the Italian Colonies, 1941–1951* (1952); A. Pelt, *Libyan Independence and the United Nations: A Case of Planned Decolonization* (1970); M. Khadduri, *Modern Libya* (1963); S. Pankhurst, *Ex-Italian Somaliland* (1951); A. and R. Pankhurst, *Ethiopia and Eritrea* (1953); and R. Lewis, *Eritrea: Africa's Newest Country* (1993).

SECTION SEVEN

Appendices and Maps

Appendix 1
Dates of Independence
of African Nations

Botswana	30 Sept 1966
Burundi	1 July 1962
Cameroun	1 July 1960
Central African Republic	13 August 1960
Chad	11 August 1960
Congo Republic (formerly French)	15 August 1960
Congo Democratic Republic (Zaire)	30 June 1960
Dahomey	1 August 1960
Gabon	17 August 1960
The Gambia	18 Feb 1965
Ghana	6 March 1957
Guinea	2 Oct 1958
Ivory Coast	7 August 1960
Kenya	12 December 1963
Lesotho	4 Oct 1966
Liberia	26 July 1947
Malagasy Republic	26 June 1960
Malawi	6 July 1964
Mali	22 Sept 1960
Mauritania	28 Nov 1960
Niger	3 August 1960
Nigeria	1 Oct 1963
Rwanda	1 July 1962
Senegal	20 August 1960
Sierra Leone	27 April 1961
Somalia	Formed 1 July 1960 when British Somaliland, independent 26 June 1960, merged with Italian Somaliland, a trusteeship territory
Sudan	1 Jan 1956

Swaziland	6 September 1968
Tanganyika	9 Dec 1961
Togo	27 April 1960
Uganda	9 Oct 1962
Upper Volta	5 August 1960
Zambia	24 Oct 1964
Zanzibar	9 Dec 1963
Zimbabwe	18 April 1980

Appendix 2
Modern and Colonial Names
(where they differ)

Modern	Colonial
Bangladesh (1947–71, East Pakistan)	Part of India
Benin	Dahomey
Burkina Faso	Upper Volta
Burundi	Urundi
Cameroun, Federal Republic of	German Kamerun; divided into British and French mandates, 1920.
Congo Democratic Republic (Zaire, 1971–97)	Congo (Belgian)
Congo Republic	Middle Congo (French)
Djibouti	French Somaliland
Equatorial Guinea	Rio Muni, Fernando Po etc.
Ethiopia	Abyssinia
Ghana	Gold Coast
Guinea-Bissau	Portuguese Guinea
Guyana	British Guyana
Kenya	(Differs only in pronunciation)
Kiribati	Gilbert Islands
Lesotho	Basutoland
Malagasy Republic	Madagascar
Malawi	Nyasaland
Mali	Soudan (French)
Micronesia	Caroline Islands (Spanish 1866, German 1899, Japanese mandate 1921, USA mandate 1947, fully independent, 1991)
Namibia	(German) South West Africa
Niger	Niger Territory (French)
Pakistan	Part of India. 1947 included East and West Pakistan; 1971 East Pakistan became Bangladesh.

Sri Lanka	Ceylon
Surinam	Dutch Guiana
Tuvalu	Ellice Islands
Vanuatu	New Hebrides
Zaire (See Democratic Republic of Congo)	
Zambia	Northern Rhodesia
Zimbabwe	Southern Rhodesia

Maps

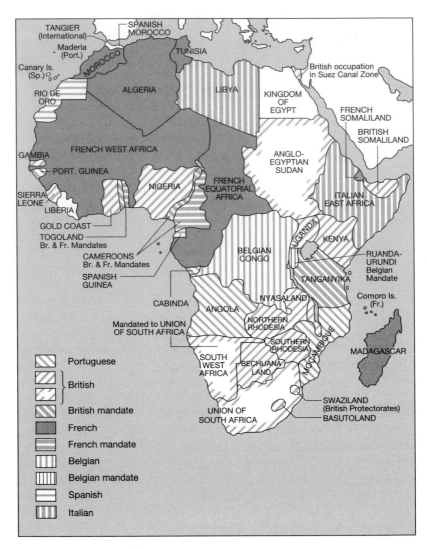

Map 1   Africa in 1939

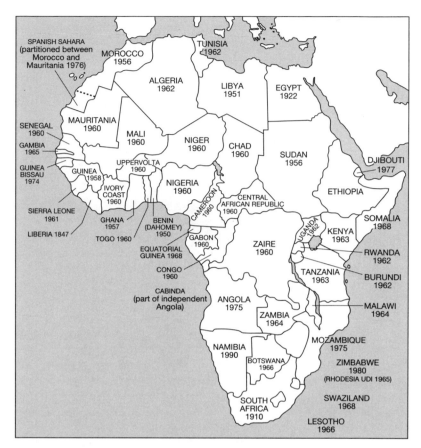

Map 2   The chronology of African independence

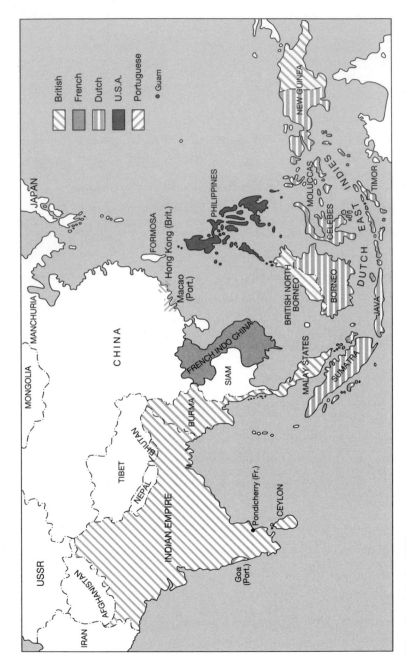

Map 3   Asia in 1939

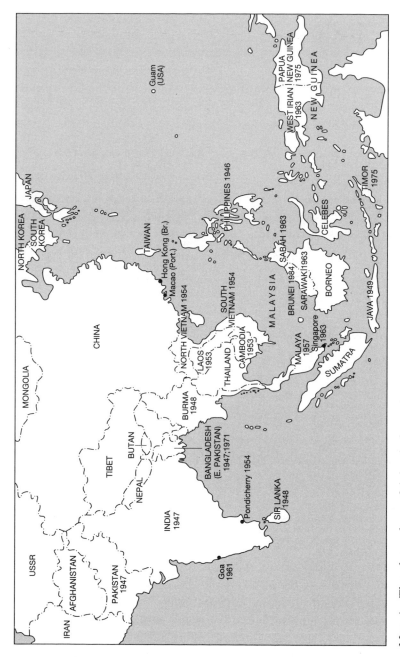

Map 4   The chronology of Asian independence

Index